Musical Pursuits

Alec Hyatt King in the Music Room of the British Museum, 1966.

British Library
Occasional Papers

Musical Pursuits

Selected Essays

Alec Hyatt King

The British Library | 1987

© (This Collection) 1987 Alec Hyatt King

First published 1987

Published by
The British Library
Great Russell Street
London WC1B 3DG
and 27 South Main Street, Wolfeboro,
New Hampshire 03844–2069

British Library Cataloguing in Publication Data

King, Alec Hyatt
  Musical pursuits: selected essays.
  (British Library occasional papers; 9).
  1. Music—History and criticism
  I. Title   II. Series
  780'.9   ML 160

ISBN 0 7123 0132 1

Designed by Alan Bartram
Typeset in Lasercomp Bembo by August Filmsetting, Haydock, St Helens
Printed in Great Britain by the University Press, Cambridge

TO ARTHUR SEARLE

Contents

Introduction | *ix*
Sources | *xii*
Acknowledgements | *xii*
List of illustrations | *xiii, xiv*

Music Printing

1 The five-hundredth anniversary of music printing:
   The Gradual of *c* 1473 | *1*
2 The significance of John Rastell in early music printing | *7*
3 Rastell reunited | *32*
4 Fragments of early printed music in the Bagford Collection | *38*
5 C G Röder's music-printing business in 1885 | *43*

Mozart in Manuscript and Print

6 The Mozarts at the British Museum | *53*
7 Mozart and Peter Anton Kreusser | *73*
8 Vignettes in early nineteenth-century London editions of
   Mozart operas | *77*
9 Oldman, Einstein and the Wandering Minstrels | *99*

Libraries and Collections

10 Frederick Nicolay, Chrysander and the Royal Music Library | *107*
11 The Quest for Sterland – 1
    The London Tavern: a forgotten concert hall | *119*
12 The Quest for Sterland – 2
    Sterland, the Harmonic Society and Beethoven's fourth
    symphony | *126*
13 The Quest for Sterland – 3
    Don Giovanni in London before 1817 | *137*
14 The Library of the Royal Philharmonic Society | *151*
15 The Wandering Minstrels and their archive | *178*
16 William Barclay Squire, 1855–1927: music librarian | *187*

Index | *200*

Introduction

Despite their apparent diversity, most of the essays in this volume have one feature in common – their origin in my study of music or musical literature, single items and collections, in the British Library. This arose in the course of my routine duties as Superintendent of the Music Room in the British Museum (after 1973, the Music Library of the British Library) and again later while I was working as an honorary consultant after my retirement in 1976. From time to time I came across various things which, though clearly of historical or bibliographical importance, had been strangely ignored. Generally, however, they were too complicated for fuller investigation at the time. So, with but one exception – my study of John Rastell – most of the longer pieces of research in this volume were completed during my retirement. Perhaps I should say something about the work or occasions which first aroused my curiosity.

It was in 1946, when I was cataloguing the printed music in the Hirsch Library, that I first noted a London edition of an arrangement of Mozart's operas, made by Joseph Mazzinghi, the title pages of which bore scenes from them in vignette. This was an imperfect set; the subsequent purchase of a complete one revived my interest and led ultimately to a wider exploration of the illustrations. Another Mozart rarity, purchased in 1963, was an arrangement for violin and piano of his early duet sonata K.19d. This combined a curious problem of biography with the matter of source transmission.

Mozart's personal association with the Museum first came to my attention in 1955, when I wrote *Mozart in the British Museum*, a little illustrated catalogue of the exhibition mounted to mark the bicentenary of his birth. The boy's gift of *God is our Refuge* to the Trustees in 1765 was clearly an event of some importance, but I had to defer its full evaluation in historical and musical terms for some 25 years.

The greatest gift received by the Music Room during my term of office, (and one of the most splendid ever made to the Department of Printed Books) was the Royal Music Library. Its deposit on loan in 1911 was due in no small measure to the advocacy of Barclay Squire, and it was in 1957, exactly 30 years after his death, that HM Queen Elizabeth II presented the collection outright to the Trustees to mark the bicentenary of the gift of the Old Royal Library in 1757. The results of a study of the history of the Royal Music were included in my book *Some British Collectors of Music* (1963), but one strange episode – the use of its Handel manuscripts by the famous German scholar Chrysander – appeared only in a now defunct periodical, and seemed worth reprinting here.

In the early 1960s I was asked by the Museum to write an illustrated booklet, *400 years of Music Printing*, an enormous topic to be encompassed in some 10,000 words. One of my terms of reference was to mention unique

Introduction

items in the Museum's collections. Three of these were the so-called 'Constance Gradual' of *c* 1473, and the two remarkable pieces of music printed by John Rastell in London, apparently in the 1520s. My more detailed examination of these *unica* reappears in the present volume. It was while I was working on this same booklet that a member of the Music Room staff, Mr Arthur Keyte, chanced to find on its shelves a piece of nineteenth-century music quite unremarkable in itself (though probably now very scarce), but important because it includes what seems to be a unique account of the operations of the firm of C G Röder, once the most famous of all European music engravers.

Two of the longest articles in this book are due to the fact that in 1969 I had the honour of becoming the Honorary Librarian of the Royal Philharmonic Society, in succession to C B Oldman, the former Principal Keeper of Printed Books, who died in that year. I had previously learned from him something of the importance of its archive, part of which had been deposited on loan in the British Museum in 1913, with later additions. I decided after my retirement to read through all the minutes of the Society's meetings and other papers in order to find out more about the history of its Library. The resultant article is included here, as is also a study of the elusive John Sterland, whom at one time the Society held in high regard.

A very different archive, that of the Wandering Minstrels, also attracted me, and the circumstances of its presentation to the Museum revealed yet another example of its debt to the tireless activity of William Barclay Squire, who had charge of their collection of printed music from 1885 to 1920. It seemed fitting that this volume of essays should be rounded off by my account of that very distinguished servant of the Trustees of the British Museum, who was also one of the greatest music librarians of his time.

Several articles touch on the same topic, as was perhaps unavoidable in a collection which deals largely with the resources of a single institution. But as such passages are not extensive and are generally complementary rather than repetitive, I have left them unchanged. Excision would have entailed some rather awkward rewriting with cumbrous references.

A.H.K.
31 March 1987

Notes

The text of these articles has been reprinted almost unchanged; minor errors have been corrected. References to additional or recent sources of information are given in footnotes marked with an asterisk and printed at the foot of the relevant page. The style or rank of persons remain as they were when the articles were first printed, the original date being added at the end of each, and any subsequent decease of those who were alive at the time of writing has not been recorded. Likewise, all references to the British Museum, to various sections of its library departments and the several names of their collections, stand as they were before the British Library Act of 1973.

Sources

1. The five hundredth Anniversary of Music Printing: the Gradual of *c* 1473 (*The Musical Times*, vol. 114, December 1973, pp. 1220–3)
2. The Significance of John Rastell in early Music Printing (*The Library*, fifth series, vol. LXVI, no. 3, September 1971 pp. 197–214)
3. Rastell reunited (*Essays in Honour of Victor Scholderer*, edited by Dennis E Rhodes, Munich, 1970, pp. 213–8)
4. Fragments of early Printed Music in the Bagford Collection (*Music & Letters*, vol. 40, July 1959, pp. 269–73)
5. C G Röder's Music-Printing Business in 1885 (*Brio*, vol. 2, no. 2, 1965, pp. 1–7)
6. The Mozarts at the British Museum (*Festschrift Albi Rosenthal. Herausgegeben von Rudolph Elvers*, Tutzing, 1984, pp. 157–79)
7. Mozart and Peter Anton Kreusser (*The Music Review*, vol. XXV, no. 2, May 1964, pp. 124–6)
8. Vignettes in early nineteenth-century London Editions of Mozart Operas. (*The British Library Journal*, vol. 6, no. 1, 1980, pp. 24–43)
9. Oldman, Einstein and the Wandering Minstrels (*The Musical Times*, vol. 125, March 1984, pp. 146–8)
10. Frederick Nicolay, Chrysander and the Royal Music Library (*The Monthly Musical Record*, vol. 89, January–February 1959, pp. 13–24)
11. The Quest for Sterland – 1. The London Tavern: a forgotten Concert Hall (*The Musical Times*, vol. 127, July 1986, pp. 382–5)
12. The Quest for Sterland – 2. Sterland, the Harmonic Society and Beethoven's fourth Symphony (*The Musical Times*, vol. 127, August 1986, pp. 434–8)
13. The Quest for Sterland – 3. Don Giovanni in London before 1817 (*The Musical Times*, vol. 127, September 1986, pp. 487–93)
14. The Library of the Royal Philharmonic Society (*The British Library Journal*, vol. 11, no. 1, 1985, pp. 1–24)
15. The Wandering Minstrels and their Archive (*Ars iocundissima. Festschrift für Kurt Dorfmüller, zum 60. Geburtstag. Herausgegeben von Horst Leuchtmann und Robert Münster*. Tutzing, 1984, pp. 169–77)
16. William Barclay Squire, 1855–1927: music librarian (*The Library*, fifth series, vol. XII, no. 1, March 1957, pp. 1–10)

Acknowledgements

For permission to reprint this collection of articles, as given and numbered in the above list of sources, my grateful thanks are due to: Messrs Novello & Co, London – 1, 9, 11–13; the Council of the Bibliographical Society, London – 2, 16; Dr Karl H Pressler, Munich – 3; the editors of *Music & Letters*, Oxford – 4; the United Kingdom Branch of the International Association of Music Libraries – 5; A F Leighton-Thomas Esq, Burry Port, Dyfed, editor of *The Music Review* – 7; the British Library Board, London – 8, 14; Messrs Stainer & Bell, London – 10.

List of illustrations

1. The 'Constance' Gradual. (Constance? c 1473.) British Library, Printed Books, I.B. 15154.
2a-c The three-part song 'Tyme to pas', from John Rastell's play *A new Interlude and a mery of the iiii Elements*, John Rastell: London, c 1525. British Library, Printed Books, C.39.b.17.
3a,b A fragmentary ballad 'Away Mornynge', John Rastell: London. c 1520. British Library, Music Library, K.8.k.8.
4. Water-colour of the courtyard of Montagu House. c 1842. British Museum, Department of Prints and Drawings, 1939-3-10-1.
5. Mozart's *God is our Refuge*, K.20. Autograph. 1765. British Library, Music Library, K.10.a.17.(3).
6. *The favourite Overture, Songs, Duetts, &c in Mozart's celebrated opera Le Nozze di Figaro*, for the pianoforte ... arranged ... by J. Mazzinghi. D'Almaine, London, c 1816. British Library, Music Library, h.1632.a.(3).
7. *The favorite Overture, Songs, Duetts, &c. in Mozart's celebrated Opera Il Don Giovanni*, for the piano forte ... arranged by J. Mazzinghi. D'Almaine, London, c 1816. British Library, Music Library, h.1632.a.(1).
8. *The favorite Overture, Songs, Duetts &c in Mozart's celebrated opera La clemenza di Tito* for the pianoforte arranged by J. Mazzinghi. D'Almaine, London, c 1818. The British Library, Music Library, h.1632.a.(4).
9. *The favorite Songs, Duetts &c. in Mozart's celebrated Opera Cosi fan tutte* for the piano forte arranged ... by J. Mazzinghi. D'Almaine, London, c 1823. The British Library, Music Library, h.1632.a.(5).
10. *The favourite Overture, Songs, Duetts &c. in Mozart's celebrated Opera Il Flauto Magico* for the piano forte ... arranged ... by J. Mazzinghi. D'Almaine, London, c 1823. British Library, Music Library, h.1632.a.(2).
11. *Selection of favorite Airs &c from 'Il Don Giovanni'* Arranged for two performers on the pianoforte ... by J. Mazzinghi. D'Almaine, London, c 1817. British Library, Music Library, h.321.j.(4.)
12. Painting of Giuseppe Ambrogetti as Don Giovanni in Act 2, finale, of Mozart's opera. 1819.
13. *Selections from Mozart's celebrated opera Il flauto magico or Zauberfloete, arranged for two performers on the pianoforte*. Book 4, J Power, London, c 1819. British Library, Music Library, g.382.h.
14. *Mozart's celebrated opera, Cosi fan tutte*. Preston, London, c 1828. British Library, Music Library, H.1847.m.(4.)
15. Water-colour drawings of Miss Betts and Miss Cawse in *Tit for Tat (Così fan tutte)*. 1828. National Portrait Gallery, London, 1962.J. (Kerslake, no. 739.)
16. Water-colour drawing of the London Tavern. c 1848. British Museum, Department of Prints and Drawings, Crace XXIV, sheet 21, no. 42.
17. Beethoven's fourth Symphony. Score, written by John Sterland. 1807. Title page. British Library, Western Manuscripts, R.P.S. Loan 4.5.
18. *Mozart's Grand opera Don Juan. The principal parts performed at Mr Griffin's Concert, Hanover Square, April 20 1809*. London, 1809. British Library, Music Library, Hirsch IV. 1377.b.(3.)
19. Miniature of Samuel Chappell by Thomas Overton, 1823.
20. Water-colour drawing of the Argyll Rooms, Regent Street, 1825. British Museum, Department of Prints and Drawings, Crace Portfolio XXIX, sheet 14, no. 25.
21. *Catalogue of the Library belonging to the Philharmonic Society, London*, c 1823. Title page. British Library, Western Manuscripts, Loan 48.11/2.

List of illustrations

22 *Catalogue of the Library belonging to the Philharmonic Society, London*, c 1823. p. 27. British Library, Western Manuscripts, Loan 48.11/2.
23 An untitled manuscript catalogue of the Philharmonic Society's library, begun c 1846. British Library, Western Manuscripts, Loan 48.11/3, fol.15^v.
24 Drawing of William Barclay Squire by William Strang, 1904. British Library, Music Library.

Pl. 4, pl. 16, and pl. 20 are reproduced by courtesy of The Trustees of the British Museum, and pl. 15 by courtesy of the Trustees of the National Portrait Gallery. I am most grateful to Mrs Jill Croft-Murray and to the late Commander C E Sclater DSO, for allowing me to reproduce pl. 12 and pl. 19 respectively.

Music Printing

1 The 'Constance' Gradual, c 1473. fol. 1ʳ. 308 × 220 mm.

1

The five-hundredth anniversary of music printing
The Gradual of *c*.1473

The illustration opposite (pl. 1) shows the *recto* of the first leaf of a Gradual which was probably printed in about 1473 and is therefore almost certainly the earliest music printing of any kind.[1] It is the work of an unknown printer whose press stood somewhere in south Germany. Although these statements of time and provenance may seem tentative and over-cautious, they are quite characteristic of the imperfect state of our knowledge of much that concerns early printing, especially many of the books which were printed before the beginning of the year 1501 and are now known as 'incunabula' or incunables. But while there are good reasons for ascribing this Gradual to '*c* 1473', and to 'south Germany', a later date and a more precise location have also been proposed. Accordingly, the year 1973, as the probable 500th anniversary of the book's appearance, provides an appropriate occasion to put on record all the known facts about it, to review the evidence for its conjectural date and possible provenance, to explain its technical significance, and to say something of its importance as a landmark in the history of music.

Apart from a fragment of seven leaves in the University Library at Tübingen, only one complete copy of the Gradual exists. It was acquired by the British Museum on 19 June 1846 from A Asher & Co. of Berlin, apparently at auction, and now bears the pressmark I.B. 15154. The descriptive catalogue entry[2] for the book is as follows:

GRADUALE   Undated
1ᵃ [A]D te leuai animam me am ‖ deus meus in te confido non ‖ erube scam ...
160ᵃ END: ...
[A]g nus dei qui tol lis peccata ‖ mun di Do na nobis pa cem Finit feliciter.
Folio. [a–m⁸ n¹⁰; o² p–t⁸ v¹².] 160 leaves. Text and music alternating line by line. Type: ?130. Many rough printed capitals; spaces left for the rest. The music is printed on a stave of five lines. The type-page is enclosed in lead rules at the sides, and measures about 238 × 148 mm.
    308 × 220 mm. Foliation, as far as the end of quire o, and capitals supplied in red. The titles of the various feasts, &c are written in red. The F line is ruled over in red throughout. Traces of manuscript quiring as above; quire o is doubtful and perhaps n¹⁰ + ² should be read. Old stamped leather, with scrolls inscribed abrosi keller, and a paper label.

Like many other incunabula, the book has no 'colophon' – the final statement which, at best, included the printer's name, the town he worked in, and the date. Evidence for these must therefore be drawn from the Gradual itself, and from other books known to have been printed at the same press and in the same type. There are only two such books, a Breviary and a Psalter. Of the latter, only two leaves are extant (BM I.A.15152). But there are two copies of the former, and one of them, now in the Fürstliche Bibliothek at Donaueschingen, was rubricated in 1473. Although a book was not always rubricated as soon as it was printed, the delay would not normally have exceeded a year at the most. The earliest likely date for the Breviary is therefore 1472. The chronological relation of the Breviary to the Gradual is hard to define. Although the former included an additional text-type not used in the latter, this is no evidence for priority or otherwise. But the fact that only three books from this press are known suggests strongly that it had a short life. Again, the rather primitive appearance of the type, the rough press-work and the absence of signatures combine to point to the earlier 1470s. From this evidence, considered in conjunction with the rubrication date of the Breviary, it can be argued that 1472 and 1474 are in all probability the extreme limits for the life of this press. The date '*c* 1473' for the Gradual is therefore likely to be correct within a year or so either way.

As to the location of the press, the evidence is more shadowy. It was originally assigned to Augsburg by the distinguished British Museum incunabulist Robert Procter (1868–1903). His preliminary note to the catalogue entry quoted above reads thus:

This Gradual is clearly for use in Bayern: the prominent saints are SS Laurence, George and Ulrich. As the British Museum copy was bound by Ambros Keller, it probably belongs to Augsburg ... This conjecture is supported by the fact that the watermarks, large ox-head without nostrils, with rod, crown and rosette above and cross-keys, are found in Augsburg manuscripts in and after 1472 and 1462 respectively (the ox-head further in Zainer and Bämler books of 1480–90, the cross-keys in Zainer's 1472 Isidorus, Etymologiae, I.B. 5438).

While the alleged *termini post quos* for these distinctive watermarks add some confirmation to the early date proposed for the Gradual, the conjectural ascription to Augsburg has not stood the test of time, and subsequent research by the late Victor Scholderer called it into question. The occurrence of an Augsburg binder's name on the Gradual does not suffice to show that the book was printed there, although Keller made a brief appearance as a printer some six years later. The evidence of the paper is also inconclusive because, as the research of the late Allan Stevenson[3] has shown, paper was a mobile commodity during the incunable period. In fact, though the evidence may seem to fit Augsburg circumstantially, it does not actually point to it.

Again, the prominence of certain saints appropriate to southern Germany does not necessarily identify the place of its production with any of the towns in which it could be used. This is especially so when such an identification would postulate a new centre for incunable printing. To assign the Gradual to Constance, on the analogy of the Constance Breviary already mentioned, would thus be equally hazardous. No more precise location than 'southern Germany', then, can be safely given to the printer of these books. But however vague our knowledge of the printer of the Gradual, it certainly antedates, by probably not much less than two years, the next earliest book of printed music, which is the Missal printed in Rome in 1476 by Ulrich Han (a native of Ingolstadt). This Missal is also the first book containing printed music (other than the Gerson mentioned in n.1, with its merely diagrammatic notes) which included a colophon giving the actual date of printing.

Here we must digress to consider the references made to the Gradual in Kathi Meyer-Baer's *Liturgical Music Incunabula: a Descriptive Catalogue*,[4] because this is the only comprehensive study of the subject and the only one which attempts with some authority to place the Gradual in a complete chronological and topographical sequence of liturgical printing. The following is the text of the relevant passages:

p. viii (and pl. 7): Probably the earliest book with music printed from types.
p. xi: It is printed with the type used in the Constance Breviary dated 'not after 1473', and, on the basis of the watermarks, has been ascribed to the press of Guenther Zainer at Augsburg. It may be the earliest known example of music printed with type throughout a whole book.
p. xx: [ligatures, gothic] *Graduale Constantiense*
p. xxxi. The *Graduale* set in the type of the printer of the Constance service books and published, I believe, at about the same time as the Missal printed by Han.
p. 5: [no. 15] *Graduale*: Augsburg? Zainer? ... types of the text identical with the Breviarïum Constantiense, 'not after 1473'.
p. 48: [part of a chronological list]
   after 1475 Psalterium Strasbourg Flach
   c 1476 Directorium Const. s.l. s.typ.
       Graduale. Augsburg? Zainer?
   1476 Miss. Romanum Rome Han

There are two more references, in the indexes (pp. 62 and 63), giving 'Zainer' as the printer of no. 15 (the Gradual).

Three points emerge. First, the attribution of the Gradual to Zainer is based on an unwarranted inference from the passage about the watermarks quoted above from the British Museum catalogue. Second, there is a contradiction between the statements on p. viii and p. xxxi, and again, between p. viii and the erroneous dating of the Gradual as '*c* 1476' in the list on p. 48. Third, there is an unjustified application of the adjective 'Constantiense' to both the Gradual and the Breviary, which also contradicts the attribution of the former to Zainer's press in Augsburg. It is important that all these confusing errors should not be perpetuated. The book should simply be referred to as 'the Gradual of *c* 1473'.

Nomenclature and date apart, the significant historical fact about this book is that it had been preceded by a dozen other printed liturgical works in which the music was supplied not by printing but in manuscript in spaces left blank on purpose. (For a particular reason, to be explained later, this practice continued throughout the incunable period and for some time thereafter.) Such spaces, with the notes filled in by hand, occur in the earliest of all liturgies, the famous Mainz Psalter of 1457, which suggests that the need to print music must have been recognized from the very beginning of printing. It is therefore likely that experiments, all trace of which is now lost, were made at some time during the two decades that elapsed between the perfection of the art by Gutenberg from 1450 to 1455 and the production of the Gradual. For printers must have realized that there was a wide demand for printed liturgical music and that the continued use of a mixture of print and manuscript was anomalous. Moreover, the music printing in the Gradual, though not of high quality, reaches a fair standard of competence: without a period of experiment, the formidable technical difficulties could hardly have been overcome. On the other hand, the printing of the text is irregular and has a rather primitive appearance. This suggests that two printers, of varying skill, may have been working together.

By the time the Gradual came to be printed, the design and manufacture of text types did not present much difficulty. But music type had to be developed *de novo*, from a design copied, as were early letter forms, from manuscripts. The second stage was to cut the several punches for the notes, clefs and directs, and then make the matrixes from which the font of type could be cast. All this took time, and could be done only after careful thought had been given to the size of the type in proportion to the stave lines, the text and general balance of the page. Even after the type had been designed and cut, its use in the forme was difficult. There were two particular reasons for this. One was that notes, unlike letters, had to be set and printed not along a single line but at a variety of vertical points. The second, even more complex, reason was that whereas most book-printing needed but one impression of the paper on to the inked surface of the type, all early music required two.

The process was very slow and laborious. For the first impression, the printer set in the forme the types for the underlaid text and the narrow, oblong metal blocks incised with the stave lines. He packed numerous un-inked quads into the spaces to prevent the type from shifting in the forme. After inking it, the printer then wiped surplus ink from all but the raised surfaces, put the forme in a press, laid the paper on it and took the first impression for the whole edition of each sheet. Next, having emptied the forme, he set up the type for the notes, clefs and directs, packing the interstices with even more quads than before. This had to be done with the greatest possible precision, to ensure that when the already partly printed sheet was laid on the forme again, the impression was 'registered' at exactly the right points along the stave and in correct vertical relationship to the underlaid text. This second impression, like the first, had to be repeated for the whole edition of each sheet. This was a slow and delicate process only used (and in a relatively simple way) for books when they contained initials or sections which were printed in a distinctive colour.

We can now see that the Gradual was a great achievement, the result of patient craftsmanship wedded to a new, remarkable skill. That the demand for such books increased steadily is shown by the fact that the total of incunabula with printed music ultimately reached about 270. But though music printing had spread to most countries of central and southern Europe before 1501, in many books notes or staves (sometimes both) were still added by hand until then and for some time later. This was not solely due, however, to lack of type and skill. Since the Roman use was not followed everywhere, special local needs could be served more easily if the music was added by hand. The same service book could be sold in different places.

Whether any of those who printed liturgical music also tried to solve the problems of printing polyphonic works seems doubtful. They can hardly have been unaware of the quantity available or of the need for multiple performing copies. But the technical difficulties were vastly greater than those of liturgical printing, and we have no record of any attempt to overcome them. Though there are three books containing the note forms of mensural monody, printed from type, none was the work of a printer of liturgies. The earliest was the *Grammatica brevis* of Franciscus Niger, printed by Theodor of Würzburg (1480). Here the notes, lacking staves, are used to indicate the syllabic quantities of verses in elegiac and four other Latin metres. No other example is found until *c* 1496, when mensural note shapes appear in two treatises printed in Paris by Michel Tholoze – an edition of Gerson's *Utilissime musicales regule*, and the anonymous *L'art et instruction de bien danser*. In both, the type for the notes (again, without staves) was crudely designed and the setting of it irregular and rough.

Consequently, when Petrucci began to produce his superb polyphonic partbooks barely five years later, and at first by triple impression, their technical refinement and sheer perfection of design seem almost miraculous. With Petrucci, indeed, there opens a new chapter in the annals of music printing, some 28 years after the appearance of the Gradual which set up a milestone in the diffusion of musical culture in *c* 1473.

[1973]

Notes

1 In making this statement, I have discounted Charlier de Gerson's *Collectorium super magnificat*, printed at Esslingen by Conrad Fyner in 1473. This contains five identical square notes printed in descending sequence to illustrate the mystical meaning of certain words in the text. 'This passage' (I quote my *Four Hundred Years of Music Printing*, 1968, p. 11) 'is little more than a curiosity, devoid of significance as music, to which it stands in the same relationship as would the first five letters of the alphabet, if so printed, to the words of a sentence'. In the present article, I am indebted to George D. Painter for valuable advice.
2 *Catalogue of Books printed in the fifteenth century now in the British Museum,* ii (1912), p. 401
3 *The Problem of the Missale speciale* (London, 1967)
4 Published by the Bibliographical Society (London, 1962)

2

The significance of John Rastell in early music printing

Introduction

The extant music printed by John Rastell consists of only two examples, one complete, the other a tantalizing fragment, both in the British Museum. The complete piece is a short three-part song (pl. 2a-c) which occurs in his own play, *A new Interlude and a mery of the Nature of the iiij Elements*.[1] The fragment comprises some thirty notes of music printed on a heavily cropped broadside (pl. 3a,b) which has become known from a refrain-like phrase in the text, as the 'ballad' *Away Morning*.[2] Rastell printed these pieces with a distinctive music type of which no other example is found anywhere during his lifetime, and only one later, namely in the *Goostly Psalmes* printed by John Gough about 1540. Rastell used a process by which text, staves, notes, clefs, bar-lines, time-signatures, and directs were all printed at one and the same impression. It is true that the matrices from which Rastell's music type was cast were struck twice, once with a punch cut with the staff segment, and again with a punch bearing the note or other symbol. These matrices may therefore be regarded as technically less advanced than those which Attaingnant designed for the remarkable quantity of books of chansons, tablatures, and other music which he issued in Paris from April 1528 until 1550. Nevertheless, the two pieces which Rastell printed were both the result of the single impression process. Their date is of great interest in the history of music-printing because both are likely to have been produced not later than the time when Attaingnant was first active, probably even earlier. Moreover, no dated music printed anywhere by one impression is known earlier than Attaingnant's first book.

Since, unfortunately, neither of Rastell's pieces now bears a date, both have been the subject of a wide range of conjectures, some of which were made in blissful ignorance of their implications, while others have been based on what was, to say the least, a restricted point of view. My purpose in this paper is to review these conjectures and re-examine the most cogent of them in the light of the multifarious evidence, partly familiar, partly new, which has some bearing on the matter. I wish also to pose a number of questions which have not, as far as I know, been asked before, and see if the answers help to resolve the conflict of opinion. Whatever the chronological

8 *The significance of John Rastell in early music printing*

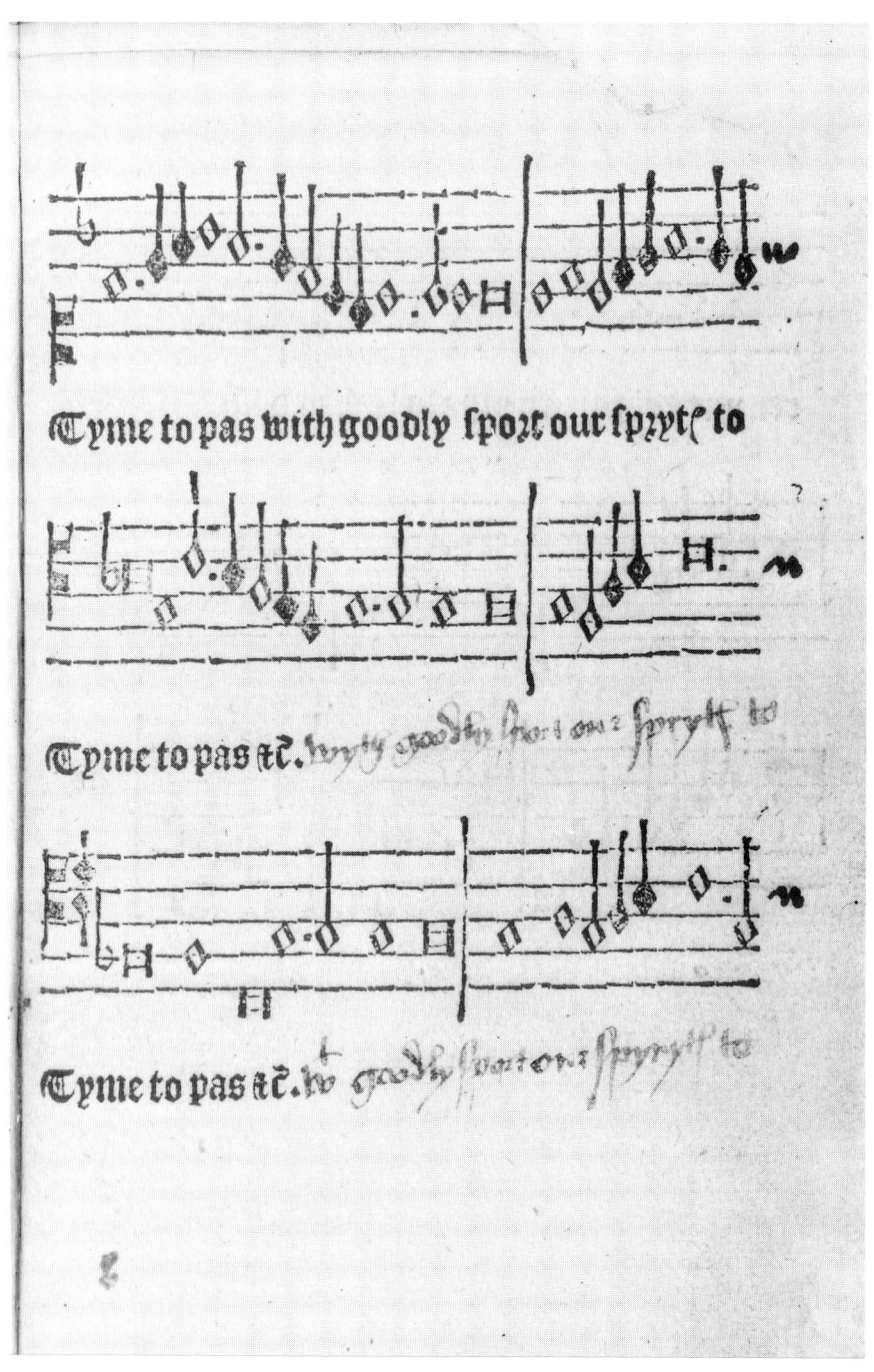

2a The three-part song, 'Tyme to pas' from John Rastell's play *A new Interlude*, etc. *c* 1525. Sig. E 5^r. 160 × 102 mm.

2b The three-part song 'Tyme to pas', from John Rastell's play *A new Interlude*, etc. c 1525. Sig. E 5ᵛ. 160 × 102 mm.

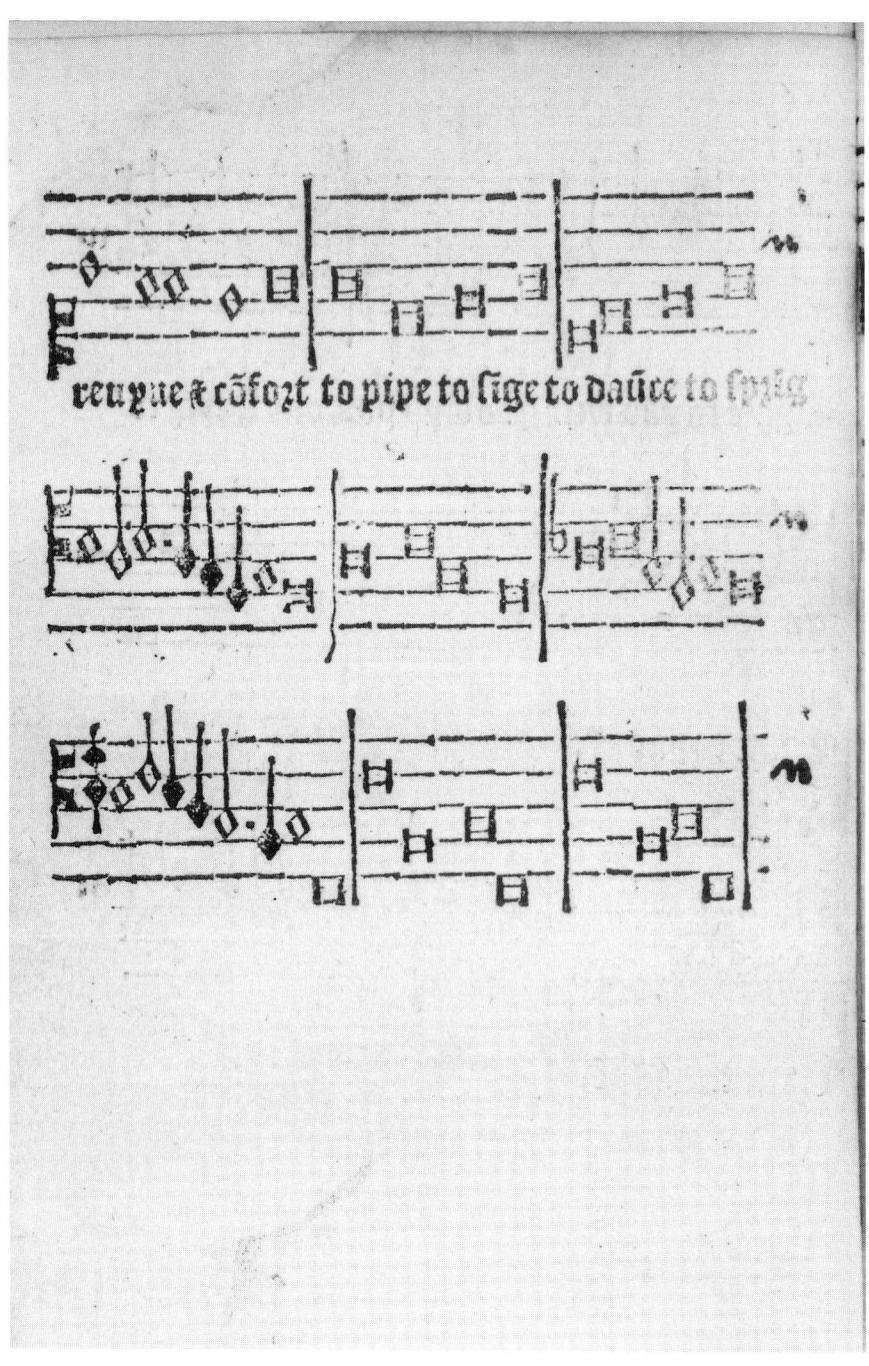

2c The three-part song 'Tyme to pas', from John Rastell's play *A new Interlude*, etc. *c* 1525. Sig. E 6^r. 164 × 102 mm.

outcome, it should at least be possible to appreciate the general significance of Rastell's music printing in its European context, remembering that in practical terms it is the result that is relevant, not the means. But before I discuss the typographical and other problems, I should like to put them in perspective by stating the limitations of music printing until Rastell's time, and then say something of the life of this remarkable man.

The first book of printed music of any kind was, most probably, the 'Constance' gradual which was published in or about 1473. This was printed by two impressions, first, the staves and the text, second, the notes and clefs.[3] For the next fifty years or so, all type-printed music, whether plainsong or in the considerably more complex mensural notation, was produced by this same process. However elegant and aesthetically pleasing the result, it was so laborious and expensive as to be uneconomic. Yet this very period was one of the most important in musical history during which many famous and prolific musicians all over Europe were composing large quantities of polyphonic vocal music and much lute music, for which there was a considerable market if only a cheaper and simpler method of printing could be invented. This required a new typographic principle, by means of which each note would be cast as a separate unit, with the adjacent portions of the stave attached to the stem and head of the note. Only thus could all the elements of a composition be set in the forme together and printed at one impression. Whoever could devise such a process would make a momentous contribution to the spread of musical culture, comparable indeed in the importance of its impact to that which the very invention of printing had made on the mind of man.

Fournier, Haultin, and Attaingnant

In 1765 Pierre Fournier wrote in his *Traité historique et critique sur l'origine et les progrès des caractères de fonte pour l'impression de musique*: 'La première impression de musique est due à la typographie. Pierre Hautin [sic], graveur, fondeur & imprimeur à Paris, en fit les premiers poinçons vers 1525. . . . Il en fit l'usage pour lui-même, & en vendit à plusieurs imprimeurs qui les mirent en œuvre.' Fournier then went on to explain the nature of type-printing at one impression, and stated that Haultin's type was first used by Attaingnant in 1530.

For nearly two centuries this statement about Haultin's invention was quoted as if it were an infallible truth. While it was sensible enough to accept the accuracy of what Fournier wrote about the well-documented seventeenth century and the typographical innovations of his own generation, a glance at the context of his remarks about Haultin should have aroused the

12 The significance of John Rastell in early music printing

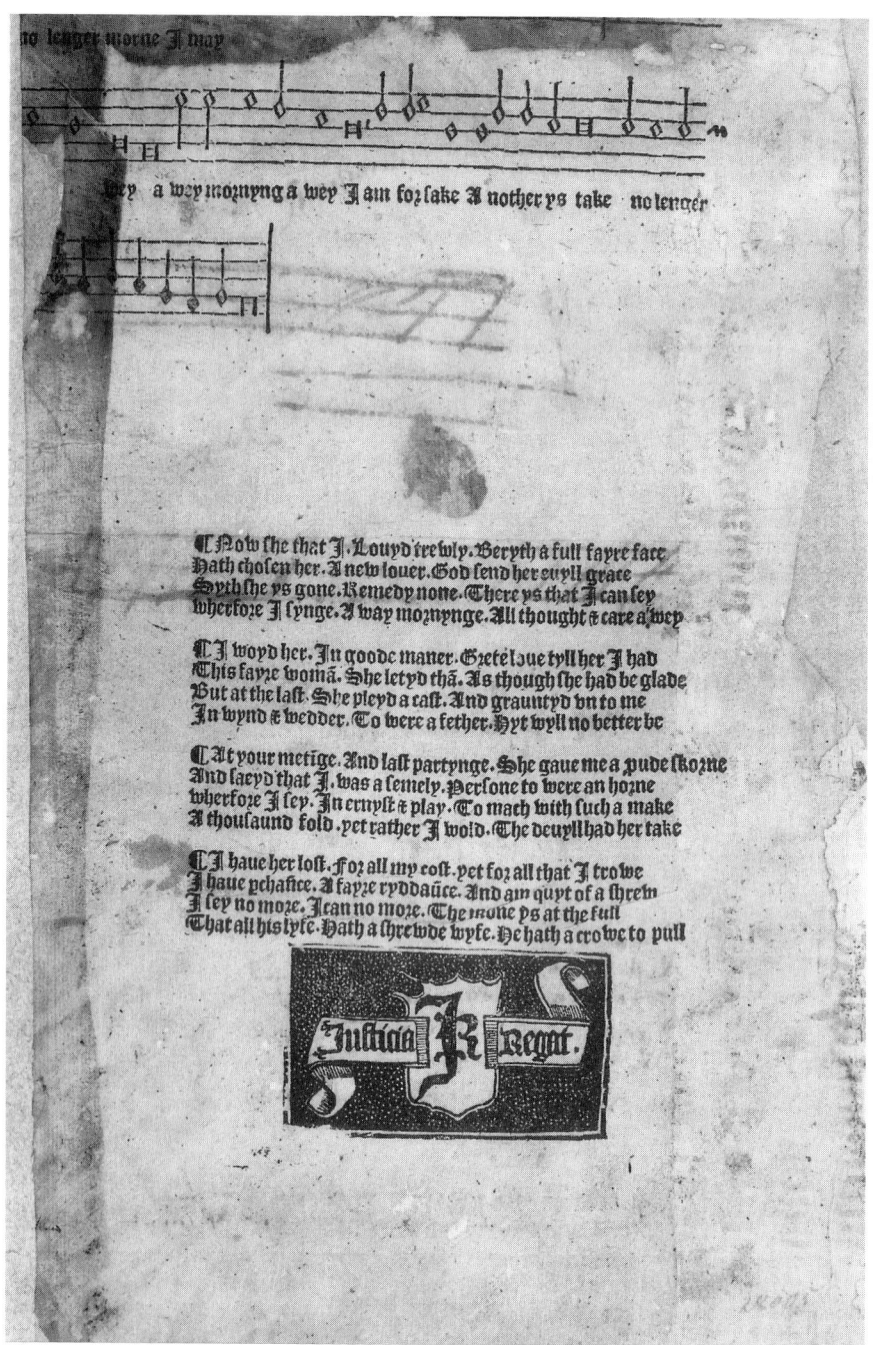

3a Recto of a fragmentary ballad 'Away mornynge', c 1520. 298 × 190 mm.

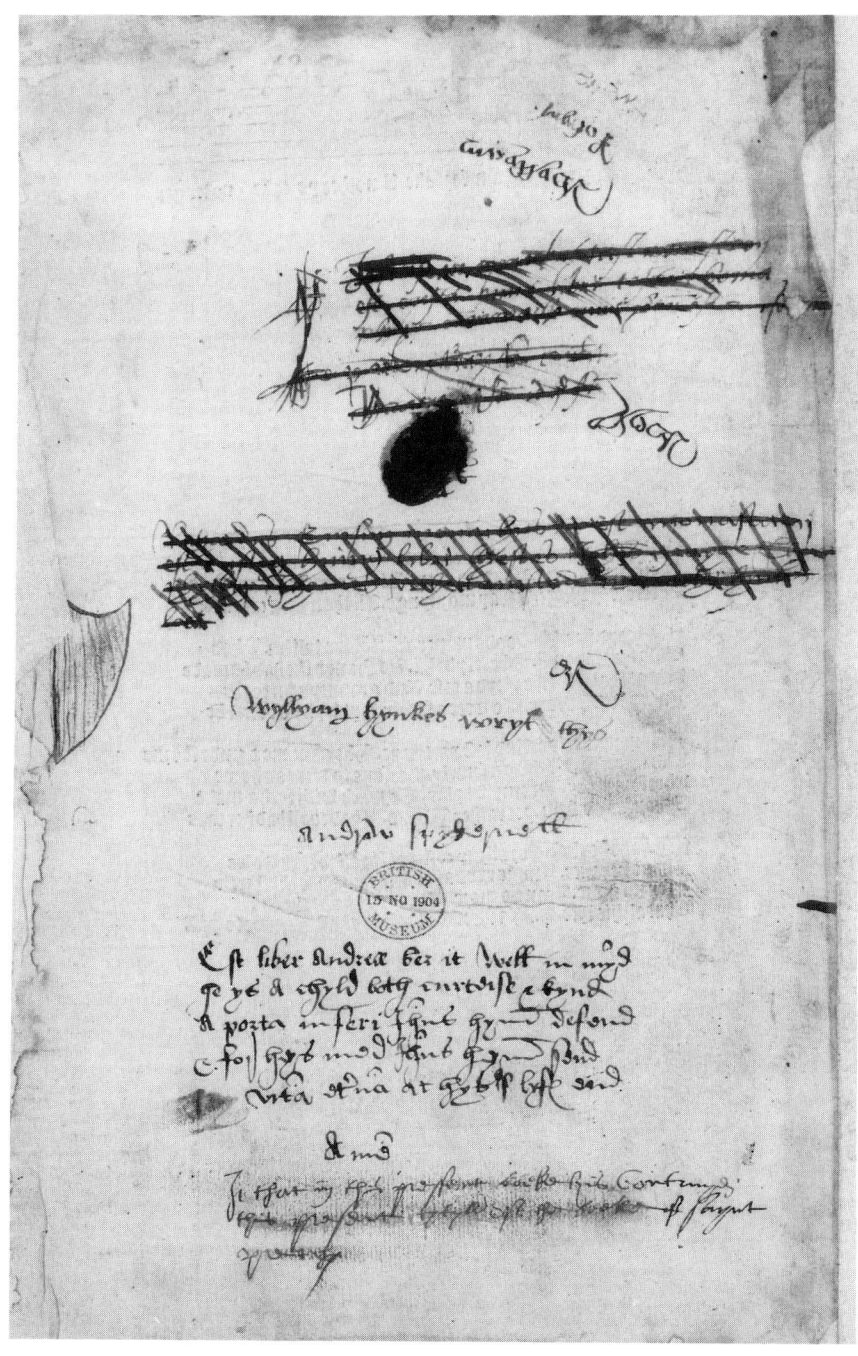

3b Verso of a fragmentary ballad 'Away mornynge', c 1520. 298 × 190 mm.

suspicions of anyone with the least knowledge of musical history. Fournier was writing at a time when the study of early music had scarcely begun to emerge from the mists of speculation which cloud the opening chapters of the histories by such eighteenth-century writers as Martini, Laborde, Burney, and Hawkins. In the sentence immediately before his dictum about Haultin, Fournier wrote: 'L'origine des notes de musique remonte au commencement du onzième siècle, vers 1028. Guy Aretin . . . en est l'inventeur'! This is simply rubbish, and is of the same order of credibility as the notion that the Creation took place in 4004 BC. While Guido's theoretical writings helped to popularize the stave, he certainly did not 'invent' notes, still less 'vers' 1028! Such a statement, standing next to the sentence about Haultin, should have cast doubts on its dogmatic value. But with one notable, long-forgotten, exception in the nineteenth century (to which I shall allude shortly), no doubts at all seem to have been voiced until the mid 1950s, when two writers expressed their scepticism independently. First, Harry Carter, in a paper read to this Society* in 1955,[4] cast a passing doubt on Fournier, and then in 1956 came an important article on Haultin by François Lesure, published in *Die Musik in Geschichte und Gegenwart*.[5] He pointed out that no book of music printed with Haultin type is extant before 1547, and that since this Haultin died in 1586, he cannot have been born much before 1520. It is necessary to repeat the facts about Haultin's so-called 'invention', because, though now discredited in specialist journals, it still stands in works of reference and other recent books. It is, for instance, found in Louis Desgrave's standard work *Les Haultin* (1960), where Fétis is solemnly quoted for the fact that Haultin began to cast music type 'vers 1524'. Again, Steele's statements about Haultin still stand in the uncorrected reprint of his book issued by this Society in 1965. Last year, Samuel Pogue gave an account[6] of Haultin's possible relationship to Attaingnant which is, to say the least, ambiguous. Most recently, the story of Haultin's 1525 invention is repeated in the tenth edition of Scholes's *Oxford Companion to Music* (1970).

Clearly, the ghost of the Haultin legend is a tenacious phantom. This must be my justification for having mentioned its appearances at some length. I hope, however, that now we have Daniel Heartz's magisterial book on Attaingnant (1969),[7] it will be laid for all time. That the ghost walked at all after 1956 is remarkable: that it was seen after 1961, inexplicable. For in that year Heartz published an important article[8] in which his main purpose was to describe a fragmentary, undated part-book which, on bibliographical grounds, could be shown to be a few months later than Attaingnant's first dated part-book. In this article Heartz quoted the complete text of a

---

* *ie* The Bibliographical Society.

privilege granted to this printer in 1531 (not mentioned by Lesure), and pointed out that the essential parts of it had been published by the great Austrian musicologist A W Ambros in his monumental history of music, as long ago as 1868![9] Even then, indeed, Ambros shrewdly asked: 'Wie kommt es, dass Pierre Hautin von seinen Typen nicht früher Gebrauch machte?' Ambros's publication of part of Attaingnant's privilege and that shrewd question that he put, over a century ago, are surely most telling. Had the older bibliographers consulted Ambros's history for the general background of early music printing, we should have been spared some pointless and confusing speculation. The reference to Ambros is doubly worth giving here because Heartz does not repeat it in his book. The salient passage of Attaingnant's rather repetitive privilege runs thus:

Having received the humble supplication of our well-loved Pierre Attaingnant, printer-bookseller dwelling in the University of Paris, stating that heretofore no person in this our realm had undertaken to cut, found, and fashion notes and characters for the printing of figural music in choses faictes or tablatures for the playing of lutes, flutes, and organs, because of the intricate conception, long consumption of time, and very great expenses and labors necessary to that purpose, the said suppliant, by protracted excogitation and mental effort and with very great expense, labour, and genius, has invented and brought to light the method and industry of cutting, founding, and printing the said notes and characters both of the said music and choses faictes as of the said tablatures for the playing of lutes, flutes, and organs, of which he has printed, has had printed, and hopes in the future to print, many books and quires of masses, motets, hymns, chansons, as well as for the said playing of lutes, flutes, and organs [and so on].[10]

This privilege, then, was granted to Attaingnant over three years after he had printed his first dated book in 1528, a piece of printing which shows such a high degree of technical excellence that we may assume that his 'excogitation' and consequent experiments took several years. As Heartz remarks, it is inconceivable that Attaingnant would have dared in his supplication to make any claim to invention if he knew (as he could hardly have failed to do) that Haultin had 'invented' the same process some six years before.

Attaingnant's first book of music was the *Chansons nouvelles en musique à quatre parties*, which he printed on 4 April 1527 (N.S. 1528).[11] It is important to note that the year (though not the month or the precise title) of this first book has been correctly given in common works of reference which first appeared long ago – in Fétis,[12] in Brunet,[13] and in Grove[14] and has been repeated in their later editions. All these facts about Fournier and Attaingnant should be borne in mind when we come to consider the implications of the dates that various authorities have assigned to the music printed by Rastell, to whom we may now return.

Rastell's career

Besides being a printer, Rastell led a full and adventurous life of many parts which merits consideration here only in so far as his character and activities may have some bearing on his printing of music. Most of what is known about him is to be found in the first chapter of A W Reed's *Early Tudor drama*.[15] Rastell was born in London about 1475, and was partly educated in the Middle Temple. At some date before 1504 he married the sister of Thomas More, and soon after moved from London to Coventry where he became active in business and litigation. He served as coroner for nearly two years, and had close associations with wealthy Coventry citizens who were 'merchants of the staple of Calais'. By 1512 he had returned to London, and served through the French war of 1512–14, during which he was partly responsible for the transport of artillery. (He served also, intermittently, in the later French campaign of 1523–5, as a trench-maker.) At some time in 1515–16 Rastell went to France to procure the font of secretary type which he used in printing his law-books.

In March 1517, probably inspired by the adventures of Hythloday in his brother-in-law's *Utopia*, Rastell sailed from Greenwich on a voyage to Newfoundland, taking among his company 'Thomas Bercula, printer'. But the crew mutinied, the ship put in at Waterford, and in due course, after returning to London, Rastell prosecuted the master mariner concerned on 15 November 1519. From the summer of 1517 to some time in the summer of 1519, Rastell remained in Ireland, and it is generally agreed, from internal evidence in the *Interlude*, that he wrote the play while he was away.

When the great banqueting hall was built on the Field of the Cloth of Gold in the summer of 1520, Rastell had a good deal to do with the construction and decoration of its elaborate roof. He was responsible for another decorated roof, also in 1520, at the Round-House in Calais. His expertise in pageantry (which Reed believes was fostered during his years spent in Coventry) was put to good use in the production of the great spectacle which was mounted in London in 1522 when the Emperor Charles V went in state with Henry VIII to St Paul's Cathedral. On this occasion, Rastell is said to have provided verses which were used during the shows.[16] Five years later Rastell was responsible for building another decorated roof, this time for the banqueting hall erected at Greenwich, in which a pageant with music was prepared for the entertainment of the ambassadors sent from France to arrange a marriage for Princess Mary. The music included songs rendered in English by two singers.[17]

At Michaelmas 1524 Rastell took a lease of some land in Finsbury Fields, facing on to what is now Old Street, and built a house with a large, permanent stage in the grounds, the earliest recorded in England. It is possible that the *Interlude* was revived for performance on it, and if so it was probably for a public audience. In 1529 Rastell became a Member of Parliament, and then again went to France for several months. The rest of his career was occupied with public affairs and litigation, in addition to printing, though on a diminishing scale. Rastell must now have been much saddened by the imprisonment and death of More, and gradually succumbed to ill-health and trouble. He was himself committed to prison late in 1535, because of his opposition to a Royal Proclamation in the matter of tithes, and died there in the following summer. Not long before, in one of his letters to Thomas Cromwell, after complaining how his printing business had shrunk, Rastell wrote thus: 'Syr, I am an old man, I loke not to lyff long, and I regard ryches much as I do chyppes, save only to have a lyffing out of det; and I care as much for worldly honor as I care for the fleying of a fether in the wynd.' Such was the pathetic disillusion of Rastell's last years.

His career as a printer was generally thought to have begun about 1512, with Linacre's *Progymnasmata*. But recently it has been put back to about 1505, to which period the preliminary typescript of the new STC assigns his printing of More's translation of *The Lyfe of Johan Picus, Earl of Myrandula*. Thus Rastell printed books for some three decades, for the last came off his press only a few years before he died. The total number of his publications now extant, complete or fragmentary,[18] amounts to about thirty-five. Over half of these consist of law-books and yearbooks, as befitted his profession. The remainder bear eloquent testimony to his versatility and remarkable range of sympathies. There were nine or ten works of literature; two of social history; one each on card-playing, grammar, prediction, and astrology (now lost); and one liturgy. Only two fragmentary leaves of the liturgy survive, none, unfortunately, with music. Yet it is hardly surprising that such a varied output should extend to music, and we may be pretty sure, since the type was expensive, that Rastell printed more separate pieces of it than the fragmentary 'ballad' which we now have.

Plomer[19] states that Rastell learnt the art of printing in France, in some house from which later he found a printer named Guérin to work for him in London. In order to print some of his law-books he procured, as I have mentioned, a font of secretary type from Rouen. Rastell who must have known northern France well, read and probably spoke French. But versatile and resourceful as he was, it seems unlikely that Rastell could read music, well though he understood its use in ceremony and pageant. For in early Tudor England musical literacy was still very limited. Still less then would Rastell have been able to set up music type himself. Nevertheless, he clearly laid some store on this side of his printing business, for in his will[20] he bequeathed to his wife Elizabeth 'my house in St Martyns, with my presse, notes and letters comprised in the same'. Here, the word 'notes' must surely have been used in the sense of 'musical notes', as it was, a little later, by Merbecke and Day.*

It would not, however, have been difficult for Rastell to have obtained advice on the technical aspects of music among his friends and his family circle. In the small world of the court at London he can hardly have failed to know the musicians of the Chapel Royal, and so would have known those who were at the Field of the Cloth of Gold even before that event. Rastell's brother-in-law, Sir Thomas More, was married twice, each time to a lady of some attainments in music. Gittern and viol are prominent in Holbein's picture of the More family, both in the artist's sketch of 1527 and in the first Locky copy of *c* 1590.[21] The Mores' friends included Erasmus, who had been trained at Utrecht Cathedral school for two years as a choirboy under Obrecht. In 1522 or 1523 Rastell's daughter married the future dramatist John Heywood, who was already a noted singer and virginals player, and no mean composer as well. A little later, Heywood became the friend of such famous musicians as John Redford and William Forrest. Bearing in mind these facts about Rastell's own musical background and associations, we can now turn to the two pieces of music which he printed.

The Interlude

The bibliographical history of the *Interlude* is inseparable from that of the *Abridgement of the Statutes* with which it was bound up, probably soon after publication. Since I have fully discussed elsewhere[22] the history of the two books and their relationship, I shall confine myself here to the essential facts. The *Interlude* is the earliest of the Garrick plays now in the British Museum. It is imperfect, lacking sig. D and all after sig. E. The fly-leaf bears two notes, which I have proved to be in the hand of the eighteenth-century antiquary Andrew Gifford, reading, on the recto: 'An Interlude of the Four Elements &c by John Rastel. Puta [*sic*] Anno 1519', and, on the verso: 'The Interlude was bound with Rastel's Abridgemen^t. of the Statutes 1st Impression dated 25th Oct.11.Hen. 8th, ie. 1519'. The copy of the *Abridgement* found its way into the library of the Bristol Baptist College, at whose sale in 1961 it was acquired by the British Museum. There can be very little doubt that this is the copy once bound with the *Interlude*, for several reasons. The latter bears, on sig. E1, the name 'John Pulley 1541' (fig. 1); the *Abridgement*, on sig. Miii verso, has another signature, 'J. Pulley 1633' (fig. 2). The writer of the second

---

* See also R J Roberts, 'John Rastell's Inventory of 1538' *The Library*, 6th series, vol. I, no. 1, March 1979, pp. 34–42

inscription was also named John, and was the grandson of the former. Both were members of the same family, resident from the mid fifteenth century onwards at Bridgnorth in Shropshire. The two books also share a wormhole which penetrates the last leaf of the *Abridgement* and the first of the *Interlude*, at the identical place in the inner, lower margin. Moreover, the offset of Rastell's larger device, from the last leaf of the *Abridgement*, matches exactly, as to margin and spacing, the now faded impression on the title-page of the *Interlude*. It seems unlikely that the two books reached Bridgnorth separately and were bound there. More probably, they were bound in London, soon after publication. The style of the younger Pulley's signature suggests that he was trying his quill in imitation of his grandfather's.★

Let us now look at the various dates assigned to the *Interlude*, and then examine the circumstantial evidence provided by the book itself. Dibdin put it as early as 1510, about which Duff (*DNB* article on Rastell) wrote: 'this is probably too early and "1519" ... is more likely to be correct'. The first British Museum cataloguer, not now identifiable, put [1520?], which was later altered to [1530?], and this still stands today. Steele[23], assuming that the extant copy of the book was printed by Gough, using Rastell's types, gave [John Gough 1539?]. (One wonders if Steele knew that Rastell bequeathed his music type to his widow.) But Steele admitted that if Rastell had originally printed the *Interlude* in about 1520 he would have had 'the honour of introducing one-printing music types'. Unfortunately, and inexcusably, Steele gave '1530' for the date of Attaingnant's first book, with an incorrect title. Squire, in his 1912 catalogue, simply followed Steele's attribution to Gough. In a later article in *The Library* (IV, ix [June 1928], 90), Steele defended 1539, repeating his assertion that one-impression music printing was generally agreed to have been invented by Pierre Haultin in 1525 and first used by Attaingnant in 1530. Rather strangely, Steele did not then mention the 'ballad'. But two years later, Isaac did bring in the 'ballad' for comparison.[24] He refuted Steele's theory about Gough, but did not attempt a date.

It was Greg who tried to bring some sense into the matter. In an article in *The Library*,[25] he considered the *Interlude* and the 'ballad' together. He too found it unlikely that Gough printed the extant copy of the former, and concluded cautiously thus: 'On the whole, I see no way of advancing beyond the position that the *Interlude* and 'ballad' were probably printed by Rastell between 1526 and 1530 inclusive, with some preference for the earlier years of the period. If that is so, Rastell's use of his particular species of music type was almost certainly independent of, and very probably anterior to, that of Attaingnant in Paris; but it would in no way affect the claim of Haultin to

★ Dr A I Doyle believes that both signatures and both dates are mid seventeenth-century.

⸿ with argyng here theyr foly...
⸿ That is not worth iij. strawes
⸿ I loue not this horeson losophers
Nor this great conyng extromers
⸿ That tell how far it is to the sterres
I hate all maner conuyng
I wolde ye knew it I am Ignorance
A lorde I am of gretter pusans
Than the kynge of ynglande or fraunce
ye the grettyst lord lyuyng
⸿ I haue seruautṛ at my retynew
⸿ That longe to me I assure you
Here with in ynglande
That with me yngnorance dwell styll
And terme of lyfe cotynew wyll
A boue v C. thowsand

Sen.   Goggṛ naylys I haue payed so of the
yng.   why man what eylyth ỹ so to blow   (tro
Sen.   For I was at a shrewd fray
yng.   Hast thou any of them slayn than
Sen.   ye I haue slayn them euery man
       Saue them that ran away
yng.   why is any of them skapyd & gone
Sen.   ye by goggṛ body euerychone
       All that euer were there.
                        E.j.

John Pulley
1541

Fig. 1

wollys &c. or ellys the pryse. The one half to the kyng / and the other half to the mayre of the staple the whiche mayre for his discharge shall haue an accion of det at his pleasure of the goodꝭ or ꝑ value. And if the customer within. viij. dayes after the request to hym made by ꝑ pte wyll nat delyuer suche a certyficat / he shall forfeyt to the pte £.li. Prouyded that no pson robbid vp ꝫ ꝑ s̄c ꝫ that prouyd by dew profe shalbe greuyd by this statute / all though that he bryngꝫ nat in his certyficat. And that prouyded also that the wollys woll fell morlyngꝭ or shorlyngꝭ growynge betwene the waters of Tese and twede / northumberland / comberlande / westmerlande / durham / rychmoūde shyre / and northaldertoñ shyre may be shyppyd in the porte of newcastell vpon tyne to passe at theyr pleasure / this acte nat withstandynge. The. iiij. E. iiij. ca. ij.

¶ If any shyp any wollys at newcastel ꝑ be nat of the growyng betwene tese ꝫ twede or of ꝑ coūtes of northumberlande / comberlande / westmerlande / durham / rychmoūde ꝫ northaldertoñ shyres he shall forfeyt the dowble value / and he that wyll se w by accion of det shall recouer ꝑ one half ꝫ the kyng the other half / wherin nother proteccyon nor wager of lawe shall lye. And euery issue

Fig. 2

have been the inventor.' In 1939, Greg, while still tending to 1525 as the date of Haultin's 'invention', expressed himself rather differently[26] regarding the date of the *Interlude*: 'It is likely to be after 1525, and about 1525–7 seems the most likely date.' Similarly, in 1939, Bruce Pattison, in a far-ranging paper 'Notes on early music Printing' read to this Society,*[27] supported the rejection of Steele's theory about Gough, and dated the *Interlude* 'about 1526', but gave yet another wrong date, 1529, for Attaingnant's first publication. Finally, the date given in the preparatory typescript copy of the new STC is [1526?].

Of all those I have mentioned, Greg alone paid any attention to the text of the *Interlude* as evidence, and only to a limited degree. Let us reconsider the circumstances. Rastell returned from Ireland with the manuscript of his play, not much later than the summer of 1519. He devotes a pungent passage in the play to inveighing against the mutineers who halted his expedition, and even when writing the lines must have been planning the court action which he brought against the master mariner in November 1519. Rastell was nothing if not an opportunist. Surely the passage should be regarded as a piece of topical propaganda for his own just cause, and he must have been anxious to get it into print as soon as possible. The passage would have been stale and pointless if printing had been delayed until 1525 or later. Greg argued against an early date for the *Interlude*, on the grounds that Rastell 'did not himself resume active production before 1525–6'. This seems to me dubious, for two reasons. If Rastell could print the *Abridgement* (a book of 112 leaves) between the time of his return and 25 October 1519, he could surely have printed the *Interlude* as well at about this time. (Steele, by the way, records a tradition that the *Interlude* was licensed to Rastell on 25 October 1520.) Moreover, we simply have not enough accurate information about the dates of much of Rastell's possible output from the early 1520s (in which we must include the Dartmouth fragments, not known to Greg in 1930) to justify an assertion that he ceased printing for any particular period. Even if he were out of the country, he could have delegated much to his workmen.

There are two more pieces of evidence in the text of the play which, though admittedly rather less cogent than the allusion to the mutiny, nevertheless contribute something. One is in the lines 'Tyll nowe within this xx yere, | Westwarde be founde new landes' – a clear reference to Cabot's discoveries in 1497. This, too, is a topical allusion which would have continued to lose its point the longer the printing was delayed. The other evidence concerns the three-part song 'Tyme to pas', which is one of five songs all of which occur in sheet E. This episode coincides with the entrance

* *ie* The Bibliographical Society.

of Sensual Appetite, a low character of a type often associated with song and dance in these early Tudor plays. It is quite clear that here Rastell intended a cumulative musico-dramatic effect. Before and after 'Tyme to pas', he printed stave lines where a song was to be sung, leaving them blank from lack of time rather than of type. At another point he printed the words of the ballad of Robin Hood, to be sung by Ignorance with a 'burden' by Humanitie. Further, in the margin of sig. E6ʳ, there is a stage direction, in a contemporary hand, which reads: 'Sēsuall appetite must sȳg thys song and hys cūpanye must answer hym lykwys.'

But, as I have already suggested, Rastell himself was not musically literate. What then did he do when he came back from Ireland with the manuscript of his play in his baggage? We may reasonably suppose that at the centre of this musical episode he had simply indicated that a part-song should be sung. Most probably he would have gone to some musician friend and asked him to provide one. What the friend provided is most interesting, for it is a very close musical parody, in three parts, of a four-part song then current in London. It is found in the so-called 'King Henry VIII's manuscript' in the British Museum. Add. 31922, in which the text is different and begins 'Adew madame et ma mastres'. An edition of this manuscript in its entirety was published by John Stevens in *Music at the Court of Henry VIII*.[28] Stevens pointed out the parodic relationship between the three-part and the four-part songs. The date of Add. 31922 falls between about 1515 and 1525, and since some of the songs also survive in other manuscript sources, they must have been known to a fairly wide public. But the popularity of this kind of song was probably short-lived then as now. Rastell's musician friend based the three-part song so closely on the four-part one that the purpose of parody is inescapable – it must have been intended for an audience then familiar with the original. But parody depends in the first place on topicality. If the printing of the *Interlude* were delayed until 1526 or 1527, this allusion too might have lost some of its point.

It might seem idle to speculate as to who, of the various musicians Rastell could have known, provided the parody. One possible name is that of Dr Robert Cowper, a composer of considerable repute, who wrote, among other works, a madrigal in a play which William Cornish presented at Windsor in 1522. Three songs by Robert Cowper appear in Add. MS 31922. This Cowper is also of interest in this context because his brother, Dr William Cowper, was vicar of Bridgnorth in Shropshire from 1515 to 1525 or later. At least this suggests one possible channel through which the copies of the *Interlude* and the *Abridgement* came into the possession of John Pulley in Bridgnorth by 1541.

The Broadside

The history of the so-called 'ballad' is less complicated, but equally interesting and instructive. It was offered to the British Museum on 26 September 1904 by Ludwig Rosenthal Antiquariat (of 16 Hildegardestrasse, Munich) for £2 10s., and was described thus on the invoice: '1 (Music Fragment) Broadside from an English music print from (about 1510).' The then Keeper of Printed Books, G K Fortescue, reported the offer to the Trustees in the words: 'A fragment in the musical type used by John Rastell in printing "The Interlude of the Four Elements", *c* 1530, the second book printed with musical type in England. Neither the words nor the music of this fragment are known.' After the Trustees had duly sanctioned the purchase, the sheet was catalogued by Esdaile under 'Rastell', as the presumed author of the words (for which there is no evidence) with the date [1520?], and the title slip was revised by A W Pollard. This date still stands, unaltered, in the Museum catalogues and elsewhere.[29] This conjectural date was reasonable enough considering that neither Esdaile nor Pollard had any knowledge of the problems of early music printing. The heading chosen seems extraordinary. It is also remarkable that Squire, who was expert in the subject, should have taken over both heading and date into the Music Catalogue without at least noticing the implications of the twenty-year gap between the date and that assigned to the *Interlude*.

The verso of the 'ballad' offered a line of investigation which Greg noticed but did not pursue. He observed that it had 'evidently come out of a binding'. In fact, the sheet was used as a paste-down for what was probably the left-hand front end-paper of a book which was once in the library of Westminster Abbey or, perhaps, of Westminster School. It bears eighteen irregular lines of writing, by several hands, of which the top eight have been scratched out. But most of what is not legible under a glass can be deciphered with ultra-violet light, and the whole runs as follows:

Wyllyam Robyns

John [one word illegible] monachus westmonasteriensis
Est custos huius libri teste Thoma
Phyllyp [rest of line illegible]

[two lines illegible]

Richardus Empson monachus Westmonasteris̄
est custos huius libri testibus Johannes Grace
Thomas Phyllyp, Thomas Whetamsted monachi huius
loci

Wyllyam Hynkes wryt this

Andrew Spyderswell [? Spykerswell]*
Est liber Andreae ber it well in mȳd³⁰
he ys a chyld both curteise & kynd
A porta inferi Īhus hym defend
& for his med[?] Īhus hym send
vitā aetnā at hys lyfes end
Amen

Note that in thys pressent boeke is conteyned
this present tytyll of the boke of Saynt
Peter

Of all those names only four – Grace, Empson, Whetamsted, and Phyllyp – are found in the Abbey records.³¹ All were alive in the 1530s. If only one of them had succumbed to the rigours of monastic life in about 1525, the chronology of Rastell's music-printing would have been one stage clearer. As it is, we only know that the notes on the leaf were written before the dissolution of the monastery in 1539 – too late a date to be of interest here.

The format and music of the broadside

So there remain the evidence of the sheet as a bibliographical entity and the additional, intricate evidence provided by the music on it. There is a watermark, a unicorn, near the top left-hand corner. The chain-lines are horizontal. The thirty notes present a curious problem, because the melodic style and the sequence of intervals (and the lack of them, as found in the six repeated notes at the end of the stave) are quite uncharacteristic of the vocal line of a single-voice song. On the other hand, the notes make musical sense, in harmonic terms, once it is realized what they really are – the tenor part (as the final cadence shows) of a song for two, or perhaps, three, voices. This knowledge helps to determine the size of the sheet, which was a broadside of about 11 to 12 inches wide and 17 to 18 inches high. Apart from this fact, the music cannot possibly have been a song for only one voice, because a reconstruction of the total original stave length, based on the proportionate relation of extant text syllables to notes, would produce a sheet quite incompatible in shape and dimensions with the place of the watermark and the area of the margin. Clearly then, the description of the sheet as a broadside 'ballad' is rather misleading, because, however appropriate in a literary context, it is less so in a musical one when 'ballad' – in any period – connotes a work for solo voice.

* A I Doyle reads this name as 'Spyderwell', and corrects 'aetnā' (in the penultimate line of this inscription) to 'et[er]na[m].'

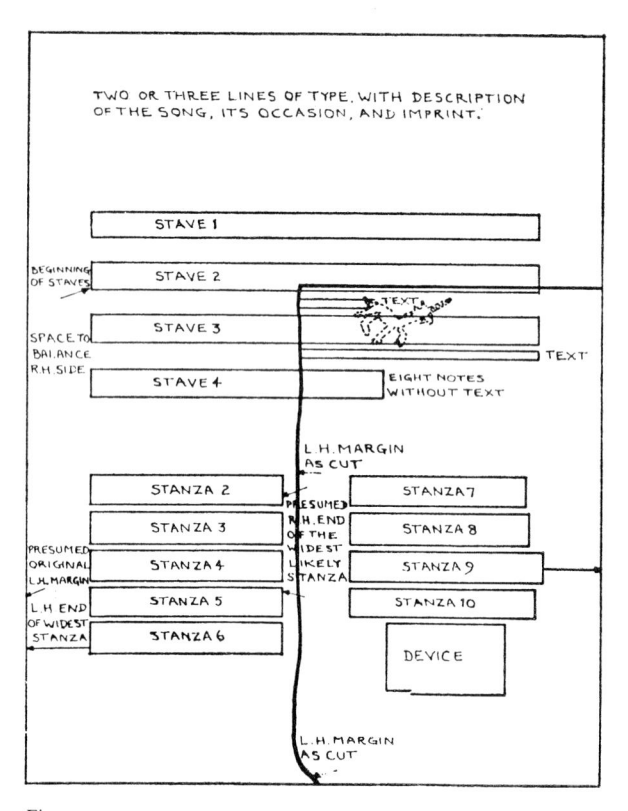

```
                TWO OR THREE LINES OF TYPE, WITH DESCRIPTION
                OF THE SONG, ITS OCCASION, AND IMPRINT.


                    ┌─────────────────────────────┐
                    │         STAVE 1             │
                    └─────────────────────────────┘
         BEGINNING  ┌─────────────────┐
         OF STAVES  │     STAVE 2     │
                    └─────────────────┘
                                        ╱TEXT╲
         SPACE TO   ┌─────────────────┐                          ┐
         BALANCE    │     STAVE 3     │                          │ TEXT
         R.H.SIDE   └─────────────────┘─────────────┐            ┘
                    ┌─────────────────┐  EIGHT NOTES
                    │     STAVE 4     │  WITHOUT TEXT
                    └─────────────────┘
                                  L.H.MARGIN
                                  AS CUT
                    ┌─────────────────┐         ┌──────────────┐
                    │    STANZA 2     │ PRESUMED│   STANZA 7   │
                    └─────────────────┘ R.H.END └──────────────┘
                    ┌─────────────────┐ OF THE  ┌──────────────┐
                    │    STANZA 3     │ WIDEST  │   STANZA 8   │
         PRESUMED   └─────────────────┘ LIKELY  └──────────────┘
         ORIGINAL   ┌─────────────────┐ STANZA  ┌──────────────┐
         L.H.MARGIN │    STANZA 4     │         │   STANZA 9   │
                    └─────────────────┘         └──────────────┘
         L.H END    ┌─────────────────┐         ┌──────────────┐
         OF WIDEST  │    STANZA 5     │         │   STANZA 10  │
         STANZA     └─────────────────┘         └──────────────┘
                    ┌─────────────────┐
                    │    STANZA 6     │         ┌──────────────┐
                    └─────────────────┘         │    DEVICE    │
                                                └──────────────┘

                                 L.H.MARGIN
                                 AS CUT
```

Fig. 3a

Because of the loss of the clef on the left-hand side of the sheet, we cannot be certain whether the extant notes are from the lower part of a two-voice song or from the middle or lower part of a three-voice song. Therefore two alternative reconstructions are possible, as in fig. 3. In the two-voice version, I believe that all the staves ran above the level of the first stanza, and that the space under the staves on the now lost left-hand part of the sheet was filled with four or five more stanzas of text, so printed as to balance the stanzas with Rastell's device under them. In the three-voice version, it must be assumed that the total number of stanzas was only five: the third voice would have been printed on the lower part of the lost portion of the sheet.

In either case, the parts were printed in sequence, as were the parts at the end of 'Tyme to pas', and not in score as on its first three pages. Each part would have had untexted sections where in performance the accompanying instruments continued to play while the voices were silent. Although this style of music was generally old-fashioned by the 1520s, it still lingered on in England which was backward by European standards. Whether the song

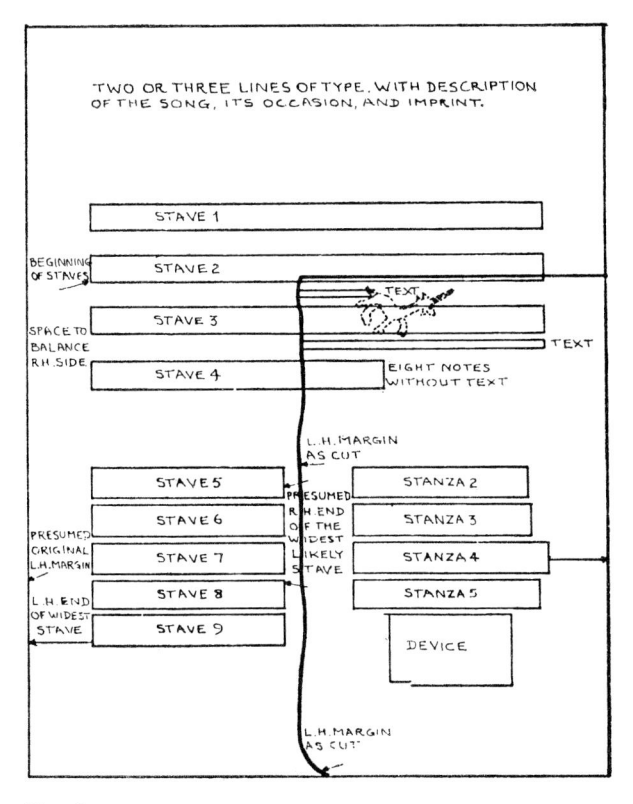

Fig. 3b

was for two or for three voices, the broadside as a whole was quite an adventurous piece of printing which did credit to Rastell's workmen. The top of the sheet, above the stages, would have borne a description of the song, a statement of the occasion for which it was printed, possibly the name of a composer, certainly an imprint and perhaps a date – in all, two or three lines set right out to the full type width.

The sentiments expressed in the surviving verses of the broadside (Plate 2b) shows that the poem was of the type in which a lover reviles the lady who had been false to him. Such sentiments are not uncommon in early Tudor verse: similar poems are found in Francis Lee Utley's collection *The Crooked Rib*.[32] The text of Rastell's broadside seems not to be noticed in the literature on the poetry of the period.

The format and content of the broadside suggests that Rastell may have printed it for a special occasion, such as the musical festivities which formed part of the great entertainment held, as I have already mentioned, at Greenwich in 1527. The chronicler of that event remarked particularly that some songs were sung in English by two singers. This, of course, proves nothing about the date of Rastell's broadside. But it does show that the sort of music which it bore was heard on notable ceremonial occasions. Since there is no record of such festivities in the last eight years or so of Rastell's life, it is at least likely that the broadside was connected with some occasion which took place after 1519 and before 1528. Greg, as we saw, placed both the broadside and the *Interlude* 'Between 1526 and 1530 inclusive, with some preference for the earlier years of the period'. The preliminary typescript of the new STC dates the broadside [1526?] which is, I think, too late. This presumably derives from Ferguson's researches and was probably based on the evidence offered by the alleged wear of the block from which Rastell's smaller device was printed. But since only four of his productions bear this device, and none of these are dated, it seems rather tenuous evidence from which to assign to precise a date to the broadside. Rastell may, after all, have had more than one block for each of his devices, especially if, as Samuel Redgrave states,[33] he was himself sufficiently expert in wood-cutting to produce the many elaborate cuts which illustrate his own book *The Pastyme of the People*. I have not been able to find the source for Redgrave's statement, but the ability to design and cut blocks would not be surprising in a man of Rastell's capacities.

Summary and conclusions

Let me try to summarize the evidence for dating, ask some final questions, and then consider the general implications. Greg's modified opinion on the *Interlude* was that 'about 1525–7 seems to be the most likely date' and with this, the preliminary typescript for the new STC, which gives [1526?], is in virtual agreement. If Greg had had occasion to express a second opinion about the broadside, I think he would probably have placed it within the limits he set for the *Interlude*. The slight circumstantial evidence which I have adduced would put the broadside nearer to 1525 than to 1528. But in the case of the *Interlude* the evidence seems to me much stronger. I think Greg erred on the side of caution, and I believe for circumstantial reasons that the play was first printed at some time between about November 1519 and the middle of 1520. But I can offer no irrefutable proof of this. The Garrick copy of the play may, of course, not have been of the very first printing, though the manuscript stage directions and the manuscript addition to the text of 'Tyme to pas' suggests that it was probably of an early printing, if not of the first. But even if I am wrong, and leaving out the broadside because of the less definite criteria, there still remains the consensus of Greg's second opinion with the revised STC date of [1526?]. Rastell must then have printed mensural music from type certainly two, and probably eight, years before the first Attaingnant's books appeared in April 1528.

Where did Rastell get his music type? In this crucial matter, it seems relevant to quote a sentence from the preface written by Harry Carter and Christopher Ricks in their edition of Edward Mores's *Dissertation upon English Typographical Founders*:[34] 'Between the death of Caxton and the appearance in 1567 of John Day's Anglo-Saxon Letters it is doubtful whether any type is first found in English printing.' These words may be taken to apply even more forcibly to the complex sorts needed for music type, bearing in mind also their restricted use. Although Rastell obviously had among his workmen someone who could set music type, it is unlikely that any of them had the technical skill to cut music punches from which matrices could be struck and type cast. He must therefore have procured it from some European source.

Rastell's long connections with northern France, and his employment of a printer from Rouen, suggest this part of Europe as the most likely source. But we should not overlook the Low Countries as another possibility. Yet from neither country does any music survive printed in this type, nor does it resemble any other extant face used there or elsewhere.

We have, then, in Rastell's type a unique survival of a font which was probably cast in northern Europe, somewhere between the Rhine and the Seine. As I suggested earlier, the need for one-impression music-printing must have been generally recognized early in the sixteenth-century, and it is not unlikely that success was achieved by some small, local printer of whom all trace has now been lost. Nevertheless, an existing source from which to procure type quickly must have been known to Rastell when he returned from Ireland early in 1519, perhaps even before he left on his voyage in 1517. For inventive as he was, he simply would not have had time, between the spring and late autumn of 1519, to conceive the idea himself and go abroad to find a type-caster to do the job. The process of trial and error must have taken place some years before the printing of the *Interlude* and long before Attaingnant began his 'excogitation'.

Although, as I have said, no other music printed from them survives, a discovery of Donald Krummel's shows that twice-struck matrices were still used on the continent nearly thirty years after Rastell died. The Royal Library at Brussels has a psalter of 1564 (printed by Claes van den Wouwere at Antwerp)[35] in which the stave-lines clearly show through the centres of the notes. This example can hardly represent a late, solitary revival of the process. It must surely be regarded as the sole known survivor from a period of some twenty-five years during which music type was being produced in Antwerp from the two kinds of matrices contemporaneously. (The use of once-struck matrices for music began there in 1540.) It seems likely that twice-struck matrices had been used to produce music type elsewhere in the Low Countries even earlier, in Rastell's time.

Let us return briefly to Attaingnant. If the twice-struck matrix was invented in northern France, he could hardly have failed to know about it. Perhaps he felt he could legitimately ignore it in his privilege, because of its technical inferiority. If, however, the invention had taken place in or near Antwerp, he might never have heard of it, and in any case safeguarded himself by having the phrase 'in this our realm' included in his privilege statement.

After so much speculation, it is satisfactory to conclude with the wider facts about Rastell's place in the history of music printing as it stands at present. He can be credited with several achievements: the earliest mensural music printed in England; the earliest broadside with music printed from type anywhere in Europe; the earliest song printed in an English dramatic work. Rastell also made the first attempt at printing a score, by any process in any country. Rough as it is, and based on the metre of the words and not the tempo of the music, it is some seventeen years earlier than the next, much improved, piece of score printing, which is found in Lampadius's *Compendium musices* (Berne, 1537).[36] Yet who knows what new material may not appear in the *International Inventory of musical Sources* when the dozen volumes which will be devoted to the alphabetical series of printed music have all been published, by the mid 1970s? Then some of this inquiry may have to be undertaken all over again.

It is now nearly eight years since I first began to look at these two pieces of Rastell's music printing. Faced with their perplexing ambiguities, I have often felt that they were, in the words of Sir Thomas Browne, 'begotten only to distract and abuse the weaker judgements of scholars, and to maintain the trade and mystery of tyopgraphers'.

[1970]

Notes

1 Pressmark, Case 39.b.17. I am much indebted to Mr Nicolas Barker, Mr Harry Carter, the late Professor Thurston Dart, Professor Daniel Heartz, Mr Donald Krummel, Mr Howard M Nixon, Mr Julian Roberts, and Miss Pamela Willetts, for a variety of enlightenment or correction which they generously gave me, either in discussion or by correspondence. Roger Coleman's preface to his edition of the play (privately printed, CUP, 1971) offers an excellent discussion of its chronology.
2 Pressmark, K.8.k.8.
3 It is generally agreed that in some of the first part-books issued by Petrucci from May 1501 onwards, even three impressions were used.
4 'The Types of Christopher Plantin', *The Library*, v, ix (1956), p. 175.
5 Vol. 5, cols. 1827, 1828. Another short, but important article sppeared in *Encyclopédie de la musique*, ed. F. Michel, in collaboration with Lesure and Fédorov, 1959, tom. II, p.431.

6 *Jacques Moderne* (Geneva, 1969), p. 40 no. 3.
7 *Pierre Attaingnant, Royal Printer of Music. A historical study and bibliographical catalogue*, University of California Press, 1969.
8 'A new Attaingnant book and the beginnings of French music printing', *Journal of the American Musicological Society*, XIV, no. 1 (Spring 1961), pp. 9–23.
9 *Geschichte der Musik* (Leipzig, 1868), iii. 192, 193 n. 2.
10 Quoted, by kind permission of Professor Heartz, from his article referred to in note 8.
11 Complete lists of his entire output, from 1528 to 1550, with exact dates, are given in the article on him by Vladimir Fédorov in MGG, vol. I (1949–51), cols. 766–70, and, with full bibliographical details, in Renouard, *Imprimeurs & libraires parisiens du XVIe siècle* (Paris, 1964), tom. I, pp. 114–54.
12 *Biographie universelle des musiciens*, Brussels, 1835.
13 *Manuel du libraire* (Paris, 1862), tom. 3, cols. 1116–18.
14 *Dictionary of Music*, part 1, vol. 1 (1878), article by Franz Gehring.
15 Methuen (London, 1926), pp. 1–28, with much documentary information in appendices I–VIII. Some additional facts, and some corrections, are given in Sydney Anglo's *Spectacle, Pageantry and early Tudor Policy* (Clarendon Press, Oxford), 1969.
16 Glynne Wickham, *Early English stages* (London, 1950), i. 81.
17 Reed, p. 18.
18 Cf. Ray Nash, 'Rastell Fragments at Dartmouth', *The Library*, IV, XXIV (1944), 63–73.
19 'John Rastell and his contemporaries', *Bibliographica*, ii (1896), 437–51.
20 H R Plomer, *Abstracts from the Wills of English Printers and Stationers from 1492 to 1630*, 1903, p. 5.
21 Stanley Morison, *The Likeness of Thomas More*, edited and supplemented by Nicolas Barker, London, 1963, pp. 22, 81.
22 'Rastell reunited', see infra pp. 32–7.
23 *The earliest English music Printing*, 1903, pp. 5, 6, 36.
24 *English and Scottish printing Types*, 1930, section on John Rastell.
25 IV, xi (June 1930), 44–56, 'Notes on some early Plays'.
26 *A Bibliography of the English Drama*, i. 85, no. 6.
27 *The Library*, IV, xix [March 1939], pp. 389–421.
28 *Musica Britannica*, xviii, Stainer & Bell, for the Royal Musical Association, 1962, pp. 13, 14, 102. Cf. also Stevens's *Music and Poetry in the early Tudor Court* (London, 1961), pp. 456, 464.
29 eg John Stevens, *Music and Poetry in the early Tudor Court* (London 1961), p. 448. The date 'c 1516' in Humphries and Smith, *Music Publishing in the British Isles*, p. 268, is based on a misunderstanding of the tentative chronology attaching to Rastell's smaller device. So, too, is the wrong information in Grove, fifth edition, vol. vi, p. 930.
30 Mr J C T Oates has pointed out that his *Catalogue of fifteenth-century Printed Books in the University Library, Cambridge* (1954), no. 4059, p. 671, mentions a similar inscription in Lefevre's 'History of Jason', and *The Book Collector*, 1967, p. 507, gives another, later, example.
31 E H Pearce, *The Monks of Westminster*, Cambridge University Press, 1916. The other names do not occur in the Westminster School lists.
32 Columbus, 1944.
33 *Dictionary of the Artists of the English School* (London, 1878), p. 348.
34 Oxford, 1961, p. lxvi.
35 Bernard Huys, *Catalogue des imprimes musicaux des XVe XVIe et XVIIe dièclès (du) fonds général de la bibliothèque royale de Belgique* (Brussels 1965), no. 361. Pressmark II.13.006. A.L.P.
36 Cf. Edward Lowinsky, 'Early Scores in Manuscript', *Journal of the American Musicological Society*, XIII, nos. 1–3 (1960), pp. 126–71.

3

Rastell reunited

In 1779 David Garrick bequeathed to the British Museum his magnificent collection of some 1200 English plays, the earliest of which is entitled *A new Interlude and a mery of the Nature of the iiij Elements*, here referred to as the *Interlude*. This is a unique but unfortunately imperfect copy, which lacks sig. D and all after sig. E, including the colophon which would probably have given the printer's name, possibly that of the author, and (almost certainly) the date. The author has been proved to be John Rastell who can be shown, on typographical grounds, also to have printed the book. But the date remains uncertain, and has been the subject of much speculation ranging at different times from '*c* 1510' to '1539?' The date is, however, of great importance, not only because of the play's early position in English drama, but also because it contains a three-part song which is undoubtedly the earliest mensural music printed in England from type at a single impression.[1]

The earliest bibliographical listing of the *Interlude* is found in Edward Capell's manuscript catalogue of the Garrick plays written in 1773,[2] where it is number 188. Capell dated it 'about 1519', adding a footnote 'See a note bound up with it'. The *Interlude* has long been studied by writers on English drama.[3] A recent acquisition by the British Museum sheds some new light on its history, and as neither the book nor its printer is perhaps generally familiar, a brief account of both may not be out of place.

Rastell, who was born about 1475 and died in 1536, was active as a printer from 1512 onwards. There survive from his press some forty books, mostly of legal, literary, historical and dramatic interest. In addition, he led an active life as lawyer, controversialist and adventurer. The fullest account of him is given in A W Reed's *Early Tudor Drama*.[4] Reed was able to show that Rastell wrote the *Interlude* while he was in Ireland in the winter of 1517–18, but left vague the possible date of publication.

The *Interlude*, like a number of other books printed by Rastell, has no title page, nor indeed any conventional title at all. The descriptive title, on sig. A1, reads thus:

A new interlude and a mery of the nature of the iiij elements declarynge many proper poynts of phylosophy naturall, and of dyuers straunge landys, and of dyuers straunge effects & causis, which interlude yf ye hole matter be playd wyl conteyne the space of an hour and a halfe, but yf ye lyst ye may leue out muche of the sad mater as the messengers pte, and some of naturys parte and some of experyens parte & yet the matter wyll depend conuenyently, and than it wyll not be paste thre quarters of an hour of length.

Blanks have been supplied in place of sig. D and there are seventeen blanks after sig. E. The fly leaf bears the notes alluded to by Capell, in a hand which appears to be of the mid-eighteenth century, on the recto: 'An Interlude of the Four Elements &c. by John Rastel. puta [sic] Anno 1519', and on the verso 'The Interlude was bound with Rastel's Abrigem^t. of the Statutes 1st Impression dated 25th Oct. 11 Hen. 8th'. Sig. E 1 bears the signature 'John Pulley 1541'. On sig. A 1 there is a somewhat murky offset of Rastell's larger device (McKerrow 37).

After Reed, the most detailed account of the *Interlude*, with special reference to its date, was given by Greg, who had seen the notes on the fly-leaf but did not quote them. Nor did he mention Pulley's signature. In an article, 'Notes on some early Plays', Greg considered the *Interlude* together with a fragmentary ballad also printed by Rastell, and summed up as follows: 'On the whole I see no way of advancing beyond the position that the interlude and the ballad were probably printed by Rastell between 1526 and 1530 inclusive, with some preference for the earlier years of the period. If that is so Rastell's use of his particular species of music type was almost certainly independent of, and very probably anterior to, that of Attaingnant at Paris; but it would in no way affect the claim of Haultin to have been its inventor'.[5] Later, in *A Bibliography of the English Drama*,[6] Greg expressed himself rather differently about the printing of the *Interlude*: 'It is likely to be after 1525, and about 1525–7 seems the most likely date'.

This then, in outline, was the general background against which from 1961 onwards, while I was collecting material for my booklet *Four Hundred Years of Music Printing*,[7] a number of questions began to take rather hazy shape in my mind. More recently, when I started a detailed study of Rastell's place in the history of early music printing, the questions came into sharper focus, and may be posed in these terms:

1. When did Garrick get the *Interlude*?
2. Assuming that the notes on its flyleaf mean exactly what they say and consequently that the offset was made by the verso of the last leaf of the *Statutes* –
a) What happened to the *Statutes*?
b) When were this book and the *Interlude* bound together and when were they separated?

c) If the *Statutes* could be traced, might it perhaps shed any light on the date when the *Interlude* was printed?

d) When did the *Interlude* become imperfect?

The starting point was the fly-leaf of the *Interlude*. The one certain and easily established fact was that the writer of the notes was not Garrick. Whoever he was, and whether the owner or not, he saw the two books bound together, or knew they had been. The *Statutes* had been owned by Joseph Ames, and was described by him, with liberal quotation, in the first edition of his *Typographical Antiquities*.[8] The handwriting on the fly leaf of the *Interlude* was demonstrably not his, and he did not mention the play in the 1749 edition. But it does appear in the second edition, by William Herbert,[9] and more details were given by Dibdin in the third.[10] Two other facts complete the puzzling picture: the *Statutes* is listed without location by Proctor,[11] and does not appear in the STC. Where then was the book?

This question was answered at a Sotheby's sale of 28 November 1961 when the *Statutes* was auctioned (lot 375) as one of over 100 books from the library of the Bristol Baptist College. It was purchased by the British Museum, and now forms part of the collections of the State Paper Room.[12] It contains two bookplates, one plain, with the name of the Society, the other decorative, with the motto 'meliora spero' and the legend 'Andrew Gifford of the Museum'.

The book is almost perfect, lacking only sig. 1, 1, 2. At the foot of Sig. A 1 there is the manuscript signature 'Ames'. Sig. M i recto and M ii verso bear the signature 'J Pulley', and sig. M iii verso the signature 'J Pulley 1633'. There are a few other notes and some figures of no relevance. The recto of the last leaf bears Rastell's larger device which, in the spacing of the margins and other details, corresponds exactly to the offset on the *Interlude*. The book is printed in textura 93 a, the type which he used for the *Interlude* and for other books.

Perhaps the most curious feature of the two books is the two signatures 'John Pulley' and 'J Pulley', written at an interval of ninety-two years.* Reference to G W Marshall's *Genealogist's Guide* showed but a few entries for this mercifully uncommon surname, and only two with the initial 'J', both of whom are found in a family tree printed from a Visitation of Essex in 1634.[13] The first, a John Pulley of Bridgnorth, flourished in the early sixteenth century, and the second, his grandson, also John, in the early seventeenth. Despite the lack of precise dates, these holders of the name lived at

---

*For a different interpretation of the two Pulley signatures and dates, see note ★ on p. 19 above.

about the right time to be considered as the successive owners of the *Statutes*. Their wills, the earlier proved in 1583, the later in 1654, are in Somerset House, but mention no bequests of books. I have failed to find out anything about the Pulleys, especially about the earlier John, which might connect the family with Rastell. The fact that neither Pulley appears in the registers of the Inns of Court, of Oxford or Cambridge, suggests that both were of the country gentry. It is remarkable that the younger was clearly copying the style of his grandfather's signature. One or two leaves of the *Statutes* bear pen flourishes in the lower margin which suggest that the younger Pulley was trying his quill in imitation of his ancestor's calligraphy. The signatures make it certain that the *Interlude* and the *Statutes* were first bound together not later than 1541 and probably in Rastell's lifetime. Clearly, they remained so until a later owner decided to separate them, and only then were the notes written on the new fly-leaf of the *Interlude*. The recovery of the *Statutes*, with the bookplate of Gifford, provided a new line of investigation as to their date and writer.

Andrew Gifford (1700–1784) was well known as a numismatist and book collector. He entered the Baptist ministry in 1730, and worked as an assistant librarian in the Department of Printed Books in the British Museum from 1757 until his death – a late entrant, even for the eighteenth century. He was able to indulge his acquisitive instincts because he married a wealthy woman as his second wife. He bequeathed his coins and books, valued at 1000 guineas, to the Baptist Society in Bristol where his father and grandfather had served as ministers.[14] Although no letters or papers of Gifford's are now extant in the library of the College, comparison of the notes in the *Interlude* with four autograph letters elsewhere,[15] shows that the hands are identical.

After the death of the younger John Pulley the *Statutes*, with the *Interlude*, passed at some time early in the eighteenth century into the possession of Ames, who wrote his name at the foot of the first leaf of the *Statutes*. It may be suggested that Ames, when describing the *Statutes* in the first edition of his *Typographical Antiquities* (to which Gifford subscribed), omitted the *Interlude* simply because if the latter lacked all the leaves it does now he regarded it as a fragmentary 'adespoton'. Ames died in 1759. The fact that the *Statutes* do not appear in the Ames sale catalogue of 1760 proves little except that not all the books in his collection were auctioned. He may well have known Gifford, and perhaps gave him the two books during his lifetime. The phrase 'of the Museum' on Gifford's bookplate has no bearing on the date of acquisition. We cannot tell exactly when he separated the books and wrote the notes on the fly-leaf of the *Interlude*, but it cannot have been later than 1765.[16] As Gifford's name does not occur in Garrick's extensive correspondence, we do not know whether the two men were acquainted. But it is interesting that notes in Gifford's hand can now be identified in a number of other early plays in Garrick's collection.[17]

This reconstruction appears to take account of all the bibliographical data, but though we now know the answers to Questions 1 and 2a, the other problems are still unsolved. Regarding the date, the offset provides no certain evidence that the *Interlude* was printed soon after 1519. A search for broken letters common to both books has proved negative. There are other matters which might affect the *terminus ante quem*: the identity of the three-part song with an earlier four-part version extant in manuscript; the typographical relation of the song to the fragmentary ballad printed by Rastell; the considerable musical interests of his family; the place of music in his work as a provider of pageants and as owner of the earliest theatre known in London; the character of his music-type and its possible relation to sources in northern France and his own connexions with it.

All this lies beyond the main purpose of this enquiry. But whatever cumulative evidence further study of these topics may produce affecting the date of the *Interlude*, there remains the fact that Greg made a reasoned case for it not being printed later than 1527. If he was right, then Rastell had used one-impression music type, however crudely, at least three months before Pierre Attaingnant printed the earliest known dated music by this process – the first of his long sequence of *Chansons* which appeared in Paris on 4 April 1528. To establish Rastell's place in the history of European music printing would require prolonged investigation on the lines indicated above. Meanwhile it is gratifying that two of his books have come together again, if not between two covers as they once were, at least in the same library.

[1970]

Notes

1 Robert Steele, *The Earliest Music Printing*, 1903, p. 5, 6, believed that the extant copy of the *Interlude* was not of the first printing, but was a reprint issued by John Gough, *c* 1539. Steele was refuted by Frank Isaac, *English & Scottish Printing Types*, 1930, in the section on John Rastell. Isaac had the advantage of drawing a comparison with Rastell's ballad, which was not known until 1904.
2 BM pressmark 643.1.30, now Case 39.b.17.
3 Edited by J O Halliwell for the Percy Society, 1848; by Robert Dodsley, in W C Hazlitt's edition, *Old English Plays*, vol. 1, 1874; in facsimile by J S Farmer as one of the *Tudor Facsimile Texts*, 1908. The full text of the play is also given in a thesis by Julius Fischer, *Das ,,Interlude of the Four Elements"*, Hft.5 of *Marburger Studien zur Englischen Philologie, 1903*, and by bibliographers, but its interest is by no means exhausted.
4 Methuen, London, 1926, pp. 1–28, with much supplementary information in the appendices.

5 *The Library*, ser. 4, vol. 2, June 1930, pp. 44–56. It should also be noted that 'the claim of Haultin' (never put forward by Haultin himself) has been shown to be pure legend: the inventor was indubitably Attaingnant. See Daniel Heartz 'A New Attaingnant Book and the Beginnings of French Music Printing', *Journal of the American Musicological Society*, vol. XIV, no. 1, 1961, pp. 9–23.
6 The Bibliographical Society, 1939, vol. 1, p. 85, no. 6.
7 Trustees of the British Museum, 1964, second edition 1968.
8 1749, vol. 1, p. 143–5. He stated that books marked with an asterisk, as is the *Statutes*, were in his own possession.
9 1785, vol. 1, p. 342.
10 1810–19, vol. 3, p. 105.
11 *Handlists of the English Printers*, Bibliographical Society, pt. 2, 1896, p. 3. Presumably Proctor took his information from Ames.
12 Pressmark B. e. 11/1.
13 *Harleian Society Publications*, vol. XIII, p. 472.
14 Information from the DNB and from an anonymous booklet, *Bristol Baptist College. 250 years 1679–1929*, [Bristol, 1930]. As a corroborative detail, it may be mentioned that an early catalogue of the College's library, *An Alphabetical Catalogue of all Books in the Library, belonging to the Bristol Education Society*, Bristol, 1795, lists the *Statutes* on p. 37.
15 Two in the British Museum, Add. MSS. 6210, fol. 94, and 28537, fol. 252–4; one in the library of the Society of Antiquaries, which Mr Hopkins, the Society's librarian, kindly allowed me to examine; and one in the Bodleian, Mus. Bibl. 8⁰ 50, dated 27 March 1754.
16 Thomas Percy, *Reliques of ancient English Poetry* (London) 1765, p. 124, quoted the title of the play, and wrote 'Mr. Garrick has an imperfect copy'.
17 I owe this information and that given in note 16 to Mrs Dorothy Anderson.

4

Fragments of early printed music in the Bagford Collection

Although the name of John Bagford has received some attention in connection with early English music, it is probable that he and his remarkable collection are unknown to most of those now interested in the subject. It may, therefore, be appropriate to give a very brief account of his life and general aims before passing to the musical contents of the collection. Bagford, born in 1650 or 1651, was a shoemaker by profession who early developed an enthusiasm for the history of printing and soon became known to various noble bibliophiles, including Robert Harley, Earl of Oxford, Sir Hans Sloane and John Moore, Bishop of Ely. Being regularly employed by them on commission as a collector of rare books, Bagford had fine opportunities of picking up many specimen pieces illustrative of his own particular interests. In 1707 he published 'Proposals for printing an Historical Account of that most universally celebrated, as well as useful art of Typography', but when he died in 1716 this vast project had not taken shape.

The collection, which included much manuscript material, was purchased by the Harley family to augment their great assemblage of manuscripts which was sold to Parliament in 1753 and formed part of the foundation collections of the British Museum. Ultimately, in about 1895, the printed part of the Bagford fragments was transferred to the Department of Printed Books. Their pressmarks remain those of the Harleian collection, namely Harl. MSS 5414, 5419, 5892–5998. It is principally in 5936 that the items of musical interest, truly extraordinary in their diversity, are to be found.

During the nineteenth century it was fashionable in bibliophilic circles to abuse Bagford as an ignorant 'biblioclast'. Blades, Didbin and other men learned in books blackened his memory with the accusation that he had built up his collections by pillaging title-pages and odd leaves from rare volumes. More recently, however, strong arguments were advanced against this idea.[1] There now seems little reason for not accepting Bagford's own statement (Harl. MS 5910, iii, 120) that he picked up these leaves from binders' waste, damaged copies, fragments and other sources that he encountered during the wide searches undertaken on behalf of his patrons. While there is nothing to suggest that Bagford had any particular interest in or knowledge of music printing, it is noteworthy that the musical contents of Harl. 5936 are practically confined to English specimens, whereas the collection as a whole ranges far and wide over European presses. But in any case our concern here is not so much with these fragments in their typographical as in their historical aspect. Since no collector can imagine all the uses to which posterity may put his material, we may doubt whether Bagford was aware of the full importance of his musical gleanings. Not all the contents of these volumes call for mention here. The following list, given in order of the volumes in which they are bound and the folios on which they are pasted, is of little-known or unique pieces only.

1) 5927. f.20 recto.
Quintus. Musica Sacra:. to sixe voices. Composed in the Italian Tongue, by Giovanni Croce. Newly Englished. At London, printed by H.L. for Mathew Lownes. 1611.

The title-page only. No copy of this edition is known. Cambridge University Library has the Sextus part only.

2) 5936. f.118 verso.
The oration of Maister John Bull, Doctor of Musicke, and one of the Gentlemen of hir Maiesties Royall Chappell. As hee pronounced the same, bee-fore diuers Worshipfull persons, th' Aldermen & commoners of the Citie of London, with a great Multitude of other people, the 6. day of October 1597. In the new erected Colledge of Sir Thomas Gresham Knight, deceased: Made in the commendation of the saide Worthy Founder, and the excellent science of Musicke. Imprinted at London by Thomas Este.

Title-page only. This is the only leaf of this book at present known to survive. It was seen by Barclay Squire and used in his article on Bull in the second edition of *Grove*. Squire omitted, however, to notice that the verso of the leaf bore a fairly clear offset of the first page of the text. With the aid of a mirror, most of it can be deciphered. It runs as follows:

It is written, Right worshipful, that the Eagle onely soaring aloft into the clouds, looketh with open eye upon the Sun: such a quick sighted bird should now bee in this place who flying thro' heaven might fetch [?] Apollo's harp and sound unto you the prayse of heavenlie Musick. My Master liueth and long [may he] lyve, and I his scholar not worthy in yours & his present to speak of this Art and Science. Beare, I pray you, with all my defects of knowledge, and you shall finde that dilegence shall recompense the [three words illegible]. One starre is not so light as another, yet as by a faint light you may see your way, so by my simple knowledge may you in some form[?] learne this Science: & although I am not, as it were, winged to flye to the hill Parnassus, there to sing with the Muses a part in the praise of Musick, yet give me leave, I pray you, [first two words illegible] to shew you the foundation and foundress...

3) 5936. f.125. verso.
The Pleasant Companion: or new Lessons and Instructions for the Flagelet. By Thomas Greeting, Gent. London, Printed for John Playford, and are to be sold at his shop in the Inner-Temple, near the Church. 1675.

Title-page only. The only complete copy known is in the Bodleian.

4) 5936. f.126 verso.
Country Dances: being a Composition Entirely New; and the whole cast different from all that have yet been publish'd: with a bass and a treble to each Dance. Also, the newest French Dances in use, Entry's, Genteel and Grotesque, Chacons, Rigodoons, Minuets, and other Dancing Tunes. By Thomas Bray. London: printed by William Pearson, next door to the Hare and Feathers in Aldersgate-street, and sold by John Young, Musical-Instrument-seller, at the Dolphin and Crown, at the West end of St. Paul's Church-yard, 1700.

The title-page only of an unrecorded edition. A copy of a 1699 edition is in the library of the English Folk Song and Dance Society.

5) 5936. f.127. verso.
The Compleat Tutor to the Violin containing very plain & easy Directions for young Beginners, with variety of the Newest Tunes, particularly those performed at the Ball at St. James on the King's Birth-day last. All the newest French-Dances and Minuetts Now used at the Dancing Schools, severall New Ayres perform'd at both the Theatres, and Flourishes in every Key By Mr. John Bannister. To which are added Six Country-Dances never before Published. The whole fairly Engraven on copper Plates. London Printed for John Young at the Dolphin & Crown at ye West-End of St. Paul's Church-yard and Tho. Cross in Catherine-Wheel-Court on Snowhill. 1699. Price one shilling & sixpence.

The title-page only. No copy of this tutor is known. The title was quoted by Pulver[2] but only in a short and incorrect form taken from a contemporary advertisement.

6) 5936. f.128. verso.
The Compleat Instructor to the Flute the second Book containing very plain & easie directions for young Beginners, with variety of ye newest & best Tunes, particularly the Dances, song Tunes & ye rest of ye Musick in the Jubilee. Also All ye Minuets, Boreys, Regadoons, Marches, Trumpett Tunes and song tunes, now in use, to which is added ye newest French Dances Perform'd at ye Ball at St. James^{es}, on ye Princes Birthday last. London Printed & sold by I. Young ... price one shilling & sixpence. 1700.

The title-page only: otherwise unknown.

7) 5936. f.131. recto.
Directions for the Flagellett. wth 20 severall lessons fitted to the same Instrument. Written & engraven by Tho. Swain gent: 1657. sold by Robert Pawzett att the Bible in Chancery lane.

This fragment comprises four leaves: (i) a frontispiece, identical with that to the second edition, 1682 (1683) of Greeting's Pleasant companion: verso blank. (ii) Title-page, as above, verso blank. (iii and iv) printed on both sides, giving: description of time values, fingering and method of holding the instrument; address to the reader, followed by "explanation of all the lines markes characters". No complete copy of the book is known. Swain appears to be otherwise entirely unknown; the publisher Robert Pawlett is otherwise known only as having issued political pamphlets.

8) 5936. f.142 recto.
A Curious Collection of Musick-Books, both vocal and instrumental (and several rare copies in three and four parts, fairly prick'd) by the best masters... The collection is to be sold by Henry Playford, *etc.* 4 pp. [1690].

9) 5936. f.143 recto.
A Catalogue of all the Musick-Books that have been printed in England, either for Voyce or Instruments. London, Printed and are to be sold by John Playford. [1653].

10) 5936. 143 recto-145 recto.
A General Catalogue of all the Choicest Musick-Books in English, Latin, Italian and French, both Vocal and Instrumental. Composed by the best masters in Europe, that have been from these Thirty Years past, to this present Time: With all the plainest and easiest Instructions for Beginners on each particular Instrument. Sold for Henry Playford, at his shop in the Temple-Change, Fleetstreet, and are to be had here and in most of the cities and Publick Places in England, Ireland, and Scotland. [*c.* 1697.]

11) 5936. between ff.51 and 52.
A Catalogue of Ancient and Modern Musick Books, both vocal and instrumental with divers treatises about the same, and several musical instruments. As also a small collection of books in history, divinity and physick, which will be sold in Dewing's Coffee-House in Popes-Head Alley near the Royal Exchange, on Thursday, December the 17th, 1691.

16 pp. in all: pp. 3–11 music.

These four catalogues may be taken together, as unique copies of great importance, providing a primary bibliographical source for the history of English music publishing. They have, fortunately, been described and analysed in detail by William C Smith in two articles in *The Musical Times* (July and August 1926) entitled 'Playford: Some Hitherto Unnoticed Catalogues of Early Music'. They are also studied in the introduction to *Music Publishing in the British Isles* by C Humphries and William C Smith (1954).

12) 5993. f.15 recto.
A Breefe Introduction to the Skill of Musick for Song & Violl by J P London. Printed 1654. Sould by Jo: Playford at his shop in the Inner Temple.

The title-page only. Two complete copies were known to Kidson[3], both in private libraries, one English, one American. The English copy is apparently no longer available for study. This is the first edition of one of the most famous of all English theoretical works on music.

Rare though many of these books of music are, it is not impossible that complete copies of them may yet come to light. But none of Nos. 1, 4, 5, 6, 7 have been discovered by the *British Union-Catalogue of Early Music*. This suggests how grateful we should be to Bagford for preserving evidence that such interesting editions once existed.

[1959]

Notes

1 See W Y Fletcher, 'John Bagford and his Collections' in *Transactions of the Bibliographical Society*, Vol. IV, 1898; A W Pollard, 'A Rough List of the Contents of the Bagford Collection', Vol. VII, 1904; Robert Steele, 'John Bagford's own Account of his Collection of Titlepages, etc.' in *The Library*, Ser. 2, Vol. VIII, 1907.
2 *A Biographical Dictionary of Old English Music* (London, 1927), pp. 37, 38, with the date 1698.
3 'John Playford, and 17th-century Music Publishing', in *The Musical Quarterly*, 1918, p. 521.

C. G. Röder's music printing business in 1885

In the second half of the nineteenth century, Germany led the world in music-printing. It is all the more curious how scanty, even in German, is the literature about the great firms engaged in the industry which served music publishers in many parts of the world. By far the largest of the music printers was the firm founded in Leipzig by Carl Gottlieb Röder (1812–1883). Röder's did indeed issue a sumptuous book, *Festschrift zur 50 jähriges Jubelfeier des Bestehens des Firma C. G. Röder* (1896). It consisted mainly of an outline history of music-printing, by Riemann, followed by a brief description of the firm, all in highly technical German. The article on Röder in MGG gives a few other references, which do not appear to add a great deal.

The more interesting, therefore, is a very detailed account in English which has come to light in a long-forgotten piece of music now in the British Museum. Its title-page reads as follows:

THE TWELVE MONTHS OF THE YEAR

12

PIANOFORTE PIECES

composed

BY

THEODOR KIRCHNER

and published as a

SOUVENIR OF THE INTERNATIONAL INVENTIONS EXHIBITION

LONDON 1885

BY

C. G. RÖDER

Engraver & Printer of Music

LEIPZIG

Ent. Sta. Hall

Copyright of the publisher

This little work (BM pressmark d. 161. d. (3.)) was received by deposit under the Copyright Act on 1 August 1885. (In passing, it may be mentioned that the musical part of this publication is remarkable for twelve plates showing the antics of two winged cherubs throughout each month of the year.) After the music, comes the following account of Röder's growth and activity, here reprinted verbatim and faithfully to the spelling and capitalisation of the original.

C. G. RÖDER

ENGRAVER AND PRINTER OF MUSIC

REUDNITZ–LEIPZIG.

———

TELEGRAM ADDRESS: RÖDER, NOTENDRUCKEREI, LEIPZIG.

AGENT FOR GREAT BRITAIN MR Wm. WITT, LONDON W., 6 ARGYLL STREET,

OXFORD CIRCUS.

———

The following few notices of the Origin and gradual development of this establishment will be gratifying, as they testify what can be accomplished by energy and perseverance and strict attention to business.

The founder, Mr C. G. Röder, commenced business in 1846 in a very small way; as the son of a small baker, he had been obliged at an early age to look out for himself, but his endeavours were not successful, until, when 26 years old, he learnt to engrave music, which was the first step in the right direction, and gradually led him to that honorable position, which he occupied up to the end of his life.

Without any means, and assisted by only one apprentice, he started in business on his own account, as a Music Engraver and Printer on the 21st of October 1846. He was not at first very successful in business, but as his superior method gained favor it also gained him more customers, and as he continued to give great satisfaction the number of his customers gradually increased, and the business was now established on a sure basis. In 1853, Röder was enabled by the assistance of a friend to purchase, and amalgamate with his own, another business (Paez) and to remove to more extensive premises in the Tauchaer Strasse. He selected only the most talented artists and best workmen, and their number was increased by his apprentices, who had benefited by his good teaching and example; his reputation spread rapidly and orders increased from far and near. It was soon obvious that the above premises would not be sufficiently large to carry on the ever increasing business, and Röder resolved to build a more convenient factory according to his own plans. Before, however, this idea could be carried out, a most important change took place. Röder, finding that he could not execute his orders with sufficient promptness with the 24 hand presses already in use, had in 1860–61 made several attempts to render the lithogr. steam printing machines (constructed by G. Sigl, of Berlin and Vienna) available for the purpose of printing music. After repeated endeavours he finally succeeded in overcoming all obstacles, and also to ease the minds of his printers, who were afraid the new method would endanger their earnings. The earlier productions of the new process were not quite perfect, but with great trouble and perseverance the shortcomings were remedied and in 1863 the first steam press was started, and thus the way opened for the printing of those cheap editions, which later on, were to have such enormous and hitherto unheard of circulation. In 1864 a second press had to be added and in 1865, with increased steam power, a third one.

On March 1, 1863, Röder's Son-in-law, Mr L. Hugo Wolff entered the business. In the meantime the premises had again become too small for the ever increasing business, and Röder bought a piece of ground (Dörrienstrasse No 13); and after the necessary buildings were erected in 1867, the business was transferred there, with 4 steam presses and an engine of 10 horse power. But before long the number of steam presses had to be increased to 10, and the number of employés rose accordingly. A great lift was at that time given to the enlargement of the business by the enormous success of 'Peters' Edition' which began in 1867 by first issuing an octavo volume of Beethoven's Sonatas, price five shillings complete. The improved steam printing process now gave rise also to the printing of other cheap editions.

The new building at first contained in the three lower floors the business premises, whilst the upper floors were used for private residences, these however were required one after the other for the business, and in 1871 the entire building, with the exception of Röder's own private rooms, was devoted to the business.

On the 1st of July 1868, Röder and his employés founded an infirmary, which proved to be a great boon to all concerned, until December 1884, when a new law coming into operation, it had to be amalgamated with a public institution.

On the first of February 1871 Röder's second Son-in-law Mr Max Rentsch entered the Firm.

On the 21st of October of the same year Röder celebrated the 25th Anniversary of his establishment in business by a festival dinner followed by a ball, when not only all his employés, but also a great number of his customers assembled at the 'Schützenhaus'. On this joyful occasion, he set apart a large sum of money, which was considerably increased by the liberality of several friends, for the purpose of creating a fund for the benefit of invalids. The musical papers 'Musikalisches Wochenblatt', and 'Signale' fully reported this interesting festival in their columns.

It was also in 1871 that His Majesty The King of Saxony honored Röder, by personally inspecting his establishment and conferring on him the title of 'Königl. Commerzienrath'.

On the 15th of November 1872 Röder admitted his two Sons-in-law as partners in his firm.

In the same year another and still larger piece of ground on the Gerichtsweg was bought for the erection of the factory now occupied by the firm, and which contains 6 large workrooms (125 and 180 feet long, by 42 feet wide), a new 40 horse power engine, etc.

In 1873 Röder exhibited at the great International Exhibition at Vienna, and received the order of 'Franz Josef' and the medal for progress in Art.

In May 1874, Röder finally retired from active business, leaving the management in the hands of his two Sons-in-law.

C. G. Röder died on the 29th October 1883, having enjoyed only for a few years his retirement, so well earned after so many years of toil and incessant labour. During the first year or two of his retirement, he still continued to devote occasionally a few hours to business, until his failing eyesight rendered it impossible.

The large number of friends who attended his funeral, and the numerous notices about him in the daily and the musical papers testify to the respect with which the deceased was regarded during his long life. Honor to his memory!

A few more particulars about the Röder Establishment may be interesting. In June 1874 the removal of the business to the premises now occupied by the firm took place. Also in this, the fourth abode, the business continued to increase. Agreeably with the intentions of the founder new and approved machinery were constantly added, and the employés working continually together, have attained a high degree of perfection, and every new improvement is at once introduced, when found to be practicable.

Although it was thought that the new premises would prove sufficient for all requirements, in 1879, a new (third) wing had to be built, and in 1882 a third floor had to be added to the central block, after the erection of a new 75 horse power engine; and in 1884 another story was added to the two side wings.

In February 1881, the business of Messrs. Graichen & Riehl, letter press printers, was bought and added to Röder's business as a new branch.

The electric light introduced into part of the building in 1883 was found to be so satisfactory, that in 1884 more machines were added to carry the light through nearly all the buildings, and now the Engravers, Type printers, Lithographers and Lithoprinters work with Electric light.

To form an idea of the way in which the business is carried on, in this, the most extensive establishment of its kind in the world, it will be best to give a description of the various stages through which a manuscript has to pass before it is printed and ready for circulation.

After all necessary notices and instructions have been entered in the books kept for that purpose, the manuscript is given into the hands of the 'Engraver's preparer', whose business it is, to calculate the number of plates, and how many bars are to go on each page, paying attention to the turning over. Then the MS is sent up to the engraving department, where the foreman gives it with the requisite number of plates, to the engravers, who, after preparing the plates, measure and mark the staves on them, then draw the lines of the staves, with a tool made for that purpose, and dot the notes, each according to their respective value and position in the scale. To the dots are then added, with the help of a ruler, the perpendicular tails, and the text or words are marked in according to the MS with a pencil. After this the heads of the notes, the brackets, clefs and text are stamped in. As this proceeding brings the plate out of shape, it has to be straightened again by a polished hammer and anvil; the slurs, ties, bar and ledger lines, marks of expression, crescendos or diminuendos are then engraved by hand and the chips removed by a triangular scraper; after which the engraving is completed.

The 136 Engravers, now employed at Röder's, finish about 200 plates daily, or 60,000 a year. The Engraver's department is well supplied not only with all necessary tools, but also with all available works for instruction or reference.

The finished plates go then to the Corrector's press, and one copy is pulled off for the Corrector, whose duty it is, carefully to compare the proof with the MS and to note any mistakes made by the Engraver, who then has to correct the same, by hammering the plates at the faulty places from the back, to remove the wrong notes and to produce a smooth surface, after which the right notes are punched in. Should many corrections be necessary, part of a plate has sometimes to be cut off and another piece to be soldered on. In such cases another proof has to be taken, and the corrector has again to examine it. When required, the corrected proof is also sent for revision to the composer or publisher. Three correctors attend to this department. The plates are now ready for printing, and according to the edition required, they are delivered to either the department of printing by hand, or by steam.

There are now eight hand presses going, each served by two printers, one of whom, has to ink the plate and the other to pull it through the press. This is done by first laying the plate on the press table, putting the moist paper on the plate, covering both with an elastic cover, and then pulling the whole through iron cylinders. This hand printing is now only used for very small editions, or for 'Editions de Luxe'.

By far the largest part of Music printing is done by steam, even when the editions are as small as 50 Copies. There are 26 Steam presses of various dimensions constantly at work, and they are worked after this manner: – After an impression has been taken from the plates by a hand press on transfer paper, this impression is transferred by another handpress on to a smoothly prepared Litho Stone, which is then cleaned and etched, after which it is ready for printing.

These transfers for the steam presses are done in 7 divisions, each of 2 Music printers, 2 Lithographers and 3 cleaners. The grinding with sand and water and the polishing of the Litho Stones by 14 machines occupies 12 men, who can finish about 300 Stones daily.

After the transfer has been prepared as above, the stone is handed to the printer in the steam press room, and it his duty to superintend the inking and moistening of the stone, and also the printing. The paper is put in its proper position, marked near the roller, in single sheets by a girl, whilst the machine in motion takes hold of it, and after a turn of the cylinder on the transfer stone, it is withdrawn on the other side by another girl and then the printing is completed.

From 3000 to 5000 imprints can daily be taken by each press. These presses are managed by 1 foreman, 26 printers and 52 girls.

The requisite paper is provided from the paper store room, and it takes 5 men to count and deliver it. Before it is used, it has to be moistened by machinery, and has to lay one night to get properly saturated.

The glazing is done by four large calendars and one smooth hot rolling machine. These machines are worked by 8 girls and 2 men. The hand press printed Music is however glazed after the printing by two hydraulic presses, worked by 4 men.

For cutting the edges of the paper there are four machines.

The plates are made on the premises. They are cast by two men in two moulds and then planed into shape by two machines. Last year 1 000 000 pounds of metal were used for plates.

For the production of the Titles 3 Artists and 27 Lithographers are employed. The titles are either engraved, or drawn with pen or chalk on stone. The printing is done in a special department by six steam presses and fifteen hand presses.

After the printing is finished all sheets are examined by the foreman, and then the last stage to be undergone is the folding up or stitching or binding. This department has lately been completely fitted with all the most modern machinery.

The plates are then stored in the arched basement, shut off by iron fire proof doors. They are numbered like books in a library, and arranged in such order that they are at once available when required for reprinting. There are two storekeepers to attend to this business. In the adjoining basement on one side are the store rooms for the Litho Stones, in which about 25 000 Stones, each with two titles, are stored, also numbered, on shelves; and on the other side the paper stores to the value of about £7 500. The various qualities and sizes of the paper are also known by numbers.

Finally, the department for type and letter press printing has to be mentioned. It was found that often titles, or advertisements for the back of Music were wanted in type, and in order to execute these orders promptly, the firm purchased in 1881, as has been already mentioned, the letterpress printing business of Messrs. Graichen & Riehl, which at that time was worked with 4 steam presses. The extensive stock of working material and type has since then been increased by the addition of the newest ornamental type, especially by all that is necessary for Music type printing. As all modern improvements have been made use of, also this branch of the business is continually growing and orders are received not only from the Music trade, but from book publishers as well. At present there are 7 steam presses at work, one of which prints in 2 Colors. There is now about 65 000 lbs of type in use and 25 Compositors, 5 Machinists and a corresponding number of assistants male and female are employed.

To form an idea of the extent of Röder's establishment, it may be mentioned that at the commencement of this year 488 persons were employed in the various departments distributed as follows: 136 Engravers, 30 Litho printers, 30 Artists and Lithographers, 37 Engineers and Attendants, 75 layers on and takers off, 16 handpress printers, 50 transfer printers, 20 bookbinders, 15 stone grinders and plate moulders, 10 glazers, 25 Compositors, 5 Blacksmiths & Stokers, 25 Paper Storekeepers and packers, 3 Carpenters, 11 Bookkeepers and Clerks, and the following Machines are constantly at work, 7 Letterpress printing machines, 32 Litho steam-presses, 18 hand presses, 4 rolling machines, 1 hot rolling machine, 14 Stone polishing machines, 2 hydraulic presses, 4 paper cutting machines, 2 planing machines, besides several auxiliary machines, worked by an engine of 75 horse power and two boilers, another boiler being now in course of construction.

The present members of the firm can look with genuine satisfaction at the results of their management of the business, which they have carried on in the spirit of the founder C. G. Röder. The productions of their establishment are to be met with in all parts of the world, for not only German publishers have their music printed at 'Röder's' but also publishers in Belgium, Holland, Denmark, Sweden, Norway, Russia, Greece, France, Spain, England, and North and South America.

Always anxious to take advantage of all new inventions and improvements the firm trusts also in the future to give satisfaction to all who will honor it with their patronage.

Leipzig, March 1885.

★   ★   ★

So lucid is this account that little comment is really needed. The firm of 'Paez' is possibly the Karl Paez of Berlin mentioned in Eitner's *Buch- und Musikalien-Händler*. The whole gives a fascinating picture of dynamic nineteenth century enterprise coupled with benevolent paternalism. The statistics of employees given in the 1896 Festschrift show how the business expanded, even in eleven years. The principal categories are: engravers, 202 (in 1885, 133); machinists, 45 (37); handpress printers, 39 (16); artists, lithographers 46 (30); compositors, correctors, 40 (25); storekeepers, 39 (25); bookkeepers 34 (11). The firm probably continued growing right up to the First World War, but from the 1920s onwards, Röder's declined with the general decline in music-printing. During the Second World War, the firm miraculously survived three heavy raids on Leipzig, and is still in existence.★ Since it now works little for Western Europe, but mostly for East Germany and Russia, it is difficult to judge either the quantity or quality of its production. In any case, music-printing from engraved plates and lithographic stones used on the vast scale developed by Röder's in the later nineteenth century is gone for ever. But the record occasioned by the London exhibition of 1885 remains as a vivid monument to the firm's greatness.

[1965]

★ How much of its post-war activity is in music-printing is not made clear in the articles in MGG and the *New Grove*.

Mozart in Manuscript and Print

6

The Mozarts at the British Museum

One of the most remarkable musical events of the mid-eighteenth century was the hazardous journey which Leopold Mozart undertook with his wife and children, right across Europe, between 9 June 1763 and 29 November 1766. When they left Salzburg, Wolfgang Mozart was under seven and a half years old, and Maria Anna (Nannerl), his sister, barely twelve. The risks Leopold took in going so far from home with such young children were considerable. But he had a profound faith in providence, and the ultimate reward, more in terms of the development of his son's latent genius than of material gain, was certainly great. The city which offered more musical diversity than any other in Europe was London, and here the Mozarts made the longest sojourn of their whole journey. During their stay of sixteen months, which lasted from 23 April 1764 to 24 July 1765, Wolfgang greatly enlarged his musical experience, and himself composed a good deal, including chamber works, pieces for keyboard, symphonies, operatic arias, and one other vocal work.

Most substantial biographies mention that in July 1765 Leopold visited the British Museum with his family and presented to its Trustees the manuscript of a four-part composition *God is our Refuge* (K. 20), headed 'Chorus by Mr. Wolfgang Mozart. 1765'. Although a few books add vaguely that the presentation also included Wolfgang's 'published sonatas' (or some such phrase), the majority do not, and no one has examined in detail all the curious circumstances of this visit to the Museum and its background. In this account I hope to shed some new light on the whole matter by correlating all the ascertainable facts, and by trying to answer some of the questions which they raise. I also propose to consider what the presentation really comprised, and to say something about its subsequent handling and location within the British Museum. Some other points which have not been generally appreciated may be stated here. Mozart's visit to the Museum was the first known to have been paid to it by any musician, and the resultant gift (of what was then modern music) undoubtedly the earliest of its kind received by the Trustees. Moreover, the Museum was the only national institution which ever solicited and received a gift from Mozart.

By way of preamble, it is necessary to cite the five contemporaneous sources which mention either the visit to the Museum, or the presentation, or both. The first two occur in the travel diaries *(Reiseaufzeichnungen)*[1], which Leopold Mozart and Nannerl kept during the family's journey. Among Leopold's London entries, none of which bears a date, there is the following:

The Rev. Mr. Planta and his family in the British Museum. [More will be said of Mr. Planta later.]

Nannerl's entry, also undated, is a good deal longer, and formed part of an excited record of the marvellous things she saw in London:

... The British Museum, in which I saw the library, the antiquities [This must be what she meant by 'Antiquadik'], birds of all kinds, fishes, insects, and fruits [etc.].

The third source, hitherto entirely unpublished, is in the archives of the British Museum. Since the early visitors' books have not survived, there is no official, written record of the Mozarts' visit. But the result of it is mentioned twice, in the extant documents. The minutes of the Standing Committee of the Trustees contain the following entry for 19 July 1765:

Lord Cardross having presented a portrait of Queen Elizabeth, Mr. Mozart a copy of the printed music of his son, and Dr de Or a copy of his Theological Inaugural Dissertation printed at Leyden 1765
Ordered
that thanks be returned for the same.[2]

This minute corresponds to the sentence from the Trustees 'Book of Presents', which forms part of an entry for 19 July 1765:

A copy of the Printed Music of his son: from Mr Mozart. Omitted in the Donation Book.

This sentence does not occur in the original book, but is added in the blank left hand column of a later transcription of it, watermark date 1840, with an asterisk referring to another under the words 'Lord Cardross'.)

Next comes the best known of the sources – the acknowledgement which the Trustees sent to Leopold Mozart, still preserved in the Mozarteum at Salzburg. It reads thus[3]:

Sir,
I am ordered by the *Standing Committee* of the Trustees of the British Museum, to signify to You, that they have received the *present of the musical performances of your*

very ingenious son, which You were pleased lately to make to Them, and to return you their Thanks for the same

July 19 1765.

This acknowledgment is an engraved form, with blank spaces in which the words italicised above were added by hand. This wording was characteristic of the eighteenth century. (The library departments of the Museum continued to use a similarly worded form of acknowledgment until 1973, when they were absorbed in to the British Library.)

The fifth and last source is a newspaper report from London, which was reprinted by Nissen.[4] Though no copy of the original now seems to be known, there is no reason to doubt its accuracy. The full text, including Nissen's heading, reads thus:

The *Salzburger Zeitung* of 6 August 1765 contains the following, of 6 July.

The very famous clavier maker Burkard Thudy [*sic, ie* Tschudi] of this city, a Swiss by birth, had the honour of making for the King of Prussia a wing-shaped instrument with two manuals which was very much admired by all who saw it. It has been regarded as particularly note-worthy that Mr Thudy connected all the stops (*Register*) to a pedal, so that they can be drawn by treading, one after another, and the decrease and increase of tone may be varied at will, which *crescendo* and *decrescendo* has been long wished for by clavier players. Mr Thudy has moreover conceived the good notion of having his extraordinary instrument played for the first time by the most extraordinary clavier player in this world, namely by the very celebrated master of music Wolfg. Mozart, aged [seven or] nine, the admirable son of the Salzburg Kapellmeister, Herr Mozart. It was quite enchanting to hear the fourteen-year-old sister of this little virtuoso playing the most difficult sonatas on the clavier with the most astonishing dexterity and her brother accompanying her extempore on another clavier. Both perform wonders. The British Museum has not only asked for the sonatas that were printed in Paris and made known here[5] together with the portrait of this gifted family, so as to add all such things to the rarity of its amazing collection, but has also received by special request some original manuscripts by this infant prodigy, among which is a short four-part chorus set to English words.

A close examination of these five sources raises a number of complicated questions, some of which clearly originate in the family's visit to the British Museum. But before trying to answer them, we should consider the significance of what Leopold and his daughter wrote in their diaries in relation to the regulations of the Museum and its general character, as they were in July 1765 – barely twelve years after its foundation and some six and a half after it opened its doors to scholars and visitors on 15 January 1759. We need also to know something about the Museum staff, and in particular about the 'Rev. Mr. Planta'.

4 The south-west aspect of the courtyard of Montagu House, showing the entrance to a staff residence where, probably, the Rev Andrew Planta received the Mozart family in 1765. Water-colour by John Wykeham Archer, c 1842. 245 × 350 mm.

Montagu House, the first home of the British Museum, was constructed from 1686 onwards by an unknown French architect on the foundations of an earlier mansion, built by Robert Hooke, and destroyed by fire on 18 January of that year.[6] The high front wall had but one entrance gate. This wall ran right along the line of the Museum's present frontage in Great Russell Street, and was backed by an interior colonnade that faced into the spacious courtyard. (Pl. 4) The main body of the great three-storied house, running east and west, contained the collections, and in the wings[7] flanking the courtyard were lower ranges in which the principal staff, with their families, were obliged by statute to reside. Montagu House was thus well suited for the stringent security required by the Trustees. From its inception the Museum was an enclosed society, rather in the manner of an Oxford or Cambridge college, with the additional immense responsibility of a national treasure house.

The *Statutes and Rules* in force when the Museum was first opened to the public decreed emphatically (para. 12) 'That no children be admitted into the Museum'.[8] Clearly therefore Leopold Mozart was a privileged visitor in that he was invited to bring with him his gifted son and daughter. But we should remember that while the Museum housed the beginnings of a great library, its collections also included then a remarkable range of objects, amassed by Sir Hans Sloane relating to scientific and natural history. In this context also, the Mozart family and its gift would have been welcome, for had not the *Public Advertiser's* announcements of the children's exhibitions at the *Swan and Hoop* tavern described them as 'prodigies of nature'?

The higher staff of the Museum in post at this time was as follows[9]:

Principal Librarian	Gowin Knight MB
Under Librarians	Charles Morton MD
	Matthew Maty MD
	Samuel Harper MA
Assistant Librarians	Andrew Gifford DD
	Andrew Planta DD
	D C Solander
Keeper of the Reading Room	Richard Penneck DB

It is clear from this list that the Rev. Andrew Planta was not one of the more senior members of the staff. Why then was it his name and not that of a senior officer which Leopold noted in his diary? A likely reason emerges from a brief summary of Planta's career.[10]

Andrew (born Andreas) Planta came of an old Swiss family whose recorded origins in the Engadine went back to the twelfth century. He entered the church in 1741, and became pastor at Castasegna in Bergell, where he preached in Italian, into which language he made a translation of the psalms that was published at Strada in 1742. Besides his theological repute, Planta was also a noted mathematician. In 1745 he was appointed a university lecturer at Erlangen, where he received a doctorate. Later he became a tutor in the household of the Markgräfin of Ansbach, the sister of Frederick the Great. The court gave Planta leave to travel to England, where, in 1753, he became pastor of the German reformed church in London. His reputation as thinker and teacher induced George II to nominate him as a librarian in the British Museum in 1757, the year when the King gave the Old Royal Library to its Trustees. Planta was elected FRS in 1770.

A salient point in the summary of Planta's career is that German was one of his native languages. Since it seems very unlikely that any other member of the Museum staff spoke fluent German, he was the obvious choice to receive the Mozart family. For although Leopold had some command of English, his wife[11] and Wolfgang would have had little, if any, and Planta would have been an essential interpreter for their tour of the Museum, after which he offered the visitors hospitality in his residence. This must be the meaning of Leopold's words 'and his family'.

We can now turn to the implications of the report sent from London to the *Salzburger Zeitung*. Its last sentence states unequivocally that the gift was made in response to a request from the Museum. But at that time the Trustees as a body had no interest in music whatever, and no one on the staff of the library had any knowledge of it. (Nearly eighty years were to elapse before the first music catalogue of any kind was published.) It is therefore inconceivable that the Trustees collectively would have sent a formal request: consequently we should look outside for an initial individual link between Leopold Mozart and the Museum. Leopold himself provides this in a letter written on 9 July 1765 to Lorenz Hagenauer, his landlord in Salzburg. At the end of a vivid passage describing the second of two disastrous London fires, he wrote: 'Mr Birch, one of our acquaintances and friends, lost three fine horses, two carriages,' etc. At a point in his travel diaries considerably earlier than the date of that letter, Leopold made this entry: 'Mr and Mrs Birchs [sic], Nordfolk [sic] Street in the Strand'. This address, which can be verified from numerous documents among the Hardwicke Papers in the British Library, confirms that it was the Rev Thomas Birch DD (1705–66), who lost his horses. He was both a Sloane Trustee and one of the first group of Trustees of the British Museum elected in 1753.

Birch, whose interests lay in literature and antiquities, was known as an active and zealous member of the Board. Among his close friends was Matthew Maty, whom he appointed his executor. Both were Fellows of the Royal Society, elected respectively in 1734 and 1750, and Maty succeeded Birch as editor of the *Philosophical Transactions*. It was to Maty that the Hon Daines Barrington[12], elected FRS in 1767, having made his famous examination of Wolfgang Mozart's precocious genius in June 1765, addressed his findings in the conventional form of a 'letter' for publication in the *Philosophical Transactions*. (Inexplicably, the 'letter' was not written until 1769, and by the time of its publication in 1770 London had forgotten all about the Mozarts.) Another FRS with strong musical interests was James Harris, elected in 1763: he was appointed a Trustee of the British Museum on 3 May 1765.[13] That Harris knew Birch much earlier is shown by a letter written to him in 1738 (now Add. MS 4309, f. 36).

We shall probably never know how Leopold met Birch. But we may be fairly sure that it was through some such channel, among the membership of the Royal Society, within the close-knit world of London's learned men, that Leopold was made aware that the Museum would be interested in a presentation as a token of his son's genius. At any rate, it seems likely that the idea was canvassed informally among a few of the Trustees so that when the gift came formally to their notice, it would not be entirely novel. This provides a possible explanation of the way in which the suggestion reached

Leopold Mozart. It may well have seemed to him that it was an official request from the Museum and from its Trustees as a body. What the link with the Royal Society does not explain is the form of Wolfgang's new composition included in the gift, and why it was so totally different from all that he had written hitherto.

The form and style of *God is our Refuge* has been the subject of some diverse comment. Jahn, for example, followed by Abert, described it as a 'madrigal'. Wyzewa & Saint-Foix said it was 'a real fugue', alluded to its affinity to the pieces sung by the Madrigal Society[14], but also remarked on the influence of 'old English church music'. Similarly, Erich Schenk[15] wrote of this work as a 'precipitate of the archaising tendency of English church music'. The sixth edition of Köchel (1964) described it as both a 'motet' and a 'sacred madrigal'. *The New Grove* lists the piece as a motet. Karl Pfannhauser[16] went a good deal further, and said that *God is our Refuge* belongs to the type of short anthem, 'which, in the context of the anglican Communion Service, was sung as an Introit'. Besides conjuring up this liturgical chimaera, Pfannhauser suggested that the style of Mozart's little piece was inspired by that of Jonathan Battishill's *O Lord, look down from heav'n*, which is in G minor, the key Mozart used for his 'chorus'. According to the date on the autograph Battishill completed his work on 5 June 1765.[17]

That Mozart heard it in the last two or three weeks of this month, and was inspired by it, as Pfannhauser conjectures, cannot be proved or disproved. But there is another area of speculation which suggests that Mozart did not compose *God is our Refuge* after any liturgical model at all, or for any liturgical purpose, but followed a contemporary English fashion for setting a sacred text for a secular performance. As basis for this, we should take into account the facts, which show that one of those versed in this kind of composition, and a regular performer of it, was a Trustee of the British Museum, and that some other performers were known to Leopold Mozart.

The body which specialised in such performances was the Noblemen and Gentlemen's Catch Club, founded in November 1761. Among its founder members were the Earl of Eglinton and the Earl of March, both of whose names appear in Leopold's travel diary, as does also that of the 'Comte Carracioli' (The Marchese Domenico Carraciolo di Villa Marina, to give him his correct style and orthography), the Neapolitan ambassador in London, who was elected in November 1764, and was active at the Club's meetings throughout 1765. Among those elected in 1762 was James Harris. The minutes[18] recorded that early in 1763 it was 'resolved that Mr Harris be desir'd to examine all the prize catches and give his opinion how far they are consistent with the rules of the competition and counterpoint'.

Many of the pieces sung by the Club are preserved in the published anthologies edited and dedicated to its members by Edward Thomas Warren (afterwards Warren-Horne), the secretary from 1761 to his death in 1794. Other pieces, some published, are in the manuscript volumes preserved with its archives now in the British Library. From the Club's earliest years this music included, besides catches and glees, canons set to sacred words, English, Latin and Italian. It is true that *God is our Refuge* is not in canonic form, but rather an exercise in free vocal polyphony, not intended primarily for performance. Since, however, *God is our Refuge* was Wolfgang's first composition in this style, and his earliest vocal piece, a model must have been brought to his notice. And how more naturally than through the agency of James Harris?

For in the light of the facts, it is possible that Harris, in his influential capacities as FRS, Trustee of the British Museum (like Leopold Mozart's friend the Rev Thomas Birch), and connoisseur of the correct manner of composing catches, had some part, perhaps a leading one, in conveying to Leopold an example of the manner in which Wolfgang might compose this short piece, as a sample of his musical skill. For Leopold is most unlikely to have devised this himself. Still less would he – let alone his son – have taken the initiative in choosing the text. For though we may now regard *God is our Refuge* as a non-liturgical secular piece, not a sacred one, it is highly improbable that Leopold found, or asked for, a copy of the English authorised version of the psalms, read it through, selected the first verse of no. 46. and said to his son: 'there it is, my child, this is the text that will please the Trustees of the British Museum. Set it in four parts'. This improbability is increased by the avowed distaste which Leopold, as a devout Roman Catholic, expressed for Protestantism and all its works.[19] At any rate, when the Mozart gift came before the Trustees, Harris was in the unique position of being able to speak in favour of it, both as a member of the Board and as something of an expert in the contrapuntal style of composition.

We can now pass to the authorship of the report sent from London for publication in the *Salzburger Zeitung*. From the text we can make various deductions. The author (let us call him 'Mr X')
1. was musical
2. knew Tschudi's remarkable instrument and understood its mechanism
3. had a good command of German
4. had, almost certainly, met Leopold Mozart and his family, and probably heard the children play
5. knew about the gift to the Museum
6. had some contact in Salzburg

Besides these points, there is one other extraordinary fact to be deduced, not from the text, but from the date at its head, 5 July. This coincided with the day of meeting of the Standing Committee of the Trustees, but it was exactly a fortnight *before* the meeting, on 19 July, at which the Mozart gift was reported and accepted. (The words 'have received' must mean that the gift was delivered to the Museum some days before the date of the report. It should be added Trustees' meetings then took place every fourteen days). The minutes of the meeting of 5 July do not mention the gift. So 'Mr X' not only knew the particulars of the gift in advance, but was also certain that, by the time his report appeared in print on 6 August, the gift would not have been rejected by the Trustees as a body.

It is tempting to equate 'Mr X' with Leopold Mozart, for the report seems to read like his triumphal valediction. The tone of the passage about the children, and the exclamation 'Beyde thun Wunder' (Both perform miracles!), are redolent of the letters that he wrote from London to Hagenauer who certainly passed on their contents to the circle of friends eagerly awaiting news from their far-away countrymen. But there is one decisive argument against Leopold's sole authorship – the partly imprecise statement of Wolfgang's age, 'seven or nine', which the Salzburgers would have known exactly.[20] The discrepancy can perhaps be explained if Leopold had a collaborator who accepted the continual understatements of Wolfgang's age as given in the London press. (Barrington ascertained the correct age, but, as mentioned on p. 58, did not publish his account until 1770.) Leopold's collaborator must have been someone who not only knew German but also knew in advance about the gift to the Museum. Among all the names given in Leopold's diaries, there is only one who meets both these requirements – Planta. He, however, was not, as far as is known, musical.[21] Is it possible that Leopold proposed the report and drafted an outline, to which Planta added the official details but left vague the details of Wolfgang's age? We know that Leopold was very busy at this time preparing for departure: perhaps he never saw the final text.

This is, of course, speculative. But the fact remains that someone in the British Museum was a party to the written disclosure of information about a presentation over a fortnight before its acceptance. Then, as now, the Trustees' business included much that was highly confidential. Even though the text of the report was intended only for foreign readers, the very act of putting it into writing was irregular. It seems inconceivable that this could have been done with the approval of the Principal Librarian or with the authority of any of the Trustees. These and other foregoing speculations may now be combined with the certain facts and dates to produce the chronology appended to this essay.

Whoever 'Mr X' was, his account of the presentation made to the Trustees needs some amplification. (It is unfortunate that because their minute of 19

July – 'printed music' – is so incomplete, and the phrase in the acknowledgment – 'musical performances' (see note 18) – so vague, neither is of any practical value.) The 'sonatas printed in Paris' appeared as op. 1 and op. 2, with the imprint 'Aux addresses ordinaires'. They comprise respectively K. 6 and K. 7, and K. 8 and K. 9. But in addition there was a copy of *Six sonates pour le clavecin Op. III* (K. 10–15), which were engraved in London at Leopold's expense in January 1765. (The fact of its inclusion will be discussed below.)

The portrait of 'this gifted family' was that engraved by Jean Baptiste Delafosse after the water-colour painting by Louis Carrogis de Carmontelle in Paris in 1763. Leopold had this print made for use as publicity. It shows Wolfgang seated at a harpsichord, Nannerl standing behind it, while Leopold stands behind his son and plays the violin, his legs awkwardly crossed.

The 'four part chorus with English words' is *God is our Refuge* – Mozart's sole setting of a text in this language. But according to 'Mr X', this was not the only manuscript in the presentation. His words, 'some original manuscripts, among which...', are unmistakably precise. If 'Mr X' meant what he said, what other works could have been presented? Excluding the keyboard pieces in the so-called 'Chelsea note-book', Köchel lists with numbers fourteen works written by Mozart during his London sojourn. The manuscripts of five of them (now including the symphony K. 19a) survive in various libraries, the remainder being lost. These latter are mostly on a fairly large scale, *eg* symphonies, and were perhaps hardly suitable for presentation. But there is another group, not numbered in Köchel, but taken from the list of his son's compositions which Leopold drew up in 1768. This group is there described as 'Fifteen Italian arias, partly composed in London and partly in the Hague'. Only two of these survive, *Va dal furor portata* (K. 19c/21), written in London and *Conservati fedele* (K. 23), written in The Hague. One of the other ones written in London might well have been suitable for inclusion in the presentation. Since, however, nothing of this kind can now be traced in the Department of Manuscripts, 'Mr X's' emphatic plural must remain an unsolved mystery. Was this an exaggeration of Leopold's, or did someone else – perhaps Planta – make a mistake?

To bring this affair to its historical conclusion, it is instructive to see how the items in the Mozart gift were handled within the British Museum and how used by some visiting musicians. For several generations they seem to have caused the staff some trouble. In the 1760s there were but three departments – of Printed Books, of Manuscripts, and 'Artificial and Natural Productions'. Drawings were the responsibility of the Department of Manuscripts, while prints formed part of Printed Books. 'Prints and Drawings' were later made a sub-department of the Department of Antiquities, and did not become a separate department until 1836. Let us then first consider the case of the print after Carmontelle.

An inventory of the Department of Prints and Drawings was taken in 1837, and is extant. But the original copy of the Carmontelle engraving cannot be traced in it. (The two copies now in the collections bear respectively the registration numbers 1864-6-11-50 and 1926-2-14-4.) In 1863 the distinguished Viennese scholar Carl Ferdinand Pohl came to London to collect material for his two books *Mozart in London* and *Haydn in London*, published in Vienna in 1867 with the collective title *Mozart und Haydn in London*. Pohl worked for well over two years in London, and for much of that time in the Museum: in the preface of his Mozart book he acknowledges the assistance of Frederick Berridge, who was then Attendant (2nd class) in the Department of Manuscripts.[22] On p. 137 Pohl paraphrased the last part of 'Mr X's' report, to the effect that Leopold's gift to the Museum included the family portrait engraved by L. Carmintel [*sic*]. Up to 1863 no writer on Mozart, not even Jahn, had named the artist or the engraver, and in his letter of 1 April 1764 Leopold had given the latter's name as 'Mechel'.[23] Pohl, while sometimes weak in matters of nomenclature, was a most conscientious scholar, who scrutinised all the original documents he could find in the Museum. It is most unlikely that he had seen a copy of this engraving elsewhere. Though Pohl confuses the engraver with the original painter, and misspells the latter's name, his very mention of it shows that he had seen the copy purchased from a dealer named Lonsdale in June 1864, when he was working in the Museum.

God is our Refuge (Pl. 5) lay in obscurity for sixty-seven years, until Vincent Novello brought the work to light. In 1829 he and his wife visited Mozart's widow and sister in Salzburg and then went on to Vienna. Novello's main purpose was to collect material for a biography of the composer, which in fact he never completed. Even before his travels he had purchased a copy of Nissen's pioneering book, which contains what seems to be the earliest mention of *God is our Refuge*. It was almost certainly this which sent Novello to the Museum in search of the manuscript. The copy which he made of it[24] on 24 June 1832 is a most interesting document. A long note on his titlepage gives the date and says that he found the manuscript only 'after a very long search'. (Whether the left hand margin was damaged by then is not stated.) Novello continued: 'There are several of his earlier works (printed) in the Museum Collection; and, amongst others, the set of sonatas which he dedicated to the Queen of England: but it is remarkable (&, in my opinion, a very reprehensible neglect) that Mozart's name does not once appear in any of the Museum Catalogues'. At the foot of the second – now partly mutilated – page of his copy of the music, Novello wrote another note. It repeats some of what he wrote on his title page, and adds that the manuscript 'is contained in a Volume bound up with Mozart's sonatas op. 1. and op. 2. & other pieces... the book is [?marke]d on the back A. n°. 227. and opens, not upright but, longways. It is quite wonderful how M[ozar]t has hit off the [?antique] Church style in this early [composition]'.

As a souvenir of his visit Novello left the following note, written in ink on a slip measuring 65 × 100 mm: 'The above curious and interesting composition is in Mozart's own hand-writing. The circumstance of his having written it for the express purpose of presenting it to the British Museum, at the time that he visited England, when he was about 7 years old, is recorded in his Life by Nissen (vide page 79)'. Faint words in pencil on the blank lower right hand portion of the manuscript (visible, rather curiously only to the naked eye and not under a magnifying glass) show that Novello began writing his note in that space, but was clearly then stopped by authority. When starting his note afresh in ink he kept the word 'above', though it was no longer applicable. Oliphant added a few words in pencil: 'The handwriting of Vincent Novello. T.O.'

The extant copies of the catalogues then in use within the Department of Printed Books show that Novello was perfectly correct about the absence of Mozart's name. It was another ten years before it appeared in any catalogue at all, and then not in one of printed books but of manuscripts. In 1842 the Trustees issued Thomas Oliphant's *Catalogue of Manuscript Music in the British Museum*, which includes an entry for *God is our Refuge* as No. 239 on p. 98. This simply states that 'this composition... is attached to the printed copy of the 'Sonates pour le clavecin... Oeuvre 2... Preserved in the General Library of Printed Books', which really tells us less than Novello's notes.

But some twelve years after Novello's visit, another English musician, Matthew Cooke[25], came to the British Museum, and made the second – hitherto unrecorded – copy of *God is our Refuge*. As he was a professional copyist, he did this for someone else, probably for a member of the Glazebrook family, which included several clergy with musical interests: their armorial bookplate is found in the volume containing the collection of church music, in which the manuscript is now bound. The volume was purchased by the British Museum Music Room in 1958; the pressmark of the manuscript is G. 518. c. (33). The copy is written on paper watermarked 1843, and was probably made soon after that date. It is of no textual value, but is historically interesting. Cooke put the missing letters of the named voice parts in square brackets, which shows that the left-hand margin of the original had been damaged before the time of his visit. (Novello did not copy these words.)

On a sheet opposite his copy Cooke added a long note, which begins: 'In

5 Mozart's *God is our Refuge*, K.20, partly in his hand, partly in his father's. 1765. 240 × 295 mm.

the general library of printed books at the British Museum will be found, by the subjoined reference Select Case' etc. $\dfrac{\text{C. 21-d.}}{1-2}$
This tells us that the volume which Novello saw had been moved for security to one of the series of locked cases devised by Panizzi. Cooke went on to quote both Novello's small note and the pencilled words added by Oliphant. As Cooke expanded the initials 'T.O.' to 'Thomas Oliphant', he may well have known him and had his help in finding the book.

The next person to study the manuscript was the percipient Pohl. He examined the volume containing it in October or November 1863, and described what he found not in his book *Mozart in London* but in an article in the *Allgemeine Musikalische Zeitung*[26], in which he included the first publication of *God is our Refuge*. He wrote thus: 'The leaf has been trimmed, drastically and unevenly, by a clumsy hand, so that part of the writing has been lost. The following note is affixed to the upper edge[27]; [then follows the text of Novello's small note. Pohl continues:] This Mozart autograph is bound up with the following printed compositions: two sonatas dedicated to Madame Victoire de France; two sonatas dedicated to the Comtesse de Tesse; Air with variations (? K. 264, Lisa dormait); Allegretto, la bergere Silimene [sic] (K. 359); Arietta for piano in G minor (K. 30 [in fact K. 360]) – the last three all published in London'. These London editions can only have been those of Longman & Broderip. The Museum's copies were all unstamped, and are most probably those received by copyright at or near the time of publication in 1787, and must have been selected by Oliphant (whose unmistakable numbering they still bear) to make up a volume of suitable thickness.

Pohl gave no pressmark, but the volume must still have borne the one recorded by Cooke. For Hughes-Hughes's *Catalogue of Manuscript Music in the British Museum*, vol. 1, 1906, p. 159, gives the pressmark as Case 21. d. 31, the third mark having been added, as throughout the library, in the 1870s or 1880s. In that same year 1906 Squire moved it from the General Library to the Music Room. He extracted the English editions, had them rebound with four other Longman & Broderip editions of Mozart keyboard works, and replaced them at e. 490. b. (1). Squire made up a new volume comprising the two books of the Paris sonatas and the manuscript preceded by Novello's note pasted on a new blank leaf, so that, apart from the latter, the whole was again as Novello had seen it in 1832. Squire added a generous padding of blank leaves to make the book thick enough to be lettered across the panels of the spine and had the volume bound in full red morocco, with the date 1906 stamped in gold on the back doublure. He placed it at K. 10. a. 17, where it still is. In all these processes Squire – in breach of long-established departmental practice – destroyed all the titleslips written by Oliphant, though the latter's distinctive 'K' marks survive on the titlepages of the printed music. Fortunately, thanks to the keen observation of Novello, Cooke and Pohl, much of the history of this part of the Mozart gift can be reconstructed.

There remains the 'odd man out' – the copy of the *Six sonates pour le clavecin ... Oeuvre III*, which still bears the pressmark, h. 60. (7), given to it by Oliphant, whose title-slip also survives. How can we be certain that this copy – the only one in the general collections – was included in the Mozart gift? When Novello noted its presence in 1832, he had no reason to think that it was, but mentioned that op. 1 and op. 2, both oblong folio, were bound with *God is our Refuge*. Now op. III is an upright folio in format, an important difference which prevented it from being bound with the other works, and before long caused it to be kept apart from them. Lack of proper documentation contributed to the severance. Certainly by the time that Oliphant catalogued it, in about 1843, all knowledge of its earlier association was lost. But the evidence can be deduced from the archival catalogues, and is also preserved on the titlepage which bears, in pencil, an old pressmark 2 CC f at the bottom right-hand corner.[28]

This shows beyond all doubt that the piece was originally stored uncatalogued on a shelf in one of the rooms in Montagu House allocated, broadly speaking, to printed books on the arts and sciences. The use of this room for such books can be verified from examination of the staff copy of the 1787 catalogue (now preserved at Cup. 407. e. 7, 8), which has a large number of shelf-marks added by hand. This reveals the crucial fact. 2 CC f was also used for a number of the Garrick plays which were received by bequest in 1780 – for instance Beaumont and Fletcher's *The Scornful Lady*. But practically all these plays are in small quarto format. It is inconceivable that valuable vertical space would have been wasted by storing an unbound tall music folio on the same shelf as plays in small quarto. The Mozart sonatas must therefore have been in the Museum before 1780, and were then moved to an unmarked shelf where they joined a small but steady accumulation of other uncatalogued printed music.

This is borne out by the fact that the Book of Presents records nothing of a musical nature between 1765 and 1780, apart from two gifts of theoretical works made by Sir John Hawkins on 30 May and 23 October 1778. Furthermore, the Mozart sonatas op. 3 bear a yellow, lozenge-shaped stamp – yellow was then used for donations – identical in size, tinge and impression to those on Mozart's op. I and op. II bound with *God is our Refuge*. Who else but Leopold would have presented op. III at this time? It seems likely that when he did so, he gave it separately at a second visit to the Museum, after 5 July. This would explain why the notice in the *Salzburger Zeitung* did not mention op. III, and suggests a reason for the curious phrase 'omitted in the Donation Book' quoted above (p. 158). The logical conclusions are, first, that though four-fifths of the Mozart gift was in the British Museum before 5 July, it was not laid before the Trustees on that day; and second, that even though the minutes of 19 July refer to 'the printed music', *ie* op. III, the Board must then also have seen the other items. For the comprehensive phrase, 'the musical performances', used in the acknowledgment, could hardly have referred to op. III alone.

It is ironical that what is instrinsically the most important item in the Mozart gift – *God is our Refuge* – is also the most ambiguous. For this manuscript is not quite what it purports to be. The keen-eyed Pohl was slightly puzzled. In his AMZ article he commented on the astonishing technical skill shown by a composer of tender years, and also remarked that the words were 'more painted than written, with anxious precision'. If Pohl's remark was intended to convey a faint suspicion of doubt, he was proved right a century later. For the palaeographical study of Mozart's handwriting undertaken from the 1960s onwards by Wolfgang Plath has shown that right up to about 1772 Leopold Mozart often literally had some hand in his son's compositions. This is exemplified in *God is our Refuge*.

The sixth edition of Köchel describes the manuscript as 'autograph', but if this means that the entire sheet is solely in Wolfgang's hand, the statement is incorrect. For it was indisputably Leopold who wrote the title, heading and date, and, most probably[29], drew the first two of the three braces. As to the remainder, Wolfgang certainly wrote the notes (which, after all, are what matter) and drew the bar lines. He probably wrote the clefs, the key signatures and tempo markings. But the writing of the words, in both the text underlay and the indication of the four staves, is puzzling.

We know all too little of the boy's orthography in his childhood. But we can be certain that in the summer of 1765, when he was barely nine and a half, his natural writing, in a German hand, would have been far less well-formed and secure than his sister's, of whose hand, at the age of fourteen we have specimens in her travel diary. This shows that her writing was spidery and uncertain in direction. From this we may infer that Wolfgang's roman hand was far weaker in all respects. How much more difficult, therefore, would it have been for him to write a text in English, which he can hardly have understood at all. For the understanding of a language is an essential concomitant to writing it firmly and consistently. But it is most unlikely that, apart from a few words of musical expression in Italian, Wolfgang understood anything but German. It is therefore a fair assumption that his writing of a text in any other language was ill-controlled and disjunct.[30]

Looked at in this light, the writing of the words of *God is our Refuge* seems rather less problematical. The first line is most revealing. The ink is light brown, and the strokes are uneven, with varying direction, and the joins between the letters uncertain. This is particularly noticeable in the word 'trouble'. Comparison of this single word with its recurrences on the lower staves suggests very strongly that they cannot have been written by one and the same hand. Moreover, the firmness of the writing in all but the first line of words is matched by the colour of the ink, which is consistently dark brown.

On this basis, the process of composition was probably something like this. Leopold copied out the English text, very neatly, line by line. Wolfgang composed the music, and wrote down the notes. But his unfamiliarity with English caused him to allow insufficient vertical space for the words towards the end of the first four staves. (Hence the meandering bar-lines.) Under Leopold's guidance, however, he improved this as he went on. When

Wolfgang began to add the words, drawing them after his father's exemplar, his tentative effort became so awkward that he gave up at the end of the first line and Leopold took over, writing in a firm neat hand, with well controlled syllabic breaks, and placing the syllables as carefully as possible under the notes. The whole 'ductus' is so firm that it cannot be the writing of a young boy, even if we suppose that he took a rest after the first line, wrote the text on a practice sheet, and then started again.

This theory is strengthened if we look at Leopold's travel diaries. The entries for the later part of the time he spent in Paris contain many names written not in his German hand but in very careful roman script. All the entries from his London sojourn are in the latter. On pages 22, 29, 30–32, 34, 36–8 and 43 of Schürig's facsimile of 1920, we can find examples of distinctive single letters and letter groups – 'b', 'p', 'ble', 'hel', 'our', 'and', 'stre', 'ver' and so on – which are identical with the corresponding forms in the text of *God is our Refuge*.[31] Any superficial resemblance between the portion of the manuscript written by Leopold and that by Wolfgang is due to two facts – that Leopold's careful roman often has a rather juvenile appearance (especially when he writes unfamiliar names), and that since he himself taught his son to write, the boy naturally modelled his own roman hand on his father's. All this suggests that this manuscript should be described as a 'composite autograph'. It seems doubtful whether Leopold was trying to lead the Trustees to think that the composition was entirely in Wolfgang's hand. Since, as already remarked, they were all unmusical apart from Harris, and since none of them could have seen Leopold's or Wolfgang's handwriting before, there would have been little point in a conscious attempt to mislead. Harris, indeed, would only have been interested in the boy's musical capacity.

In 1956 Dent wrote: 'the appearance of the manuscript suggests that it was not a fair copy of an already composed work but was written down on the spot in the Museum itself'.[32] It was probably the entry in Leopold's diary recording the visit to Planta which led Dent to form this rather fanciful notion. For all the evidence suggests that, whatever passed between the Planta family and the Mozart, *God is our Refuge* was not committed to paper within the precincts of the British Museum, but was written, as Pohl said, 'with anxious care', before the visit took place.

CHRONOLOGY JUNE–AUGUST 1765

June (? early): Barrington visits the Mozarts' lodgings and tests Wolfgang's musical attainment.
June (? mid): The idea of a presentation to the Trustees of the British

Museum suggested possibly by Barrington, either to Planta or to Birch, or to someone connected with them.

June (? third week): the invitation conveyed informally to Leopold Mozart, possibly by Birch, and *God is our Refuge* composed.

June (? last week): the Mozart family visit Planta in the Museum, and tour the galleries. *God is our Refuge*, the sonatas op. 1 and op. 2, and the engraving handed over.

July (before the 5th): Notice for the *Salzburger Zeitung* drafted.

5 July: Meeting of the Standing Committee of the Trustees: the Mozart gift not reported.

July (mid): Leopold probably visits the Museum and leaves the copy of the op. 3 sonatas.

19 July: Meeting of the Standing Committee of the Trustees: the Mozart gift accepted.

19 July: The Trustees' acknowledgment sent to Leopold Mozart.

24 July: The Mozarts leave London for Canterbury.

1 August: The Mozarts leave England.

6 August: The notice from London appears in the *Salzburger Zeitung*.

Notes

1 *Mozart. Briefe und Aufzeichnungen (MBA). Gesamtausgabe*. Gesammelt und erläutert von Wilhelm A Bauer und Otto Erich Deutsch (Kassel 1962) Bd. 1, pp. 196, 198–9.

2 For these and other details from minutes and other archival sources, I am much indebted to Miss Janet Wallace, the archivist of the British Museum.

3 Reproduced in facsimile in Roland Tenschert, *Mozart. Ein Künstlerleben in Bildern und Dokumenten* (Leipzig, [1931?]) pl. 14. Maty's name is often variously misspelt, in both English and German books, as 'Maly' or 'Marty'.

4 The original is quoted by G N von Nissen, *Biographie W A Mozart's* (Leipzig 1828), pp. 89–9. My thanks are due to Messrs A & C Black for permission to quote the English translation given in O E Deutsch, *Mozart. A documentary biography* (London, 1965), p. 48. This (like the German original) omits the last sentence, of which the translation is my own. I have also added, in square brackets, the translation of the omitted words 'sieben – oder', which precede 'neunjähriger' in Nissen. (See also note 20.) The title of the journal which Nissen gave as *Die Salzburger Zeitung* is also variously found as *Europaeische Zeitung* (Salzburg) – MBA *Komm.* I p. 132 – or, as in Deutsch, *Dokumenta*, p. 24 'Aus dem Extract-Schreiben oder Europäische Zeitung... Salzburg'. Successive editions of Köchel, under K 20, give yet another variant.

5 The German is: 'die in Paris gedruckten und hier publicirten Sonaten', *ie* only the sonatas, K. 6–9, printed in Paris, not K 10–15, as is given by a number of commentators. I am indebted to Dr Wolfgang Plath for confirmation of this significant point.

6 J Mordaunt Crook, *The British Museum* (London 1972), p. 56, and Arundell Esdaile, *The British Museum Library* (London 1940) p. 39, 40.

7 The present east and west wings, built after 1839 (Esdaile, *op. cit.*, p. 89) were used as Keepers' residences, though on a dwindling scale, until the 1960s.

8 Though repeated in the Statutes of 1759 and 1760, this rule was subsequently modified.

Acts and Votes of Parliament relating to the British Museum, 1805, chap. 8, p. 116, reads: 'No children, apparently under ten years of age, will be admitted.' Nearly 180 years later, infants only a few months old can be heard in all the galleries.

9 *Acts and Votes*, etc., 1805, pp. 126–9.
10 Peter von Planta, *Chronik der Familie Planta* (Zurich 1892) pp. 345–6.
11 *MBA, Kommentar*, I, 1971, p. 132, says that Leopold took only Nannerl and Wolfgang to the Museum. Surely Frau Mozart would have gone too. Leopold was too kind a man to have left her alone in their Soho lodgings on such a notable occasion. (Some 12 years later she complained bitterly when Wolfgang left her alone in Paris.) Nannerl seems to have had a little English, enough, as Leopold noted in a letter of 5 November 1765, to babble in it when very ill at the Hague.
12 Barrington's account of the tests he gave Mozart show that he had himself acquired some musical knowledge. He was a graduate of the Queen's College, Oxford, and made his name as a lawyer and scientist. I have failed to trace any musical activities of his within the university. Nor was he a member of the Noblemen and Gentlemen's Catch Club. Later he made a systematic study of birdsong. The article on him in the DNB quotes some rather derogatory lines by Peter Pindar, in a dialogue with Sir Joseph Banks:
Sir Joseph. Pray then, what think ye of our famous Daines?
Peter: Think, of a man denied by nature brains!
Whose trash so oft the Royal leaves disgraces,
Who knows not jordens brown from Roman vases!
About old pots his head for ever puzzling,
And boring earth, like pigs for truffles muzzling,
Who likewise from old urns to crotchets leaps,
Delights in music, and at concerts *sleeps.*
13 The date kindly supplied by Miss Janet Wallace, from General Committee Minutes, p. 536. There is some testimony to Harris's musical capacity in Joseph Corfe's dedication (addressed to the first Earl of Malmesbury, Harris's son) to *Sacred Music* (1800), which Corfe arranged and published from Harris' adaptations of madrigals, mostly Italian. Corfe acknowledges 'the great assistance which at an early age, I received from him in this Science'. Harris was a patron of Handel, and prepared the list of his works included in Mainwaring's biography.
14 In an article, 'Studien zu Mozarts Kirchenmusikalischen Werken', *ZfM*, III, 1920–21. pp. 189 ff., Wilhelm Kurthen suggested, in connection with *God is our Refuge*, that Leopold Mozart knew the Madrigal Society well. There is no foundation at all for this suggestion, which is repeated in *NMA* III, Werkgruppe 9, p. viii. The list of members in 1764–65, as given in Thomas Oliphant's *Brief Account of the Madrigal Society*, 1835, pp. 18–19, contains no names found in Leopold's travel diaries, and this is confirmed by the minute books, deposited in the Music Library of the British Library in November 1981.
15 Erich Schenk, *Wolfgang Amadeus Mozart*, Zurich 1955, p. 159, and Vienna 1975, p. 125.
16 Karl Pfannhauser, 'Mozarts Kirchenmusikalische Studien im Spiegel seiner Zeit und Nachwelt', *Kirchenmusikalisches Jahrbuch*, 43, (1959), pp. 189 ff. Pfannhauser's view that *God is our Refuge* is an Introit is repeated in *NMA* III, Werkgruppe 9, p. viii, with the editorial qualification 'am ehesten'. This is lacking in the original article.
17 The autograph seems to be lost, but the date is stated in the first edition, which appears in a collection of Battishill's music, *Six Anthems and ten Chants*, edited by John Page, London 1804.

18 This volume forms part of the Club's archive now in the Music Library of the British Library. Its pressmark is H. 2788. rr. One of the early minutes uses the phrase 'musical performances' in the sense of 'compositions'.
19 Letter of 19 March 1765, apparently refusing the offer of a post in London. 'I will not bring up my children in such a dangerous place (where the majority of the inhabitants have no religion, and where one has only evil examples before one). You would be amazed if you saw the way children are brought up here: not to mention other matters connected with religion'.
20 Throughout the sojourn in London, and later, Leopold regularly falsified his son's age to the public. On his copy of the symphony in F, K. 19a, composed early in 1765, he wrote correctly 'di Wolfgango Mozart compositore di 9 Anj'. But in an announcement inserted, in September 1765, in the '*s-Gravenhaegse Vrijdagse Courant*, he stated that the boy was 'only 8 years and 8 months old' – a year younger than he actually was. Similarly, in an Amsterdam journal of 21 January 1766, Leopold gave Wolfgang's age as '8 years and 11 months'. Leopold Mozart's authorship seems to have been first proposed by Georg Kinsky in an article, 'Mozart-Instrumente', *Acta musicologica*, 1940, vol. XII, p. 1 ff: 'Leopold Mozart may well be presumed to be the author'. But in his citation of the text from Nissen, Kinsky omitted the words 'sieben – oder'. F J Hirt, *Meisterwerke des Klavierbaues* (Olten), 1955, p. xii, did the same. It is far more surprising that Deutsch, in his *Documentary Biography*, also omitted these crucial words, although in the German original he denoted their absence by dots. Deutsch (following Kinsky?) strangely omitted also the whole of the last sentence, after the words 'Beyde thun Wunder'.
21 The only musical member of the family I have traced at this period is Duriges Planta, who contributed to a collection of Romansch hymns printed at Celerina in 1765. It was edited by G. G-B Frizzoni, with the title *Canzuns spirituaelas davart Cristo Gesu il Bun Pastor*. The preface names Planta as one of the four 'perits musicants' who selected and arranged the tunes. (Copy in B L.) Peter von Planta, *op. cit.*, p. 345, states that in his youth Joseph Planta (Andrew's son) later Principal Librarian of the Museum, used to read every day 'a chapter from the Romansch Bible' or from the 'Cudesch de Cellarina', the hymnbook of Pastor Frizzoni.
22 I am indebted to Miss Janet Wallace for the particulars of Berridge's work at this date.
23 Christian von Mechel, a Swiss engraver then training in Paris under Delafosse. He may have prepared the engraving of Carmontelle's painting under the supervision of Delafosse, who appended his signature.
24 Now British Library Add. MS 61949. I am grateful to Mr Albi Rosenthal (Otto Haas) for letting me see the manuscript before it was acquired by the Library. I am unable to explain the 'A. n°. 227' seen by Novello on the spine of the original binding. Presumably it represented some sort of shelf-mark used by the Department of Printed Books in Montagu House.
25 Cooke, like his father (also Matthew), was one of the Children of the Chapel Royal. Besides being a professional musician, the younger Cooke was a man of many parts. A copy of his professional label, probably printed in the early 1860s, is pasted on the titlepage of his MS copy of *God is our Refuge*. It states that he was a compiler of Crockford's *Clerical Directory*, editor of the *Freemason's Magazine* and other journals. The label also states: 'Transcribed Old Documents; Collates MSS or Printed Books... Verifies References; Makes Extracts from the British Museum', etc. In September 1850 Cooke applied, unsuccessfully, for the post of Assistant in charge of the collections of printed music in the British Museum (see King, *Printed Music in the British Museum*

1979, pp. 80, 107. Cooke held a ticket of admission to the Reading Room from 1840 to 1878. (Information kindly supplied from the archives by Miss Janet Wallace.)
26 The issue for 16 December 1863, no. 51, pp. 854–5.
27 The phrase 'on the upper edge' appears to mean that the slip bearing Novello's note was then (1863) pasted on to the blank upper edge of the manuscript. It is now pasted on to an oblong folio sheet of almost the same dimensions as the manuscript.
28 The suggestion, made in my *Printed Music in the British Museum* (1979), p. 52, note 24, that a pressmark of this type had been devised by Hawkins for use on his own book, was quite erroneous.
29 I am indebted to Dr Wolfgang Plath for this information, and for discussion of other palaeographical points in the manuscript. According to Alan Tyson, the 12-staff paper on which K 20 was written appears to be identical to that found in two other scores: the Symphony in E flat, K 16 (formerly in Berlin; at present in the Biblioteka Jagiellónska, Kraków), and the Symphony in E flat by C F Abel, copied by Wolfgang (Köchel Anhang A 51 – once believed to be an original work by Wolfgang and given the number K 18; this score is in the Staatsbibliothek Preussischer Kulturbesitz, Berlin).
30 This is borne out by a nearly contemporaneous example of Wolfgang's writing in the heading of the first leaf of the autograph of the aria *Conservati fedele* (K. 23), well reproduced in François Lesure's *Mozart en France* (Paris), 1956. pl. VI. The superscription, written in a mixture of French and Italian, and dated October 1765, shows how wobbly and ill-formed Wolfgang's roman hand still was: he could not even write his own Christian name neatly. A facsimile of the same leaf is reproduced, very smudgily and with loss of part of the superscription, in NMA, II, 7, Arien, Bd. I, p. XXIII. Leopold's copy of the same leaf, here reproduced below the autograph, well exemplifies both the difference and the similarity in the two hands. How this endured can be seen in a page of their joint 1769 travel diary, MBA, I. pl. VIII.
31 Equally valuable for the comparison of letter forms is the short note, in French, which Leopold wrote to Christian Mechel in Paris, probably in January 1764 (MBA no. 79). The note, with its address, is reproduced in facsimile in *Mozart. Klassik für die Gegenwart*, edited by Hartmut Heinicke (Hamburg 1978), p. 39.
32 Edward J Dent and Erich Valentin, *The Earliest Compositions of Wolfgang Amadeus Mozart* (Munich 1956), p. 11.

7

Mozart and Peter Anton Kreusser

In the issue of *The Music Review* for February 1951, which was devoted to essays in honour of Paul Hirsch's seventieth birthday, I gave an account of a previously unrecorded edition of Mozart's duet Sonata in C major, K. 19d, which Robert Birchall published in London in about 1805. I was able to show that Birchall had used the plates of an earlier issue which was printed for Hugh Andrews, and had been published by him between May and September, 1789. No copy of the Andrews edition was then known, but subsequently one was discovered by Alan Tyson, who has described it in *The Music Review* for August 1961. Wolfgang Rehm discussed this English edition of K. 19d at great length in relation to that published in Paris by De Roulléde.[1] It is not the main purpose of the present article to re-open the discussion of the merits of these two editions or re-examine the complicated points that bear on the question of priority.

In passing, however, reference may be made to that section of Rehm's argument (p. 60) which depends on the date of copies of the Birchall edition of two other Mozart duet sonatas, K. 358 and K. 381, which he states bear the watermark 1789. (These copies were then owned by H J Laufer.) That of K. 358 is now in the British Museum. The watermark is in fact 1799: 1789 would, of course, have been impossibly early, since the Act relevant to the introduction of watermark dates in paper did not become law until 1794,[2] and no dates are found in English paper before that year. Perhaps all this is rather like taking a sledgehammer to crack a ten-year-old nut. But the fact remains that this duet Sonata, K. 19d, is significant as one of the earliest works of its type written by a classical master.

It is moreover interesting to find that the early history of the Sonata did not come to an end with its publication in its original form. Indeed, two printings within a space of some fifteen years suggest that this little work enjoyed some lasting popularity in London. A recent discovery shows that its attraction was not limited to pianists. The British Museum has recently acquired a hitherto unknown arrangement of the work scored as a violin sonata. The title-page reads as follows:

A Favorite / SONATA / Composed by / A. Mozart / adapted for the / Piano Forte,

/ with an accompaniment for a / VIOLIN, / by P. A. Kreusser. / Op. V. Entered at Stationers Hall.   Pr. 4s / London, Published & Sold by the Editor No. 44 Greek St. Soho. / [Signed by Kreusser]*

The watermark date in this copy can be read, not without some difficulty but nevertheless with fair certainty, as 1802. This arrangement, which has the violin part in score with the pianoforte part, was clearly based on the Andrews (Birchall) edition. The quality of the engraving is rather poor and the spacing of the notes uneven. For the most part, Kreusser contented himself with redistributing the melody from the right hand of either keyboard part. In his arrangement, both the violinist and the pianist have about an equal share. The former, when not playing the melody, has a lot of very dull figuration.

So much for the edition and its source: what of this P A Kreusser who linked his name to Mozart's in London, and, as will be seen, often acted as his own publisher? The little that is known of his life derives mainly from two dictionaries, the earlier of which, Gerber, was certainly contemporary with Kreusser. A few supplementary details can be added from his published works.

The facts given by Gerber were taken over and expanded by Schilling, part of whose article[3] merits translation:

Kreuser, Peter Anton. Violinist and employed in this capacity since 1807 in the Chapel Royal in London. Born at Langfort [Gerber has 'Langfurth am Main'] in 1772.†... When he played in Paris, he aroused such general astonishment that he was immediately employed as first violin in the Chapel Royal there. The Revolution dislodged him also from this post, and he fled to England. Here he produced several small operettas which he had composed in Paris.... He was one of the best violinists in England.

Two points in this article require comment. Kreusser's name does not appear either in the published Calendars, or in the Royal Archives at Windsor Castle[4], among the members of the Chapel Royal or of the King's Band of Music. His operettas cannot be traced among the productions of the late eighteenth or early nineteenth century, either in Paris or in London, but admittedly the records are incomplete for this period.

Kreusser's published works shed a little light on his career. Soon after his arrival in London, he issued three violin sonatas in his opus 1. The British Museum copy has a watermark date 1796, with the composer's address given

---

* Pressmark: g. 382.r. (1.).

† Correctly, 1765. See Edith Peters, *Georg Anton Kreusser* (Munich, 1975), p. 10.

in the imprint as '15 Sherrard Street, Golden Square'. This copy has a short list of the names of subscribers. Among them were: Duseck, Dr Haydn, Janiowicz, Mr Pleyel, Mr Salomon, Baron de Dalberg. (The style and spelling are as in the original.) These names suggest that Kreusser had a fair range of musical acquaintance in London. Thereafter, he resided for some time at 44 Greek Street, whence he issued his opus 2 (*Three Sonatinas*, no watermark), opus 6 (*Three Airs*, Watermark 1813), opus 16 (*Three Canzonetts*, watermark 1805) and opus 17 (*Two favorite Airs*, watermark 1815). His *Six Waltzes*, op. 12 (no watermark) were published from 33 Rathbone Place. Kreusser's last known opus was 18, a *Military Divertimento*, printed for him by Goulding, Phipps and D'Almaine in about 1810. E Riley had printed a song by him in about 1800.

Though Kreusser published his arrangement of K. 19d some eleven years after Mozart's death, he had nevertheless an indirect family connection with the composer. In Leopold Mozart's invaluable travel diaries, the names listed for the period September 1765 to 10 May 1766, when the family was in Holland, include the somewhat cryptic phrase '2 Kreuser' [*sic*].[5] This refers in fact to Georg Anton Kreusser (1746–1810), who was a distinguished violinist and later became Konzertmeister to the Elector of Mainz, and to his brother Adam Kreusser (1727–91) a famous horn player and later Konzertmeister at Amsterdam. The former was the father of Peter Anton and Johann Matthäus (b. 1763).[6] Subsequently, Leopold Mozart wrote to his wife from Milan on 10th November, 1770; 'Kreusser junior looked us up in Bologna, that is young Kreusser of Amsterdam, whose brother is first violin there, and who came to see us constantly and wanted to travel with us'.[7] Again, Leopold wrote from Salzburg to his son on 20 November 1777, 'Konzertmeister Kreusser is the best person to help you (in Mainz)'.

When Mozart died, Peter Anton Kreusser was only nineteen years old. We know nothing of the young man's movements before he settled in Paris. But if he had travelled in Germany or had remained in or near Mainz during the later 1780s, it is just possible that he met Mozart. When the latter visited Mainz in 1790, Georg Anton Kreusser was still Konzertmeister there.[8] At the least, Peter Anton must surely have heard his father talk of the genius whose juvenile sonata was later to arouse his interest in London.

There is thus a link between Peter Anton Kreusser and Mozart, although it is as slender as the former's talent. Yet despite his limited musicianship, this Kreusser has not been wholly forgotten by posterity. The charm of his three Canzonetts, opus 16, attracted the attention of Alfred Moffat, who edited the first of them as no. 1 in the series *Old Master-Songs*, published by Augener in 1910. Moffat, an astute arranger, did not always give the sources of the works which he edited. Not only did he not do so for this piece, but he also failed to check his biographical sources. For at the head of p. 1 of the song, he gave the date of composition as '*c* 1770' – two years before Peter Anton Kreusser was born!★

[1964]

★But see † note above.

1 In Abt. 2 of the 'Kritische Berichte' to the *Neue Mozart Ausgabe*, ser. ix, Werkgruppe 24, Kassel, 1957, pp. 53–66.
2 See C B Oldman, 'Watermark Dates in English Paper', *The Library*, June–Sept., 1944, 4th ser., vol. xxv, pp. 70, 71.
3 *Encyclopädie der gesammten musikalischen Wissenschaften* (Stuttgart, 1837), Bd. 4, p. 230.
4 I owe this information to the kindness of HM the Queen's Librarian, Mr R C Mackworth-Young.
5 Bauer and Deutsch: *Mozart, Briefe und Aufzeichnungen* (Kassel, 1962), Bd. 1, p. 217.
6 Gerber, confusing the seniority of the younger generation, says that Peter Anton brought over his 'younger' brother to London, in 1802.
7 This sentence contains a contradiction in terms. 'Kreusser junior' and 'young Kreusser' can only refer to Georg Anton, but it was his elder brother Adam who worked in Amsterdam, but as a horn-player and not as a violinist. As far as is known, Georg Anton was never 'first violin' there. Before his appointment to Mainz in 1775 he studied for some years in Italy.
8 Adam Gottron, *Mozart und Mainz* (Mainz, 1955), p. 77.

8

Vignettes in early nineteenth-century London editions of Mozart operas

On 21 June 1737 the royal assent was given to a measure entitled: 'An Act to explain and amend so much of an Act, made in the Twelfth Year of the Reign of Queen Anne, intituled, An Act for reducing the Laws relating to Rogues, Vagabonds, sturdy Beggars, and Vagrants, into one Act of Parliament: for the more effectual punishing such Rogues, Vagabonds, sturdy Beggars, and Vagrants, and sending them whither they ought to be sent, as relates to common Players of Interludes.'[1] Such an Act may seem rather remote from the subject of this article. But it was a long-lived measure, and some seventy years later had two important indirect results in connection with Mozart's operas. For the Act ensured that, when these operas began to receive their earliest professional performances in England, they were originally staged in the finest opera house in London, and consequently were accompanied by an edition of the music which matched the social milieu and is of considerable historical, bibliographical, and iconographical interest.

The background and effects of this Act may be summarized briefly. It put an immediate end to the absurd, debilitating squabbles between the various factions of royalty and the nobility concerned with the production of Italian opera (which in essence meant Handel's operas) in London. The Licensing Act 'provided Drury Lane and Covent Garden with the only licenses to present drama in London, while the King's[2] held the only license to perform Italian opera'.[3] This was due to the fact that one clause of the Act provided 'that no person or persons shall be authorised... to act, represent or perform... any interlude... opera... or other entertainment of the stage... in any part of Great Britain, except in the city of Westminster, and within the liberties thereof, etc.'

It was because the Haymarket lay within the bounds of the city of Westminster that the King's Theatre was given the sole licence for Italian opera. Although, as time passed, Italian works with Italian singers were occasionally heard elsewhere – for instance, at the Pantheon in Oxford Street, in the 1770s – the tradition of the King's Theatre remained as strong as its legal right.

Then, on 17 June 1789, it suffered a catastrophic fire. In the following December, when the manager, William Taylor, applied for a new licence for

Italian opera, the Lord Chamberlain refused it.[4] Consequently, at its opening on 21 February 1791, the rebuilt house could only offer an entertainment of 'music and dancing'. Meanwhile the licence for Italian opera had been granted to the Pantheon (briefly also accorded the title of 'King's Theatre'). But after it too was burnt to a shell, on 14 January 1792, the licence ultimately reverted to the King's Theatre in the Haymarket, whose affairs were thenceforth properly regulated.[5] Gradually, a new era of Italian opera began in London, and productions of Mozart were not very far away.

The architect of the new house was Michael Novosielski,[6] who had radically altered the interior design of the old one in 1782. When the lyre-shaped auditorium was finally completed with its rectangular colonnades, it was by far the largest theatre in London, with accommodation (according to the article in the first edition of *Grove*) for 'nearly 3,300 persons'. Among European houses it was second only to La Scala in Milan.[7] As in Handel's time, the theatre was patronized by the cream of society, for whom was planned the elaborate system of boxes, divided into three sections – the Prince's Side, the Crown Gallery, and the King's Side. A vivid contemporary picture of this milieu reads as follows:

When George the Fourth was Regent, her Majesty's Theatre, as the Italian Opera in the Haymarket is still called, was conducted on a very different system from that which now prevails. Some years previous to the period to which I refer, no one could obtain a box or a ticket for the pit without a voucher from one of the lady patronesses, who, in 1805, were the Duchess of Marlborough, Devonshire, Bedford, Lady Carlisle, and some others. In their day, after the singing and the ballet were over, the company used to retire into the concert-room, where a ball took place, accompanied by refreshments and a supper. There all the rank and fashion of England were assembled on a sort of neutral ground.

At a later period ... it became less difficult to obtain admittance; but the strictest etiquette was still kept up as regarded the dress of the gentlemen, who were only admitted with knee-buckles, ruffles and *chapeau bras*. If there happened to be a drawing-room, the ladies would appear in their court dresses, as well as the gentlemen; and on all occasions the audience of her Majesty's Theatre was stamped with aristocratic elegance.[8]

This audience, passionately fond of music as it was, had long been regaled with operas by such composers as Nasolini, Fioravanti, Anfossi and Portogallo. As for Mozart, the patrons were certainly familiar with some of his keyboard music – largely variations, extracts, and arrangements from sonatas – and with a few chamber works, which had been published in London in ever-increasing quantity from about 1790 onwards.[9] Some of Mozart's songs also were popular, but his larger vocal works, especially the operas, were never heard.[10] But as the operas had been produced all over Europe within twenty years of Mozart's death in 1791, they were certainly known by repute in London where the mature masterpieces had been issued in vocal score in the first decade or so of the nineteenth century. (The last six operas were issued in vocal score by Robert Birchall between about 1809 and 1815; *Figaro* and *Don Giovanni* by Monzani and Hill, in about 1810; *Don Giovanni* by Faulkner about 1817.)

The views of the average music-lover are probably well represented by this passage from an article written in 1811 by the well-known amateur William Gardiner:[11]

> His [ie Mozart's] imagination has infused a sublimity into the opera, that now renders it the highest of all intellectual pleasures. And it is to be lamented that a great nation, like England, has not talent, or ability, sufficient to represent and perform any of the works of this great master. We are still doomed to listen to the effeminate strains of Italy, and the nursury[sic]-songs of Pucito [sic – probably an error for Puccitta], while the gorgeous and terrific *Don Juan* and the beautiful *Clemenza de* [sic] *Tito* lie unopened and unknown to thousands.

Many others certainly shared Gardiner's eager curiosity.

He was, however, wrong in one respect, for he ignored the production of *La clemenza di Tito* given at the King's Theatre on 27 March 1806. This was the first of Mozart's operas to receive a complete professional performance in England, but it seems not to have been a great success, for it was only repeated six times, and then no more Mozart operas were heard for nearly five years. The true, cumulative revelation of his operas began in 1811 and extended over the next nine years. The sequence, including revivals up to the end of the season of 1820, was as follows:[12]

OPERA	FIRST PERFORMED	TOTAL PERFORMANCES
Così fan tutte	9 May 1811	28
Il flauto magico[13]	6 June 1811	23
La clemenza di Tito	3 March 1812[14]	36
Le nozze di Figaro	18 June 1812	49
Don Giovanni	12 April 1817	63

The reception from the critics was mixed, but grew more favourable with successive revivals. This is not surprising, because even to the intelligent English amateur Mozart's idiom was far from easy and the subtleties of his dramatic power elusive. But the gradual effect was overwhelming. By 1823 even Lord Mount Edgcumbe, the most conservative connoisseur of his day, could write retrospectively:

> So entirely did Rossini engross the stage that the operas of no other master were ever to be heard, with the exception of those of Mozart and of his, only *Don Giovanni* and *Le Nozze di Figaro* were often repeated. *La Clemenza di Tito* was occasionally revived, but met with less success. It is singular how every other

composer, past and present, were [sic] totally put aside, and those two alone named or thought of. That Mozart should be admired is not at all so, for he was undoubtedly one of the greatest of masters: it is only strange that though he has been so long dead, his works should have been but so lately known and performed in this country.... His genius was not only original, it was inexhaustible: his productions are full of diversity, and all possessed of intrinsic merit. The frippery and meretricious style of modern music is to the ear like tinsel to the eye, brilliant, striking, for a moment perhaps captivating, but it will be transitory and speedily lost in the fluctuations of taste; and I think I may venture to predict, that Rossini will not long have ceased to write before he will cease to be remembered, and that his music will be thrown aside as that of so many of his predecessors and superiors already is; while the name of Mozart, with those of this two great countrymen, Handel and Haydn, will live for ever.[15]

Clearly the time had become ripe for an enterprising publisher to exploit the intense interest in Mozart aroused by the performances at the King's Theatre. The firm which took the opportunity was Goulding, D'Almaine, Potter & Co., of 20 Soho Square[16] and its editor was Joseph Mazzinghi, a prolific, fashionable musician of Corsican origin who had been appointed musical director of the King's Theatre in 1784, and composed the 'Opera Dances' performed on its stage from 1786 to 1789. Most of the music he wrote from Op. 9 onwards had been issued by this firm.[17] Mazzinghi was also music-master to Queen Caroline when Princess of Wales, a post which must have given him many connections among the aristocratic patrons of the King's Theatre. Since Goulding apparently published little of Mozart's vocal music before the sequence of opera performances began, it seems more likely that the idea for the edition of the Mozart operas was Mazzinghi's rather than his publishers'. Given the attraction of royal duchesses as dedicatees and the employment of an effective artist to provide the vignettes for the elegant title-pages, this exceptionally elaborate edition was assured of success. Though not of much musical significance, its variety shows that it was intended to satisfy the needs of diverse domestic performance.

It is likely that Mazzinghi and Goulding planned the edition as a whole,[18] probably before the end of the operatic season of 1816–17, which saw revivals of *Così fan tutte*, *La clemenza di Tito*, and *Le nozze di Figaro*. For after that season Mazzinghi was replaced as musical director by Henry Bishop. The evidence of the plan is found in the following advertisement, which is regularly printed in the edition and sets out the component groups in full (the letters [A] to [E] have been added for identification).[19]

Selections
From
Mozart's Celebrated Operas
Now Publishing.
Arranged by
J. MAZZINGHI.

[A] Le Nozze di Figaro
 Il Don Giovanni
 La Clemenza di Tito
 Cosi fan Tutte
 Il Flauto Magico or Zauberflote

Arranged in Numbers Price 6s each for the Pianoforte, Harp, Flute & Violoncello

Also the same Operas, with the same Accompaniments in One Book

[B] Le Nozze di Figaro
 Il Don Giovanni
 La Clemenza di Tito
 Cosi fan Tutte
 Il Flauto Magico, or Zauberflote

Arranged in Numbers Price 4s each for the Pianoforte, Flute & Violoncello

Also the same Operas, with the same Accompaniments in One Book

SINGLE OVERTURES.

[C] Le Nozze di Figaro
 Il Don Giovanni
 La Clemenza di Tito
 Cosi fan Tutte
 Il Flauto Magico, or Zauberflote

Arranged for the Pianoforte, Flute and Violoncello

[D] Selections from Il Don Giovanni, arranged for Two Performers on the Pianoforte, either in Numbers or One Book

[E] Batti, batti, O bel Masetto, with variations for the Pianoforte, Harp, Flute and Violoncello

Also arranged for the Pianoforte, Flute and Violoncello

At this point, one of the titles may be transcribed as an example of the standard form of the wording:

The Favorite / Overture, Songs, Duetts, &c in Mozarts / Celebrated Opera / Il Flauto Magico / or Zauberflote. / For the / Piano Forte / Flute and Violoncello / Arranged & Inscribed / To Her Royal Highness / The Duchess of Kent, / By / J. Mazzinghi. / Rushell & Co. /

The following is a table of all the parts of the edition, corresponding to the advertisement, now in the British Library's Music Library.

GROUP	OPERA	DEDICATEE[20]	PRESS-MARK	PARTS	WATER-MARK DATE
A	Le nozze di Figaro	Duchess of Gloucester[21]	Hirsch M.1281.(2)	P.F. and harp (in score), bk. 1–5	–
	ditto★		g.442.j.(15, 16)	harp, bk. 1, 4	1816
B	Le nozze di Figaro	Duchess of Gloucester	h.1632.a.(3)	P.F., flute, and 'cello, bk. 1–5	1816
	Don Giovanni	Duchess of Cumberland[21]	h.1632.a.(1)	P.F., flute, and 'cello, bk. 1–5	1816
	ditto★		Hirsch M.1281.(3)	P.F., bk. 1–7	1818
	La clemenza di Tito	Duchess of Cambridge	h.1632.a.(4)	P.F., flute and 'cello, bk. 1–5	1818
	ditto		Hirsch M.1281.(1)	P.F., bk. 1–3	1817
	Così fan tutte	Duchess of Clarence	h.1632.a.(5)	P.F., flute, and 'cello, bk. 1–5	1823
	Il flauto magico	Duchess of Kent	h.1632.a.(2)	P.F., flute, and 'cello, bk. 1–5	1823–7
C	La clemenza di Tito	Duchess of Cambridge★	h.405.ff.(2)	P.F.	none (c. 1830)
	Le nozze di Figaro	Duchess of Gloucester★	g.271.b.(6)	P.F.	1821(?)
D	Don Giovanni	Countess of March	h.321.j.(4)[22]	P.F., duet, bk. 1–4	1817
	ditto		g.382.xx.(7)[22]	P.F., duet, bk. 1–4	1816
	ditto		h.405.k.(1)[22]	P.F., duet, bk. 1–4	1817

There are no copies of any part of Group E[23] in the Music Library. Items marked with an asterisk in the above list lack any illustrated title-page.

The watermark dates show that in groups [B] and [D] all the parts for *Le nozze di Figaro, Don Giovanni,* and *La clemenza di Tito* are of the first or an early issue, while those for *Così fan tutte* and *Il flauto magico* in group [B] are of later issues, as are also the two items in group [C]. The only external date which can be fixed with any precision pertains to group [D], of which there is a review in the *Monthly Magazine* for March 1818. But there are some other pieces of indirect evidence which suggest a terminal date of 1819 to 1820 for the edition as a whole. The artist who probably supplied the vignettes died (as mentioned below) in September 1819. All the groups in the edition are found in a catalogue[24] which Goulding issued at about that time. Two other pointers are found in a composite volume at Hirsch M.1280, of which the relevant contents are included in the above list: its binding is dated 1821 on the front cover (on which is also lettered the name of the owner, H Villebois), and it has a front end-paper with the watermark date 1819.

Having set the King's Theatre productions of Mozart's operas in their historical context, and Mazzinghi's edition in its chronological and bibliographical perspective, we may now turn to the vignettes which adorn the title-pages. The identity of the illustrator is problematical and merits a digression. The name on all the vignettes is either 'Hopwood' or 'J Hopwood'. There were two artists of this name, both James Hopwood, father (c 1752–1819) and son (1795–1850).[25] Both worked largely as stipple engravers; the son was precocious and exhibited at the Royal Academy, in oils, in 1802 and 1803. The Department of Prints and Drawings in the British Museum contains 135 engraved portraits by the elder Hopwood and seventeen by the younger. Apart from a varying degree of definition, there is no great difference between their styles. But on the whole, the vignettes resemble more the work of the father.[26] If they are attributable to him, one point needs to be made. The vignette for *Il flauto magico* must have been one of his last works, because he died, after a period of illness, on 29 September. The opera was produced on 25 May 1819, prior to which, unlike the others, it had enjoyed no revival since its first production on 6 June 1811.

The subjects of the five vignettes in group [B] are:

Le nozze di Figaro, Act 1, scene 7. Susanna, Don Basilio, Cherubino, Count Almaviva (Pl. 6).

Don Giovanni, Act 2, scene 14. The Commendatore, Don Giovanni[27] (Pl. 7).

La clemenza di Tito, Act 1, scene 4. Probably Sextus, Vitellia, who gestures towards the burning Capitol, at a point in the scene when the other singers have left the stage (Pl. 8).

Così fan tutte, Act 2, scene 3. Ferrando, Fiordiligi, Dorabella, Guglielmo. But there is nothing to identify one or the other in either pair (Pl. 9).

Il flauto magico, Act 1, scene 1. The Three Ladies (attendant on the Queen of Night), Tamino[28] (Pl. 10).

84 *Vignettes in early nineteenth-century London editions of Mozart operas*

6 *Le nozze di Figaro*, Act 1, scene 7. Stipple engraving by James Hopwood. *c* 1816. 114 × 128 mm.

7 *Don Giovanni*, Act 2, scene 14. Stipple engraving by James Hopwood. *c* 1816. 112 × 135 mm.

8 *La clemenza di Tito*, Act 1, scene 4. Stipple engraving by James Hopwood. *c* 1818. 106 × 125 mm.

9 *Così fan tutte*, Act 2, scene 3. Stipple engraving by James Hopwood. *c* 1823. 116 × 140 mm.

10 *Il flauto magico*, Act 1, scene 1. Stipple engraving by James Hopwood. *c* 1825. 106 × 122 mm.

11 *Don Giovanni*, Act 2, scene 12. Stipple engraving by James Hopwood. *c* 1817. 127 × 175 mm.

The subject of the vignette in group [D] is:

Don Giovanni, Act 2, scene 12. The statue of the Commendatore on horseback, Don Giovanni. Hopwood has unaccountably omitted Leporello, who is with Don Giovanni when he first notices the statue, towards which he faces here (Pl. 11).

The vignettes were based on sketches made in the theatre during the dress rehearsal or actual performances, probably – except for *Don Giovanni* – at revivals rather than first productions. The purpose of the vignettes was to make the edition of the operas attractive to intending purchasers, who would see it on display in the windows and on the counters of music shops. The vivid little action pictures would help to recall scenes which had lingered in their mind's eye. We may guess that the choice of the scene to be illustrated was made by Mazzinghi. For the publisher, knowing little about Mozart, would hardly have decided what would or would not be effective. Though Hopwood might have sketched more than one scene in the other operas besides *Don Giovanni*, the choice would probably have been the editor's.

The iconographical value of the vignettes needs careful consideration. There is little doubt that the gestures, the vestiges of scenery, the properties (for instance, the rather insignificant serpent in fig. 5), and – as will be shown – the costumes, were all realistically seen by comparing one of them to a painting. The singer who created the part of Don Giovanni and sang in all the performances up to 1820, was Giuseppe Ambrogetti,[29] of whom there exists a splendid portrait[30] in this very role, by John Partridge (1790–1872) (Pl. 12). The face in Hopwood's engraving (Pl. 7) bears no resemblance to the animated features of the Don in the picture, in which he raises his glass to Donna Elvira who has just rushed off the stage (Act 2, finale). But his ruff, hat, and tunic (with the addition of a sash, probably introduced for the studio picture) are the same as those in the engravings. The picture also shows, as Leporello, Giuseppe Naldi[31] who also sang Figaro in the King's Theatre production of *Le nozze di Figaro*.

Here we may likewise consider the vignette of another Mozart edition,[32] a popular arrangement of *Il flauto magico*, which can relate only to the King's Theatre production of 1819 because it is on paper watermarked in that year and because no other production in Italian was staged in London within the next decade. The *passe-partout* title-page reads:

Selections from Mozart's / celebrated opera / Il Flauto Magico or Zauberfloete / Arranged (from the Original Score) for / Two Performers on the Piano Forte, / By J. H. Little / Book 4 / London. / Published by J. Power. / No 34, Strand /.[33]

The subject of the vignette is:
Il flauto magico, Act 2, scene 16. Papageno, Tamino, and the 'Three benefi-

12 *Don Giovanni*, Act 2, finale. Oil painting by John Partridge. 1819. 750 × 615 mm.

cent genii' (Pl. 13). Unusually, they wear wings because, according to the libretto, in this production they are directed to fly off at the end of the short trio 'Seid uns zum zweitenmal willkommen'.

Thieme and Becker state that the artist, Henry Corbould (1787–1844), was noted for his illustrations of the works of Byron, Milton, Homer, Shakespeare, Dryden, and Scott, and for his reproductions of classical sculpture.[34] This vignette provides a second, independent, drawing of Tamino and shows him wearing the same tunic as in Pl. 16. This, added to the identity of the costumes of the Commendatore and Don Giovanni (Pl. 7 and 11) justifies the inference that all the vignettes were engraved from accurate sketches made in the theatre.

The King's Theatre was totally destroyed by fire in 1867 and with it whatever may have remained of the scenery, properties, and costumes from its early productions of Mozart operas. These vignettes seem therefore to be the only known representation, apart from Partridge's painting, of scenes (with background details) in which two or more characters are seen together.[35]

In 1820 John Ebers succeeded William Taylor as manager of the King's Theatre and between 1821 and 1825 gave revivals of all the earlier Mozart productions except *Il flauto magico*.[36] Before long, however, Mozart's general popularity at this theatre waned and Rossini dominated the stage as he did in other European opera houses. But in London another enterprising manager still thought it worth while to defy the Licensing Act and to try to revive an opera by Mozart. This, like the productions at the King's Theatre, elicited an edition with a charming vignette on its title-page (Pl. 14), which is, however, lithographed and not engraved.

The opera was *Così fan tutte*, staged in English at the Lyceum, or the 'Theatre Royal, English Opera House', as it was known from 1809 to 1841.[37] With a seating capacity of probably little over half that of the King's Theatre, it was better suited to the small scale of this work. Its manager and licensee was the dramatist Samuel James Arnold (1774–1852).[38] Whether the idea of reviving *Così fan tutte* was due to him or to William Hawes, his versatile musical director, is not known. But fortunately the full text of the adaptation has survived in the Lord Chamberlain's plays in the British Library,[39] and contains very detailed stage directions and scene descriptions, some of which bear directly on the authenticity of the details in the vignette.

The script of the opera was submitted to the Lord Chamberlain on 14 July 1828, and was allowed on 19 July. The title-page simply bears the words 'The Tables turned', followed by Arnold's letter of submission. The title *Tit for Tat*, by which the adaptation became generally known, does not occur anywhere in the manuscript. A fortnight before the text was submitted, a

13 *Il flauto magico*, Act 2, scene 16. Stipple engraving by Henry Corbould. *c* 1819. 106 × 132 mm.

14 *Tit for Tat (Così fan tutte)*, Act 1, scene 6. Lithograph by Charles Haghe. *c* 1828. 125 × 162 mm.

poster appeared, on 30 June, announcing 'A New Romantick Entertainment ... a Comick Opera, the Musick by Mozart'.[40] The first performance took place on 29 July 1828,[41] and the twentieth, and last of that season, on 27 September. In the short revival of 1829 it was performed another five times.[42] More evidence of the opera's popularity is found in a newspaper notice[43] which mentions 'frequent calls for repetitions', and in a review of the following arrangement of some of the music – *Select Airs from Mozart's opera Cosi fan tutti*[sic], *performed at the English Opera House under the title of Tit for Tat, arranged with a flute accompaniment (ad lib) by George Perry*. This review alludes to 'many arrangements of this opera'[44] among which were two editions that are the concern of this article.

Of what may be described as the 'authentic' edition (which must be described although it is unillustrated), the British Library possesses one number only, whose head-title reads:

'One word from my Angel', / The favorite Cavatina as sung by Mr. Wood, / in the popular Opera, called / 'Tit for Tat' or 'The Tables Turn'd', as Performed at the / Theatre Royal English Opera House, / The Music Composed by Mozart, / The Poetry Written by Hampden Napier Esqre / The whole Arranged & Adapted to the English stage by / W. Hawes, / Director of the Music to the Theatre Royal English Opera House. / London, Printed by W. Hawes, 7 Adelphi Terrace / Where may be had the whole of the Music in the above Opera, *etc*.[45]

This edition is unillustrated. Of the 'unauthentic', illustrated edition, which comprised a selection only of the music and was issued with a *passepartout* title-page, the British Library has likewise one number. This title-page reads:

Mozart's / Celebrated opera, /Cosi fan tutte / Now performing at the / Theatre Royal English Opera House / No. [MS. 3] ... London / pub^d by Preston 71, Dean Str^t Soho. /[46]

The head-title, on page 1 of the music, reads:

Ye Breezes softly blowing, / The admired Trio, from / Mozart's celebrated opera / Cosi fan tutte, / ... The English Words by W. Ball. /

(The Trio is 'Soave sia il vento'.) At the foot of this page are the names of the three singers – Miss Betts,[47] Miss Cawse,[48] Mr. H. Phillips.[49]

Each edition requires brief comment. Hawes, besides being a musician of parts, was a successful publisher. That his claim to have issued the complete music of *Tit for Tat* is correct is shown by the presence, at the foot of page 1, of the number '17', which agrees with that of this aria, 'Un' aura amorosa' (here in its original key of A major), in all full scores of *Così fan tutte*. Napier[50] was an obscure versifier who seems to have been attached, at that time, to the Lyceum. As his verses 'A word from my angel' correspond exactly with those of this aria in the text submitted to the Lord Chamberlain, the statement[51] that the version was all Arnold's work requires modification.

The firm of Preston was older, more important, and more enterprising than Hawes's, and had much Mozart on its lists. This selection from *Così fan tutte* had Italian and English words, the latter supplied by William Ball, a popular and prolific writer of songs and poetry. No. 1 in Preston's selection[52] was, as it happens, 'Un' aura amorosa', with the key transposed to G major. It may also be mentioned that Preston used only Mozart's original title: presumably he regarded *Tit for Tat, or the Tables turned* as being in some way Arnold's copyright.

The stone from which the illustration (fig. 9) on Preston's title-page was printed seems to have become worn quickly. For in the British Library copy the artist's name (on the left of the picture) can only be read as consisting of a distinctive initial C., followed by a smudged H, both barely discernible on fig. 9. On the right-hand side, the printer's name is almost invisible. Fortunately another song, of about the same year[53] supplies the details. Here the vignette is clearly signed, in the same hand, 'C Haghe', and the printer is 'W. Day lith. 17 Gate Str^t'. This was Charles Haghe, younger brother of the far more famous Louis, who came to England from Belgium in 1823. The printer was William Day, whose business was then in Lincoln's Inn Fields, and whose name became linked with Haghe's to form the famous firm of Day & Haghe (1834–1865).

From the illustrator and the printer we can now pass to the picture itself and return first to the text of *Tit for Tat*, from which the following scene descriptions are relevant (Act 1, scene 6 in the original).

Fol. 171: 'A handsome Chamber in a Villa in the Suburbs of Naples – in the back an open Terrace – with Pillars & Trellice work overgrown with Vines – Roses &c – steps down to the Sea – part of the city seen on one side of the Bay – Vesuvius in the distance: ships and small Craft upon the Water'; fol. 175^v: 'A Boat comes up close under the Terrace'; fol. 176^r: Ferrando and Guglielmo descend the Terrace, get on Board the Boat which pushes off and disappears – The Girls and Alphonso leaning over the Balustrade.' And then, on fol. 176^v comes the line: 'Dora. I see them still – waving to us with their Hats from the Boat. (they wave their Handkerchiefs).'

Apart from the absence of Don Alphonso, these lines correspond exactly with the action in Haghe's drawing of the scene and with the back cloth. The scale of his work is too small for the faces to be anything but stylized, and the costumes likewise should perhaps only be regarded as approximations. That there is, nevertheless, some relation to the hats and dresses actually worn by the ladies, can be seen by comparing Haghe's work with Chalon's[54] water-

15 Miss Betts and Miss Cawse in *Tit for Tat (Così fan tutte)*. Water-colour by Alfred Edward Chalon. 1828. 330 × 198 mm.

colour of 'Miss Betts and Miss Cawse' in this opera (Pl. 15).[55] A playbill of the first night of *Tit for Tat* gives some additional details.[56]

> The following new scenery incidental to the opera... Terrace over looking the Bay – Tomkins. New and splendid scenery executed by Mr Tomkins and Mr Pitt [described in a later bill as 'scene-painters']. The dresses by Mr Head and Mrs Stillman.

Such unusually full information rounds off the scene in a most satisfactory way.

The value of the vignette on the title-page of Preston's edition is enhanced by the fact that on 16 February 1830 a spectacular fire destroyed the buildings of the Lyceum and most of its contents.[57] The verisimilitude of Haghe's drawing of the scene from *Tit for Tat* is reasonably proven. By inference this reinforces the case for the authenticity of the vignettes drawn earlier by Hopwood and Corbould. More such English vignette editions of Mozart's operas will no doubt come to light in due course, especially when the *International Inventory of Musical Sources* (RISM, series A/I) has been extended consistently beyond its present nominal limit of the end of the year 1800, and the early nineteenth-century holdings of British libraries are fully recorded.

[1980]

Notes

1 The full text of this Act, 10 Geo. II c 28, is in Danby Pickering (ed.), *The Statutes at Large* (Cambridge, 1765), vol. XVII, pp. 140–3. The Act is variously known as the 'Licensing Act' and the 'Playhouse Bill', see P J Crean, 'The Stage Licensing Act of 1737', *Modern Philology*, XXXV (Chicago, 1938), pp. 239–355; O E Deutsch, *Handel. A documentary biography* (London, 1955), p. 436, and Watson Nicholson, *The Struggle for a Free Stage in London* (London, Boston, 1906), pp. 46–97.
2 The King's Theatre in the Haymarket. Founded in 1704, it was known as the Queen's Theatre from then to 1714, and so again from 1837 to 1901. It was also, rather confusingly, sometimes referred to as the Theatre Royal, and at other times as the Italian Opera House.
3 Daniel Nalbach, *The King's Theatre 1704–1867. London's first Italian opera house* (London, 1972), p. 39.
4 The protracted and extremely complex negotiations and machinations that followed the destruction of the King's Theatre lie outside the scope of this article. They are given in some detail by Nalbach, op. cit., pp. 67–77, and summarized in William C Smith's *The Italian Opera and Contemporary Ballet in London, 1789–1820* (London, 1955), pp. 10–12, 16.
5 The conditions are found in a document entitled *Outline for a General Opera Agreement*, printed in 1792. No copy seems to have survived in any British library. It is summarized by Nicolson, op. cit., pp. 145–9, and by Nalbach, op. cit., pp. 75, 76. This *Agreement* confirmed the sole right of the King's Theatre to stage Italian opera, and lasted until the 'Licensing Act' was revoked in 1843.

6 Novosielski (1750–95) was of Polish origin, but was born in Rome. He is said to have come to London as a young man to assist James Wyatt in the building of the Pantheon, 1770–2. See H M Colvin, *A Biographical Dictionary of English Architects* (London, 1954), pp. 420–1.
7 The best contemporary descriptions are the article by J B Papworth, 'An Account of the King's Theatre, Haymarket', in John Britton and A C Pugin, *Illustrations of the Public Buildings of London* (London, 1825), vol. I, pp. 72–9, and E W Brayley's *Historical and Descriptive Accounts of the Theatres of London* (London, 1826), pp. 40–3. The authoritative modern account is in F H W Sheppard (gen. ed.), *The Survey of London*, vols. XXIX, XXX (The Parish of St James Westminster, pt. 1, South of Piccadilly), (London, 1960), pp. 223–50 and pls. 24–39. Nalbach includes a few illustrations. The site of the King's Theatre is now largely occupied by New Zealand House and the present, small, Her Majesty's Theatre. The only surviving part of the building which stood from 1789 to 1867, Nash's Opera Arcade of 1816, lies to the west of the old site.
8 Rees Howell Gronow, *The Reminiscences and Recollections of Captain Gronow. Being anecdotes of the camp, courts, clubs and society, 1810–1860* (London, 1892), vol. I, pp. 35, 36. The plan of the boxes from *c* 1790 is included in *A Descriptive Plan of the new Opera House, with the names of the subscribers to each box taken from the Theatre itself by a Lady of Fashion* [London, *c* 1791[. The plan itself is reproduced in Smith, op. cit., p. 17.
9 See Edith Schnapper (ed.), *The British Union-Catalogue of Early Music* (London, 1957), in which the British Museum's holding was included. A more comprehensive listing of early London and provincial editions of Mozart is in *RISM*, ser. A/I/6.
10 An anonymous article in the *Harmonicon* for 1831, pp. 106, 135, entitled 'Autobiography of an Amateur Singer', mentions private performances of *Così fan tutte*, *La clemenza di Tito*, *Don Giovanni*, and *Figaro*, given in three years between 1806 and 1811. (See however, chapter 13, *passim*.) Two separate operatic pieces by Mozart, the first ever heard in England, had, however, been sung as *Einlagen*, at the King's Theatre – the duet 'Crudel perchè finora' from *Figaro* in Gazzaniga's *La vendemmia* on 9 May 1789 and a quartet 'Dite almeno, in che mancai' in Bianchi's *La villanella rapita* (for which Mozart had originally composed it) on 27 Feb. 1790.
11 From an article signed 'W. G. Leicester' in the *Monthly Magazine*, XXXI, pt. 1 (1811), pp. 133–5. Gardiner, the proprietor of a stocking manufactory, befriended Haydn during his second visit to England, and had a wide musical acquaintance in England and abroad.
12 These totals are derived from the figures given for successive revivals by Smith, op. cit., who also prints a useful selection of press notices..
13 *Die Zauberflöte* was regarded in England as an Italian opera, probably to the detriment of its true character, as is reflected in the low total of performances. London audiences did not hear it in German complete until 27 May 1833, at Covent Garden. The King's Theatre performance in German on 18 June 1829 was a selection only. In this article it seems appropriate to use the Italian title.
14 This was in fact a revival, possibly using the designs of the 1806 production, but with only two of the same cast. See Smith, op. cit.
15 *Musical Reminiscences, containing an account of Italian opera in England*, 4th ed. (London, 1834), pp. 132, 133.
16 For the successive partnerships in the firm see Charles Humphries and William C Smith, *Music Publishing in the British Isles*, 2nd ed. (Oxford, 1970), pp. 158, 159. There is an excellent account of this splendid business, which continued as D'Almaine & Co., from *c* 1834 to 1866, in a very rare, beautifully printed pamphlet, *A Day at the Music Publishers. A description of the establishment of D'Almaine & Co.* [1848]. Copy in Department of Prints and Drawings, British Museum (Crace XXIX 6*, sheet 21).

17 There is some evidence of Mazzinghi's popularity in the fact that about 1800 Goulding had thought it worth while to reprint a number of his works composed before 1790 and originally issued by other publishers. A list of his op. 1–38 is in g.271.k.(3).
18 The only evidence to the contrary is found in the title-page of *Le nozze di Figaro* in group B in the table on p. 28, where below the imprint there are lacking the words 'N.B. All Mozarts Operas are intended to be thus Arranged and Published as soon as Convenient', which occur, however, on all the other title-pages in this group. This may suggest that *Figaro* was issued as a singleton before the larger plan took final shape.
19 Quoted from the copy in Hirsch M.1281.(1) – see the table on p. 82 – which has the watermark date 1817. Information from watermarks is the only guide to publication because here, as usually with music of the eighteenth and nineteenth centuries, no date at all is given. Nor were copies entered at Stationers Hall, although the title-pages claim that this was done.
20 Goulding's edition of these operas seems to be the earliest known of which all the title-pages bear both vignettes and the names of the dedicatees. The Music Library contains Schlesinger's 'Collection complète des opéras de W A Mozart', in vocal score (Paris, [1822?]), (Hirsch IV.1183 and R.M.11.g.9–15, R.M.11.f.3.(2), and R.M.11.g.3.(2)). Each of the operas in this edition has a pretty, lithographed title-page vignette, but no dedicatee. Each volume in Heckel's edition, also in vocal score (Mannheim [*c* 1820–1830]), (Hirsch IV.1179) is dedicated to Sophie zu Baden, first as Markgräfin, then as Grossherzogin. Only two of the seven scores have illustrations or vignettes. For the latter see Brigitte Hoft, 'Ein Mannheimer Musikverleger als Wegbereiter des klassischen Erbes. Karl Ferdinand Heckel und seine Wohlfeile Ausgabe sämmtlicher Opern W A Mozart's, in Roland Würtz, *Das Mannheimer Mozart-Buch* (Wilhelmshaven, 1977), pp. 187–217.
21 In *A Descriptive Plan of the New Opera House* (London, *c* 1791), the plan of the subscribers shows the Duke and Duchess of Gloucester and the Duke and Duchess of Cumberland holding boxes 14 and 15, 59 and 60, respectively. Possibly they still held the same boxes at the time of Mazzinghi's dedications, and it seems a reasonable assumption that the Duchesses of Cambridge, Clarence, and Kent also then held boxes. A list of the box-holders for 1828 (in a private collection) shows the Duchess of Gloucester then holding box 28.
22 The sequence of these three issues is uncertain. The vignette of g.382.xx.(7) has a tree on the right, which is lacking in the other two (see fig. 6). The vignette in h.405.k.(1) has been partly redrawn.
23 Goulding's catalogue (see note 24) specifies 'the Hon. Miss H Addington', as the dedicatee of 'Batti, batti'.
24 *Catalogue of Instrumental Music, published by Goulding, D'Almaine Potter, and Co . . . at their wholesale and retail warehouse, No. 20 Soho Square . . . Part I. London: printed by S Gosnell, Little Queen Street* (Hirsch IV.1106). The Mazzinghi–Mozart items are on pp. 18, 32, 36. The date [1825?] given in the *General Catalogue of Printed Books* is too late, because Potter dropped out *c* 1823. The watermark date 1819 is likely to be much nearer that of actual publication.
25 See Ulrich Thieme and Felix Becker, *Allgemeines Lexikon der bildenden Künstler*, vol. XVII (Leipzig, 1924), pp. 501–2.
26 The elder Hopwood's engraving of Stephen Hales, dated 1 Dec. 1800 (C IV. (sub. 2) P4), has under the portrait a garden scene with a temple, which resembles the manner of the operatic vignettes.
27 Hopwood's first vignette for Don Giovanni (fig. 2) shows the same moment in Act II as that of the edition of the opera issued in both full and vocal score by Breitkopf &

Härtel in 1801 and c 1810. In this vignette, engraved by Johann Friedrich Bolt (1769–1836) after Vincenz Georg Kininger (1767–1851), the Commendatore, grasping Don Giovanni's hand, wears the same type of armour and plumed helmet and carries a baton, which in Hopwood's figure, however, appears to be a roll of paper. The Breitkopf vignette is reproduced (enlarged) in Arthur Hutchings, *Mozart. The Man. The Musician* (London, 1976), pt. 2, p. 91.

28 Hopwood's vignette (fig. 5) suggests that there can have been no Egyptian element in the costumes and décor, and that the general flavour would have been vaguely classical.

29 In 1833 he gave up singing and joined the order of the Reformed Cistercians (Trappists) at Mount Melleray Abbey in Ireland.

30 Exhibited at the Royal Academy in 1819, no. 215. Partridge's picture was engraved in mezzotint, with modifications, by Henry Meyer (1783–1843). An interesting point arises regarding the three ladies seen at the supper table on the left. This seems to be their earliest recorded appearance in this scene, but it is uncertain whether they actually appeared in the King's Theatre production or whether they are an embellishment of the artist's. The background to the picture almost certainly reproduces the actual scenery, which was evidently classical. Partridge's picture, Hopwood's vignettes of *Don Giovanni* and *Figaro*, and Haghe's of *Così fan tutte*, all illustrate an interesting point regarding the costumes worn by the male characters. These all belong to a curious sartorial convention which was used, from the early eighteenth to the early nineteenth century, by both painters and designers of theatrical, ceremonial, and court costume, to evoke a vague atmosphere of the Middle Ages and the Renaissance. Its elements consist of a plumed bonnet or broad-brimmed hat, a ruff or a point-lace collar, a doublet with puffed and slashed sleeves, or a surcoat and tights. (I am indebted to Mr Edward Croft-Murray for this information and for other helpful suggestions.)

31 In 1820, the year after the picture was painted, he met an untimely end (according to *Grove*) 'in the apartments of his friend Garcia, by the bursting of a newly-invented cooking kettle, a trial of which he had been invited to witness'.

32 Press-mark g.382.tt.

33 James Hyatt Little, a composer of slender talent, was regularly published by Power, for whom, as the latter's catalogues show, he also worked as an arranger.

34 Corbould also drew some members of the British Museum staff – the Revd H H Baber, Sir Henry Ellis, Thomas Burgon, C F Barnwell, and Edward Hawkins. Thieme and Becker, op. cit., vol. VII (Leipzig, 1912), p. 396.

35 Contemporary magazines such as *The British Stage and Literary Cabinet* published some hand-coloured engravings of single singers only.

36 Reviewing a performance of 23 May 1819, mounted 'with great splendour', *The British Stage and Literary Cabinet* remarked (iii, 1819, p. 204): 'We again express the opinion that it will not become generally popular.'

37 Charles Dibdin, junior, includes 'An Account of the Theatre Royal English Opera House' in his *History and Illustrations of the Theatres of London* (London, 1826), pp. 81–6. The theatre's entrance was then in the Strand. When rebuilt, on an enlarged site, after the fire of 1830, the entrance was moved to the eastern side, in Wellington Street, where it stands today.

38 Son of Samuel Arnold, the operatic composer, who published a creditable attempt at a complete edition of Handel's works, from 1787 to 1797, the first of its kind for any great composer.

39 Add. MS.42891. Plays from the Lord Chamberlain's Office. Vol. XXVII (June–July 1828), fols. 167–219.

40 Th. Cts. (=Theatre Cuttings), vol. XLVI. Lyceum Theatre, vol. III (1827–40).

41 The date 1827 given by E J Dent in his essay on the history of the opera, in Eric Crozier (ed.), *Mozart's Così fan tutte, essays by Edward J Dent, Eric Blom, Clemence Dane* (London, 1945), p. 20, 'Sadler's Wells Opera Books', no. 2, is wrong.
42 These figures are derived from an almost complete series of posters in the Victoria and Albert Museum's Theatre Collection, Lyceum Theatre, box for 1827–30.
43 Th. Cts., vol. XLVI. Lyceum Theatre, vol. III (29 June 1829).
44 Issued in three books by Alfred Petter (no copy in BL): *Harmonicon* (1829), pp. 44, 45.
45 Press-mark H.1980.m.(42). Watermark date 1827.
46 Press-mark H.1847.m.(4). Watermark date 1827.
47 Little is known of Miss Betts, who sang Fiordiligi. She was also a composer: one song by her, *c* 1835, is in the Music Library. It was published by Arthur Betts, the elder, presumably a relation.
48 Harriet Cawse, who sang Dorabella, was a pupil of Sir George Smart. Her name is found in four programmes of the Philharmonic Society's concerts between 1830 and 1832. She took the soprano part in Beethoven's Mass in D, at its first London (private) performance in December 1832. See P J Willetts, *Beethoven and England* (London, 1970), pp. 59, 73. Cawse seems to have made her name as 'an arch and melodious Puck' in the première of Weber's *Oberon* in 1826. See J R Planché, *Recollections and Reflections* (London, 1872), vol. I, p. 32.
49 Henry Phillips, a popular bass singer, author of *Musical and personal Recollections during half a Century* (London, 1864). He mentions the great success of *Tit for Tat*.
50 Napier also provided verses for the songs in three other operas staged at the Lyceum – Ludwig Maurer's *Not for me* (*Der neue Paris*) produced 27 Jan. 1826; Ferdinando Paer's *The Freebooters* (*I fuoruscti di Firenze*), produced 20 Aug 1827; Peter von Winter's *The Oracle* (*Das unterbrochenes Opferfest*), produced 7 Aug 1826: all three, in vocal score, are in the Music Library. A copy of the verses for *The Freebooters* was in the British Museum, but was destroyed in 1941. The library of the University of Indiana has a copy of the verses for *The Oracle*. A Lyceum poster says that these booklets were on sale in the theatre.
51 For example, by Allardyce Nicoll, *A History of the English Drama, 1600–1900* (Cambridge, 1955), vol. IV, pp. 543, 601.
52 In a private collection.
53 *The Bonny Blue Cap, or 'Bold and True'. Song, written by Sir Walter Scott, composed by Geo: Luff. London. Pub^d. by the Author at his Music & Quadrille Repository. 92 Gt. Russell S^t, Bloomsbury.* Watermark date 1827. Copy in a private collection.
54 Alfred Edward Chalon (b. Geneva 1780; d. London 1860), came to England in 1789. He was a prolific portrait painter and miniaturist, and specialized in the delineation of ladies of the Court and stage.
55 J F Kerslake, *Catalogue of Theatrical Portraits in London Public Collections* (London, 1961), no. 739, (National Potrait Gallery 1962 J.) This drawing probably came from the brothers Chalon Sale, Christie's, 11–14 Mar. 1961 (copy in the V & A Library, Christie 23.xx), 13 Mar. 1861, Lot 390. 'Theatrical Reminiscences. Vol. I: a scrapbook containing admirable caricatures of celebrated singers and dancers.'
56 Victoria and Albert Museum, Theatre Collection, Lyceum, Box 1826 to 1830.
57 A E Wilson, *The Lyceum* (London, 1952), pp. 51–3.

9

Oldman, Einstein and the Wandering Minstrels

The third edition of Köchel's thematic catalogue of Mozart, prepared by Alfred Einstein and published in 1937, lists a considerable number of previously unrecorded single leaves, of various kinds, in the composer's autograph. Some had come to light in the 32 years that elapsed since the second edition of 1905; others were discovered by Einstein himself, or were brought to his notice by helpful librarians and collectors. One such leaf was that containing eight textless canons, which Einstein numbered K. 508a, and the final draft for the finale of the Piano Quartet in E flat K. 493. The leaf is headed on the left 'Uebungen in Contrapunct' in the hand of Johann Anton André, and on the right 'von Mozart und seine Handschrift', written by Nissen. It came to Einstein's notice in the British Museum, while he was working on Köchel in its library. This article is concerned not with the music[1] but with the particulars that Einstein gave about the discovery of the leaf and with his theory of its transmission. In his note on the autograph of K 508a Einstein wrote thus:

> London. British Museum. At one time owned by Karl Mozart. In one of three 'scrap-albums' containing programmes, press-cuttings, etc. of the 'Wandering Minstrels', an amateur concert society. The relevant volume was apparently presented to it by a Mr H B Heath, presumably the owner of the leaf, which was discovered by C B Oldman in 1935. Now V H Zavertal, an English band master who was acquainted with Karl Mozart and received many relics from him, sold two [sic] autographs in 1879 to a Mr Arthur Gaye of Oriel College, Oxford: 1, a quintet of four pages [?K. Anh.79/515c], and 2, contrapuntal studies, 6 pages. Our leaf was probably one of these six pages.

The editors of the sixth edition (1964) modified slightly the order of these sentences, but left the substance and details unchanged. Einstein's statements about the British Museum and the Wandering Minstrels are correct, but almost all else – whether given as fact or conjecture – is wrong or irrelevant. To show how he was led into error, we must know something about the Wandering Minstrels, what their collection contained, how and when it came to the museum and was catalogued.

The 'Minstrels' (for short) were founded in 1860 by wealthy amateurs for two main purposes – to give public orchestral and, later, choral concerts for charity, and to make music privately for their own entertainment. In the 38 years of their activity they raised over £16,500 for their first purpose. Their founding and later members were drawn from some of the oldest aristocratic families in the land, who travelled widely and had strong associations with the Foreign Office and the Diplomatic Service. The Minstrels recruited some players from the professional classes. They were also men of taste, who decided to preserve and augment a record of their work. Besides the programmes and many other details of their concerts, they collected objects of musical interest – rare prints (in the correct, art-historical sense), fine photographs, drawings and the like. They preserved them systematically in three huge albums – 'scrap albums' is a most misleading term – all beautifully bound and embellished, with decorated borders and illuminations. Each album, an elephant folio,[2] was housed in a suede-lined leather case fitted with straps and a stout handle, for conveyance to the Minstrels' private concerts, there to be displayed for the members' enjoyment.

Exactly what happened to these albums after the Minstrels ceased to exist is unclear. But there are a few certain facts. Lionel Benson, their last conductor and secretary, was a friend of J A Fuller Maitland and the latter's brother-in-law Barclay Squire.[3] In 1881 Benson married Miss Marion Fotheringham, a member of a distinguished Scottish family. It seems that, after Benson and his wife died, the albums passed to a female descendant. For on 12 July 1930 the British Museum sent to 'Miss Fotheringham Fotheringham, Forfar, Scotland' an acknowledgment for the manuscript catalogue of the music in the Minstrels' library (now apparently lost). The formal acknowledgment of this catalogue accords with the departmental practice of the time that all important gifts should be so treated, and stamped with the precise date in yellow, the colour used for presentations. This makes it all the more extraordinary that neither the Trustees' minutes nor the departmental papers contain any record of the earlier gift of the three albums. That they were a gift is proved by the yellow, 'blind' (*ie* undated) crown with which they were stamped throughout. Normally this crown was used only for trivial, unacknowledged gifts. The albums were virtually smuggled into the Music Room, a highly irregular procedure, for which only one person, Barclay Squire (who had always been an arbitrary man), can have been responsible. After his retirement in 1920, he continued to work in the Music Room on the catalogues of the King's Music Library, and though ailing was very much an *éminence grise*.[4]

It seems a fair assumption that Miss Fotheringham Fotheringham somehow knew of Benson's association with Squire, and through him offered the albums to the museum not long before his death in January 1927. Wishing to spare himself and William C Smith (his successor) the labour of an official report to the trustees, Squire had them placed in the Music Room, although they contained no music at all except the Mozart leaf and an autograph textless duet for soprano and tenor by Auber. Had the albums been placed in the General Library where they properly belonged, Squire would have become involved in the full process of formal acknowledgment, including a long report to the trustees recommending special thanks.

Now at his death Squire left unfinished the catalogue of the printed music (vol. III) in the King's Music Library, and William C Smith had to complete it, as the preface, dated May 1929, explains. To combine this completion with the annual routine meant that Smith must have put on one side for some time less urgent work such as the cataloguing of the albums. But in spring or summer 1929 he dealt with them, and wrote a descriptive entry which appeared in the annual Accessions Part of Music, no.XXXIV (1930). Examining the albums for this purpose, Smith saw the Mozart leaf (above which, written in capitals, are the words 'An original MS of Mozart') and that by Auber, and mentioned both in his description. While not a Mozart specialist, Smith knew that C B Oldman, his colleague in the General Library, was, and showed him the albums. (It is possible, though unlikely, that Smith showed the albums to Oldman before he examined them himself.) Oldman then wrote a rather different descriptive entry for the General Catalogue on a slip which the reviser dated 9/29. In the process he would have had little difficulty in identifying the draft for the theme of the piano quartet. (Oldman, 1895–1969, became one of the finest Mozart scholars of his day: he had entered the Department of Printed Books in 1919 and was its Principal Keeper, 1948–59.)

In his introduction to Köchel, Einstein says he was given a place in the Music Room – a rare concession in those days – with the catalogues and Gesamtausgaben at hand, and there, in 1934–5, he completed the last stages of his work. While he mentions Smith appreciatively, he expresses a much deeper gratitude to Oldman, who must have obtained the concession for him. Einstein refers to the 'pleasant working conditions', happily unaware of the strife-ridden atmosphere for which the Music Room was then notorious. While there, Einstein was shown the three albums of the Minstrels, probably by Oldman, because his fluent German would have been very helpful. Somehow Einstein got the idea that Oldman had himself discovered the Mozart leaf: he was also misinformed about the albums and their illuminated title-pages. He seems to have misunderstood completely the character of the archive, which perhaps was also not clear to Smith and Oldman. The wording of the title-pages is as follows:

[vol.I] Presented to the Wandering Minstrels by L A Breedon [n.d.?] 1868. An additional, decorated title-page, designed by Lord Gerald Fitzgerald, is dated

1861. The last item in this volume is of 1867.
[vol.II] Presented to the Wandering Minstrels by H B Heath. 1868.
[vol.III] Presented to the Wandering Minstrels on the reorganisation of the Society by Spencer H and Henry D Curtis. 1882.

Taken together, and in the context of the albums as a whole, the purport of the title-pages is quite clear. The albums were prepared as sumptuously bound guard books of blank cartridge paper, with gilt edges. The member, or members, named simply met the considerable cost of the binding and preparation of each volume. As named photographs and lists of the members show, Heath was an amateur violinist and like his fellow benefactors a member of the orchestra. Neither he nor they were collectors. Heath did not present the Mozart leaf to the Minstrels.

What, then, was the source of the leaf, and when did it come into the Minstrels' possession? Einstein's suggestion that it reached England via Arthur Gaye and V H Zavertal in 1879[5] is untenable for a chronological reason. Examination of the diverse dated material – letters, programmes, cuttings and the like – pasted into all three albums shows that it follows, fairly strictly, the succession of the dates. Undated items, such as photographs, whether of places of musical groups, clearly relate throughout to an immediately preceding programme or cutting. There are hardly any blank pages. It seems clear that the material was accumulated in chronological order of receipt by one of the Minstrels' officers[6] and then pasted down in batches. Being double-sided, the Mozart leaf was not pasted down, but was edged longways on to a 'swinging guard', on a page which is preceded and followed by items bearing various dates throughout April and May 1868. It follows, then, that the leaf came to the Minstrels before that date.

Its previous ownership and transmission remain rather a puzzle. On the page, above the upper short side of the leaf, there is a faint, pencil note, lightly erased (perhaps for aesthetic reasons) but still legible: 'Presented by E Manson Esq'. As none of the Minstrels' lists contain any such name, he is likely to have been a friend of one of their members. Whether or not the leaf was once owned by Karl Mozart, the nature of some of the rare or unique items in the albums suggests how Manson might have acquired it. The albums include such oddities as a rare coloured drawing, on mulberry paper, for a nineteenth-century Japanese woodblock print; a programme, in Russian with an English translation added in manuscript, of a St Petersburg concert, 1864; some Italian drawings of a type scarce outside Italy; the Auber autograph, and so on. If we remember that some of the Minstrels, and by inference their friends, travelled in the world of diplomacy and foreign business, it seems likely that many of their treasures were acquired in or near the country of origin, rather than through dealers or other sources in

England. May not Manson have bought the Mozart leaf somewhere in central Europe as a travel souvenir, and then passed it on to a Minstrel friend?

Einstein's note can now be rewritten on the following lines:

Autograph: Perhaps at one time owned by Karl Mozart. Now in the Music Library of the British Library, in the archive of the Wandering Minstrels, an aristocratic musical society, which existed from 1860 to 1898. This autograph (pressmark: K.6.e.2, f.17v) was probably first noted by William C Smith in 1929 and communicated by him in that year to C B Oldman who drew it to Einstein's attention in about 1935. The leaf was acquired, probably in Europe, by E Manson who presented it to the Wandering Minstrels, at some date in or before April 1868.

One point remains. Einstein specially thanks Oldman for having read the whole of the third edition of Köchel in proof (a gigantic labour of love). Oldman must have seen the phrase 'discovered by C B Oldman in 1935' and knew that at least the date was inaccurate. The most honest and modest of men, he would not have wished to deprive Smith of any credit for having first noted the Mozart leaf, but perhaps he felt that as Einstein had unwittingly omitted Smith's name he could hardly insert it himself.

To go into such elaborate detail in order to correct relatively minor errors of date, fact and provenance, may seem rather like wielding the proverbial sledgehammer to crack a small string of nuts. If there is a moral in this tangled tale, it is that a document should be studied in its fullest possible archival, historical and physical context. But this would have been a policy of perfection for those confronted, half a century or more ago, with the formidable bulk of the three albums of the Wandering Minstrels.

[1984]

Notes

1 Published in NMA: the canons in III:10 and the draft for the finale of K493 in VIII:22/1. The Kritische Bericht to the latter (1958) identifies the two separate hands as given above, whereas Köchel, 6/1964, under K493, repeats Einstein's incorrect statement that André wrote both. The three albums are in the Music Library of the British Library, pressmark K6.e.1–3. This leaf, like some others containing canons, and reproduced in facsimile in NMA III:10, was once folded into four.
2 The albums average approximately 46 × 33 cm; and each weighs about 8 kg.
3 Squire sang tenor in a choir attached to the Minstrels; he and Benson edited a series of madrigals, *Arion*.
4 I owe this information to Miss Hilda Andrews (Mrs G M Lees) who was working in the Music Room in the mid-1920s, under Squire's direction, on vol. II of the catalogue of the King's Music Library.

5 The source for this transaction, not mentioned by Einstein, is H G Farmer and Herbert Smith: *New Mozartiana* (Glasgow, 1935), pp. 95–105, where the text of the letters written by F X Jelinek, Archivist of the Mozarteum, to Zavertal, is given with the commentary. Zavertal, a close friend of Karl Mozart (d 1858), was born in Bohemia in 1821 and though described by Einstein as an English bandmaster did not settle in Glasgow until 1874.
6 There is internal evidence that the first two albums were assembled by Lord Gerald Fitzgerald, a cellist and a fine artist who designed the Minstrels' monogram and other ornaments. He had a special room built for their concerts in his London home. He was the Minstrels' first honorary librarian and in 1873 succeeded the Hon. Seymour Egerton, later the Earl of Wilton, as their president and conductor.

Libraries and Collections

10

Frederick Nicolay, Chrysander and the Royal Music Library

It is now nearly half a century since George v deposited the Royal Music Library on loan in the British Museum, in March 1911. While the collection thus became publicly accessible for the first time, it remained the property of the reigning sovereign until November 1957, when Queen Elizabeth II presented it outright to the nation. This crowning act of munificence marked the bicentenary of another famous presentation, that of the Old Royal Library, which George II gave to the British Museum in 1757. Thus this great music library has passed, as it were, into history. It is curious that although it has been available so long for study, so very little has been written about its own history. There are, obviously, many possible lines of approach. Here I shall confine myself to three topics: the purchase of a foundation collection of manuscripts in 1762; the life and work of Frederick Nicolay, Queen Charlotte's music librarian; and the very remarkable contribution which Chrysander is said to have made to the Handel manuscripts. Though apparently unrelated, these three topics have nevertheless a certain connecting thread in the person of Nicolay, a man of importance in his day but completely forgotten since.

The purchase of 1762 is a puzzling affair. The first mention of it in print, in 1929, seems to have originated with Barclay Squire. He, as is well known, was closely associated with the Royal Music Library and devoted most of his retirement from 1920 onwards to cataloguing it. Unfortunately, when he died in January 1927, he had only finished the volume devoted to the Handel manuscripts. But he had examined the whole collection while it was still in Buckingham Palace, he had supervised its transport to the Museum and its re-arrangement there, and had undoubtedly had access to papers relating to it which are now no longer available. It seems reasonable, therefore, to presume that some information from Squire was the basis of the following statement by Hilda Andrews in her preface to vol. II of the catalogue: 'The Miscellaneous Manuscripts in the King's Music Library, comprising rather more than a thousand volumes, were purchased by King George III in 1762 to form the nucleus of a Royal collection'. But as Squire left behind none of his notes on the history of this Royal collection, and as neither Miss Andrews, Mr William C Smith nor Mr Charles Humphries (all associated in various ways with the work on the catalogue) can now shed any light on the source of this statement, it must be re-considered from other evidence. For it would be of very great interest to know who formed this collection of manuscripts and when, what exactly it contained, and how it passed into royal ownership.

Even in the mid-eighteenth century, a collection of 'rather more than a thousand volumes' of manuscript music would not have been very cheap, and one might expect to find some record of a payment either in the Public Record Office (Treasury Papers, Declared Accounts, Lord Chamberlain's Papers), or in George III's papers in the Royal Archives now at Windsor Castle. No payment of this kind is recorded.[1] One therefore turns to the Royal Music Library as it now is, in order to survey the miscellaneous manuscripts on the shelves. In Squire's re-arrangement, cases 18 and 19 were allocated to Handel copies, and case 20 to the Handel autographs. He put all the other manuscripts into cases 21, 22, 23 and 24. Each shelf, following the general Museum library practice, has a letter and each book or each separate part in a set on each shelf has a number, called a 'third mark'. Thus, an opera in 3 acts was numbered 25.e. 26–28, a symphony in parts 26.b. 10–18. The total of 'third marks' in these four cases is 858. In interpreting the total, much depends on what was meant by a 'volume' in terms of the original purchase. As it seems unlikely that a separate trumpet part of four pages can be described as a 'volume', the total of 858 must be reduced by at least one hundred.

But whatever the interpretation of 'volume', the size of the collection purchased in 1762 did not amount to 858 or to anything like it. For this total can be almost halved if we deduct manuscripts consisting either of music composed after 1762 or copies made since then of music composed earlier. There are also nearly 50 volumes (in the correct sense) of Steffani's operas in score[2] which were almost certainly brought from Hanover to London by George I on his accession in 1714. A further small deduction can be made for pre-1762 items known to have been presented later – the volume mainly in Purcell's autograph, for instance – and for later purchases, such as that of 1779, which was closely connected with Nicolay. If, then, a purchase was made in 1762, it consisted not of 'rather more than a thousand volumes' but of something between four and five hundred, and of these, as a glance at the catalogue shows, a high proportion comprised Italian opera and operatic airs of the period *c* 1700 to 1755. It may be that the exaggerated total comes from a casual remark of some letter-writer or diarist in Court circles, but an intensive search in the sources given for the 1760s by the *Cambridge Bibliography of English Literature* has yielded nothing. To say the least, then, the official description of the purchase is an historical inexactitude.

From these largely negative speculations, it is almost a relief to turn to the incontrovertible facts of a hitherto unknown purchase and to the career of Frederick Nicolay. The first link in the chain of discovery came from a MS of Byrd's *Gradualia* in score (R.M. 24.c. 13) which bears an autograph note by Hawkins ending: 'This score I bought at Dr Boyce's sale 16th April 1779 for 14s.'. It seemed a fair chance that if a catalogue of this sale were in existence, it might identify other items now in the Royal Music Library. Mr Watkins Shaw's admirable article on Boyce in *Grove* mentions two extant copies – one in Leeds Public Library, the other in Mr Gerald Coke's collection. Photostats kindly supplied from Leeds showed the auctioneer to have been John Christie, and the descriptions of the 270 items identified at least a score of them with volumes now in the Royal collection. But as neither copy of the catalogue was marked, the only hope of finding out who acted for Royalty at the sale lay in the possible survival of Christie's own marked copy. Despite war-damage to the firm's premises, their file copies of all eighteenth-century sale catalogues had providentially survived.

A transcription of all buyers' names and prices[3] showed that the buyer of all the volumes identified was 'Nicolay'. Apart from a very few collectors, composers, and scholars, those bidding were book-dealers. In default of evidence from English musical and bibliographical reference books, it seemed safer to put 'Nicolay' with the latter group rather than with the former, and assume that he was acting for some member of the Royal Household. But a stroke of luck placed him in quite another category. A chance reference to the Royal Music copy of the unique prospectuses for Goodison's edition of Purcell[4] showed that several of them bore a MS note 'for Mr Nicolay', which in the printed lists of names of subscribers was amplified to 'Fred. Nicolay Esq., St. James's Palace'.

With this basis, a search in some fairly obvious sources, coupled with a further piece of luck, produced a satisfactory outline of Nicolay's career and environment. He was born in 1728 or 1729 in Saxe-Gotha, the eldest son of Caspar Nicolay and his wife Sapphira (*née* Schmidt). Frederick and his younger brother Christian Frederick were brought to England in 1736 when their parents travelled in the suite of Princess Augusta. From family tradition and documents[5] it seems clear that the young Frederick made his way steadily in the Royal Household. In 1751 he was appointed 'Assistant to Dancing Master' to George III as Prince of Wales, at a salary of £50.[6] and incidentally, in this same year on 3 March was admitted to the Royal Society of Musicians (as it is now called), being then about 23, which was the youngest possible age for admission.[7]

In 1761, he was appointed, at a salary of £100, Page of the Backstairs to Queen Charlotte whom, by George III's command, he had escorted to

England from Germany. Later he became her Principal Page, a most responsible position, requiring great tact and an intimate knowledge of Court and society. One of his duties, according to family tradition, was to receive at the soirées 'all the foreigners of distinction who came over to the Court of England'. Thus Frederick Nicolay would have become well-known abroad, and this would help to account for an entry in Leopold Mozart's *Reiseaufzeichnungen*[8] which gives, among the list of those to be called upon in London, 'Mr Nicolai, Cammer-Page beim König, oder Reserve (?) Unter-Cammerdiener'. Whether the Mozarts ever visited Nicolay is not known, but it is very probable that the Royal copy of Wolfgang's sonatas, Op. 3 (K.10–15 composed in London and dedicated to Queen Charlotte), was handed to the King and Queen through Nicolay. He was, moreover, a keen violinist, being a pupil of Mathew Dubourg[9] and associated with him in the Queen's Band of Music. Other members of this Band which later became the Queen's Chamber Band, were at different times, J C Bach, Abel, Kellway, Zuckert, Papendiek, Simpson and Schroeter.[10] Hence, if in no other ways, Nicolay's musical contacts were very wide. In 1791, his name is found on the list of people whom Haydn found noteworthy in London. It is not impossible that in his youth, Nicolay may have known the aged Handel; at all events, he was a great Handelian, as we shall see.

As is well known, George III took great interest in Burney's account of the Handel commemoration of 1784 and in Hawkins's history, being graciously pleased to accept the dedications of both books. Perhaps it is not surprising that Nicolay is found in close connection with his sovereign's interest, for which the evidence is provided by the daughter of each historian. Fanny Burney recorded that the King wished to see the unbound sheets of the *Commemoration* and drew up two critical notes which were incorporated by Burney into his text. She continued: 'At this he was certain the King could not be displeased, as it was with his Majesty's consent that they had been communicated to the doctor, by Mr Nicolai, a page of the Queen's'.[11] Hawkins's daughter described the scene of the presentation of her father's History thus:

he [Sir John Hawkins] awaited the King's coming from the riding-house, and was conversing with Mr Nicolay, one of the pages, who was a lover of music, when he was most agreeably surprised to see His Majesty enter the appartments, followed by the Queen. Mr Nicolay received the presented volume from the King's hand, and then ensued a conversation on the subject of the work, and of music in general, in which Her Majesty took a lively part; the King professing his decided taste for what is called the *old school*, and jocularly complaining of his inability to persuade the Queen to prefer it to the modern style.[12]

These passages show how close Nicolay stood to the musical interests of the King and Queen. The second of them sheds particularly valuable light on the Queen's taste, in connection both with the music books now in the Royal Music Library and with the additions made to it from the Boyce sale. Besides being her Principal Page, Nicolay was her librarian. This can be deduced from the note – 'This volume belongs to the Queen. 1788' – which he wrote in over 50 of her books.[13] If further proof were necessary, it is provided by Gerber, the first edition of whose ever invaluable *Tonkünstler-Lexicon* (1792) contains the following entry:

'Nicolai (Friedrich) Kammermusikus und Violinist in der Kapelle der Königin von England um 1783: hat auch zugleich als Bibliothekar, derselben Musik unter den Händen.'[14]

Was it, then, on his own initiative and judgment that Nicolay bid at the Boyce sale, and secured for the Royal Library such items as the Cosyn Virginal Book, the twelve *sinfonie* of Alessandro Scarlatti and his opera *Tigrane*, little known Italian madrigals and church music, Lully operas in score, and duets by Steffani? On the whole, it seems doubtful, for his musical sympathies seem (to judge by his own library[15] and by the music to which he subscribed) to have been rather conventional and limited. He must therefore have bid on advice, and whose better than that of Hawkins, whom he undoubtedly knew? According to Squire, writing in *Grove* I, Hawkins presented to the Royal Collection a collection of printed Italian and other madrigals: likewise, other books in the collection were once in his possession. He may thus have urged the Queen to add similar MS items at this great sale of 1779, at which he himself was present, and secured one item. Nicolay may, of course, have bid for other lots besides the nineteen which he actually purchased, for a total of £18 17s 6d. In any case, posterity should be grateful to the Queen, Hawkins and Nicolay for their respective shares in this valuable addition to the Royal Music. What became of other obviously important items in Boyce's library is as unkown as is the fate of other great collections of his and the next generation, such as Stafford Smith's which was dispersed almost without trace.

When Frederick Nicolay died in April or May 1809[16] his family doubtless looked back with pride on his career, less perhaps for its musical activities than for the position of high trust which he held for so long. Although they probably heard little about his confidential work, he may well have told them about the famous Boyce sale and about the Handel manuscripts which had passed into Royal possession some five years earlier, and in which he noted meticulously imperfections, transpositions of leaves and the like. These annotations are indisputably in Nicolay's hand and are of great intrinsic interest. They were later noticed by the most assiduous user of the Handel manuscripts, Chrysander. Though he could not identify the writer of the annotations, he conjectured[17] they were made about 1780. Chrysander could not, of course foresee, that Nicolay's notes would ultimately furnish conclusive proof of the falsity of a remarkable story which has been told about himself in connection with the Handel manuscripts in the Royal Music Library. As this story has recently had some currency, and is likely to receive more, it must be examined in detail.

Its first appearance in English occurred in the *Monthly Musical Record* for February 1953 where the 'Notes of the Day' (p. 31) summarised a passage from HJ Moser's *Das musikalische Denkmälerwesen in Deutschland*'[18]: the relevant sentences run thus:

The really heroic story [of Chrysander's Handel edition] is half-forgotten, and it is well that Professor Moser has now told it again. Chrysander began with only 274 subscribers and a small subsidy from the blind King of Hanover, who was replaced by the Prussian Government after 1866. He earned only enough to spend four to six weeks of each year in England copying the autograph scores; against the rules of the British Museum, he was after a time allowed to take them to his hotel, when he increased his working period from fourteen to sixteen hours a day, fighting sleep, by hunger, coffee and even feet in ice-cold water.

As this is admittedly only a summary, Moser's own words must be given in full, in a fairly literal translation:

In 1932, the singer Felix von Kraus gave memoirs [of which a summary follows] to Chrysander's son Rudolf, who as a pupil of Schwenninger had been Bismarck's house physician and secretary at Friedrichsruh, and who had been responsible up till now for the working Handel editions of his father. Chrysander amassed each year only enough money for four to six weeks in England, during which period he could copy as much as possible of the Handel autographs for each twelve months. As time passed, the librarian gave him secretly the score he was using to take to his hotel, outside the restricted working hours of the library. There, he increased his hours of work from 14 to 16 and ultimately to 18 hours a day, fighting off sleep with hunger and coffee, and finally by immersing his feet in cold water.

In 1887, Chrysander had acquired from Nägeli the autograph of Bach's B Minor Mass for the revision of the Bachgesellschaft, and then made it available to the Prussian State Library without a penny profit to himself. Similarly, he purchased a pile of Handel manuscripts at a provincial auction and, for the same ludicrous sum he had paid, passed on this lucky find to the private library at Buckingham Palace in London. Again, in 1861 he formed a committee in Hamburg to ensure that its City Library should acquire, for the preferential price which Victor Schölcher had made for him, the conducting scores of Christopher Smith corrected by Handel himself. No wonder, that in the end the London treasures were entrusted to him actually in Bergedorf.

Moser's account, itself being very compressed, does not help to clarify an already complicated matter, but it is only fair to point out that he did not draw the red herring of the British Museum across the trail, and that 'Notes of the Day' unfortunately introduced a cardinal error. For in fact, no Handel autographs or copies came direct into the Museum's collection from the Royal Library during or before Chrysander's time. Even if they had done so, in no circumstances whatever would he have been allowed to take them out of the Museum to his hotel.

In order to get the truth of the matter, it seemed essential to find the *ipsissima verba* of Felix von Kraus[19] but reference to German sources showed that these memoirs had never been published at all, either privately or for general circulation. I therefore wrote to Professor Moser, who kindly informed me that the source of his information was Dr Bertha Chrysander, the widow of Rudolf. She was good enough to send me from Bergedorf four mimeographed sheets headed: 'Aus den bisher ungedruckten Lebenserinnerungen von Professor Dr Felix von Kraus, München, 1932'. The first one and three-quarter pages describe a meeting between Kraus and Brahms, and are only relevant in that they establish the date of the former's meeting with Chrysander as having taken place in or soon after 1896. Since the remainder is the source of Moser's summary, I give it in full:

Later, I heard from Chrysander's own mouth the following account of his copying the Handel scores. I give it in direct speech, naturally without being able to guarantee the precise run of the words in detail. 'In order to be able to continue publication without a break, I had to aim throughout the year at putting on one side enough money to pay for the cost of the journey to England and of staying for four to six weeks. At first, I sat in the manuscript room of the music section in the royal library and copied the scores. I was always acutely conscious of the shocking waste of time and money caused by limiting my working time to the hours of the library. But soon I succeeded in being able to give the head of the section good advice and information on a few questions which were important to him. Meanwhile, too, he had got the impression that I was not an impostor, and so one day he gave me permission to take back each time to my hotel room the score which I was copying at the moment. This was most valuable to me, because the speed with which I could progress in my work now depended more on myself. So at first I wrote for 14 hours each day and that went quite well. But soon I saw that at this rate of work my money would not suffice for me to complete the prescribed quantity. Then I increased my daily stint first to 16 hours a day, and then as this was not enough, to 18 hours a day during the last ten days'.

When I asked in astonishment how he could keep that up, he replied, with the smile of a martyr: 'One can do that up to 16 hours, if one is used to work and has once found out the right method. One has to sit down at the desk at 4 a.m. without breakfast, and then write on until 5 p.m., at one stretch, without anything to eat at all. Then one can have a little bread, but nothing more. By that time, I was so weary that I had to sleep for one hour, after which I could quite well go on writing, but after another hour, I had to make some strong black coffee, because brain, eye and hand refused to obey me any more. Then I went on again. But at first the increase from 16 to 18 seemed quite impossible: generally, however, I had to have complete the quantity of work I had intended, and I found a solution by placing my feet in a tub of ice-cold water during the last two hours. This woke me up again somewhat, and so in the end I accomplished my task. Thus I took home with me material for at least two years.

During my next stay in London, I read of an auction sale of old paper which was fixed somewhere in the provinces, and because it was said that some old music would also be sold as waste paper by the foot, or by weight, I decided to go out and see for myself whether perhaps there was something useful in it. At first glance I knew what it was. For a few shillings I bought two heaps of old pieces of music, piled on top of one another from the floor up to the table, and took them with me. Next day, taking a certain volume I showed it to the head of the music section, and asked him what he thought it was. Hardly had he glanced at it when he cried: "That is a Handel autograph! Of course, our library must buy it, no matter what it costs. Where did you get it?" I said: "Of course, I too know that, and I have more than fifty other pieces". Then he said he would have to convene a meeting at once because these manuscripts ought to become the absolute property of the library as they belonged there simply and solely through Handel's historical position. I might now consider what price I required, as then they could come to terms with me. I told him he was quite right: I too thought the library had a claim to the possession of these scores. As to price, we would agree exactly, but he could leave the other gentlemen quietly at their work as we did not need them, for we could settle the matter outselves. Then I felt in my pocket and laid on the table my third-class return ticket, the receipt from the sale, and the bill for the meal. The total for all this came to less than 12 shillings. So this is my price, and I ask you to send someone with me so that I can give him the rest. As he would not be satisfied with this, I looked at him calmly and said: I hope you do not think sir, that I wish to make money out of the Handel autographs which, by a lucky chance I have been able to rescue from destruction and bring here, where they belong. At first he was silent: then he thanked me effusively. I did, however, get something·out of this affair, because thenceforth, they gave me from the library just the volumes I needed to take back to Bergedorf, so that I could work at home in peace and comfort: this was infinitely valuable to me'.[20]

In 1896 Kraus was 26, and Chrysander 70. Although Kraus does not pretend to give a verbatim account of what Chrysander said, there is no reason to impugn his good faith, or his accuracy, for he would presumably have made notes of a talk with such an important person, and put them later into narrative form. It is therefore all the more regrettable that several points in Chrysander's story are open to serious doubt, and his claim to have presented Handel autographs to the Royal Library is quite untrue. There is no reason to underrate his phenomenal capacity for hard work, but it is highly unlikely[21] that, even in mid-Victorian times, he would have been allowed to take a Handel autograph away from Buckingham Palace to his hotel. Indeed, it is doubtful whether, except at the beginning of Chrysander's visits to London, he stayed at a hotel or suffered from such acute pressures of time and money. His son-in-law, Charles Volkert states[22] that in London, Chrysander habitually stayed first with Mr and Mrs Russell Martineau[23] and later with himself.

Further, in Chrysander's time, there was no 'manuscript room' at Buckingham Palace. The official in charge ('Vorstand') would have been either Queen Victoria's Librarian (who was James N Berry) or the Master of the Music. The former would certainly not have known a Handel autograph at a glance: whether the latter might have done so depends on the date. If the year of Chrysander's alleged benefaction was before 1870, the Master was G F Anderson (a violinist; also treasurer of the Philharmonic Society and of the Royal Society of Musicians), who had no pretensions to palaeographical knowledge: if after 1870, the Master was W G Cusins, who, as is shown by his pencil notes and by his pamphlet on 'Messiah', had made a fairly close study of Handel autographs and would certainly not have authenticated without careful scrutiny two piles of alleged autographs, amounting to half as many again as those already in the collection.

The truth is, of course, that this fantastic addition to the Royal Collection, whether of autographs, or even of copies, was a myth, whether fashioned out of Chrysander's imagination, or – though this seems less likely – based on a misunderstanding on Kraus's part. For it can be proved that after 1809 (the year of Nicolay's death) at the latest, no Handel manuscripts either in autograph or, with two exceptions, in copies[24], were added to the Royal Music Library.* Apart from these, the Handel manuscripts are bound in two styles, both peculiar to the Royal Library. The first is a full, red morocco, highly polished and elaborately tooled with a pattern datable to a time between 1760 and 1770. This is found on thirty Royal volumes, including the twenty-four of the so-called 'Smith collection'. The other style is a half-red morocco, with no ornamental tooling: this, simple though it is, with marbled paper sides, is distinctive and was used by binders working between about 1780 and 1810. It is this second style which was used for the binding of the 136 volumes comprising all the Handel autographs and most of the copies.

* In 1970 the Trustees purchased from Messrs Novello & Co two volumes of Handel's anthems, which, being bound in an unmistakable gold-tooled morocco binding, were identified as having 'strayed' from the Royal collection. They are in the hand of a copyist, and now bear the press marks R.M. 19.g.1.a, and R.M. 19.g.1b.

This evidence, which being based on the study of tooling and materials, is necessarily inferential, can be strengthened irrefutably by Nicolay's notes. There are in all 53 of these, scattered throughout 38 volumes bound in the second style, 33 being autographs and 5 copies. They are written on endpapers, inserted leaves and tipped-in slips, with watermarks which can be dated to *c* 1800 at the very latest. All these sheets were trimmed to the same size as the manuscripts, into which they were bound. As those volumes which do not contain Nicolay's notes are bound in a style uniform with those which do, all must have formed part of the Royal collection before the date of his death. The only possible way of accounting for Chrysander's fantastic claim is the equally fantastic hypothesis that at some time between 1810 and about 1860, a careless member of the Royal Household allowed fifty volumes or so of Handel autographs to stray from the shelves at Buckingham Palace into the hands of some provincial bookseller, who proceeded to sell them as waste paper.

It is thus quite clear that there is no basis whatever for Chrysander's statement that it was in return for his 'gift' that he was allowed to take the autographs back to Bergedorf. If this was so, it must have been for some other reason. Mr Steffens, of Schott's, suggests that Chrysander may have made the request for this preferential treatment through Bismarck, who lived not far from Bergedorf, and whose secretary and medical adviser his son Rudolf was. The Royal Archives at Windsor contain no record of such a request from Bismarck, but this may not be conclusive.

It is unfortunate that Chrysander did not give Kraus even an approximate year for this provincial sale. May it be that he, in his old age, was giving a confused version of the purchase of the Smith copies which Schoelcher bought from Kerslake, a Bristol bookseller, in 1856? As is well known, Schoelcher sold them to Chrysander in 1868 for preservation in Hamburg. Or perhaps Kraus misunderstood Chrysander, and substituted his name for Schoelcher's. But if this is the origin of the story, here too there is an odd error of fact in the narrative. Apart from the curious point that Chrysander succeeded in keeping his railway ticket, its cost – apparently 7s or 8s at the most – was impossibly low. The earliest recorded price of a return ticket from London to Bristol dates from 1884: it was then 27s, second class (36s, first).

There is one other link in the chain connecting Nicolay, Chrysander and the Handel manuscripts. A volume of early copies, R.M. 19.d.11, containing songs from various works and harpsichord pieces, bears pencil notes in Chrysander's hand[25] on thirty leaves. This volume could never have been in Chrysander's personal possession for it is bound in the second style mentioned above, and contains Nicolay's notes on the fly leaf and inserted blanks.

Whether Chrysander used this volume in Bergedorf or in London, his treatment of it argues scant respect for Royal property.

[1959]

Notes

1. But it must be added that the papers for George III in the Royal Archives are incomplete.
2. The contemporary sets of separate parts and arias nearly double this number.
3. Made by kind permission of Mr William Martin.
4. Mentioned in my article 'Benjamin Goodison's Complete Edition of Purcell', in *Monthly Musical Record*, March-April, 1951.
5. Kindly supplied by Colonel B U Nicolay CB, a great-great-grandson of Christian Frederick.
6. BL Add.MS. 37386, f.7.
7. Information kindly supplied by Mr F E Beyer, Secretary to the Society.
8. Dresden, 1920, p. 33 (transcription).
9. *Court and Private Life in the Time of Queen Charlotte. Being the journals of Mrs. Papendiek* (London, 1887), vol. 1, p. 76. There are some half-dozen references to Nicolay in these entertaining pages, whose reliability, though often doubtful, need not be seriously questioned here.
10. Details of the members of both bands are given in *The Court and City Register* and repeated, with slight variations in *The Royal Kalendar* from 1762 to 1809.
11. *Memoirs of Dr Burney ... by his daughter, Madame d'Arblay* (London, 1832), vol. 2, p. 384, 385. Scholes, in *The Great Dr Burney* (London 1948), vol. 2, p. 71, unaccountably omits the sentence about Nicolay.
12. *Memoirs, Anecdotes, Facts, and Opinions, collected and presented by Laetitia-Matilda Hawkins* (London, 1824), vol. 2, p. 43, 44.
13. That the handwriting is his is proved by a comparison with his will (now in Somerset House) which is shown to be autographed throughout by an affidavit attached to settle a dispute on this very point, and with a letter by him in 1796 now in the archives of the Royal Society of Musicians.
14. vol. 2, col. 28. This article was translated verbatim by Choron and Fayolle in their *Dictionnaire historique des musiciens* of 1810, but seems to have been dropped by all subsequent lexicographers. Though Gerber's date for Nicolay's musical activity is a good deal too late, this brief notice confirms the general accuracy and width of his information about English musicians.
15. Sold by Sotheby's on 29 November, 1809.
16. His successor, William Duncan, was appointed on 16 May 1809 (information from the Royal Archives at Windsor).
17. In a note printed on a leaf inserted between pp. 2 and 3 of his facsimile of *Messiah*.
18. Kassel, 1952, pp. 17, 18.
19. 1870–1937: for a short time a pupil of Stockhausen, Kraus was a well-known bass singer and one of the earliest performers of Brahms's *Vier ernste Gesänge*, who became professor at the Royal Academy of Music in Munich, and producer at the opera until 1924 (information from Riemann).
20. Translated by myself, by kind permission of Kraus's daughter, Dr Felicitas von Kraus, who is preparing the complete memoirs for publication in German.

21 Information from Her Majesty's librarian, Sir Owen Morshead.
22 *Musical Times*, 1901, obituary notice of Chrysander, pp. 661–4, based on information from Volkert (d. 1929) who married Chrysander's daughter in 1886. Volkert was 'managing partner' of Schott's, London.
23 Martineau (1831–98) was a fine all-round scholar, who specialised in Hebrew, and was on the staff of the British Museum Library 1857–96.
24 The Earl of Redesdale gave two volumes to the Prince Consort in 1854; and in 1917, at the Aylesford sale, Squire purchased twenty volumes of copies, and added them by permission. There are also a few in modern bindings.
25 cf. Squire, *Catalogue of the Handel Manuscripts*, p. 32. He must have known Chrysander's hand well, and his opinion is confirmed by comparison of these notes with the facsimile in *MGG*, vol. 2. cols. 1415, 1416, an autograph card in the British Museum and similar notes in a RCM Handel copy, deposited in the British Museum [returned to RCM in 1966].

11

The Quest for Sterland – 1
The London Tavern:
a forgotten concert hall

In the course of its long history, the City of London has known innumerable inns and taverns, which were as varied in style and structure as they were in duration. (Though many were destroyed, by neglect or fire, there was some tradition of rebuilding on the original site.) Their uses, also, differed widely over the centuries. To modern ears, the word 'tavern' suggests rather small premises, dingy perhaps, used mostly for drinking, and occasionally offering convivial entertainment. But this was not always so, especially from about the mid-eighteenth century onwards when some taverns were elegant and spacious buildings which, besides providing lavish banquets, also served a remarkable range of social and other purposes, including music. One such was the London Tavern.

Almost unknown to works of musical reference, it is however mentioned briefly in the Athlone History,[1] but one looks in vain for its name in Robert Elkin's *The Old Concert Rooms of London* (1955), a still very useful book in which he described the musical uses of part of similar buildings such as the Crown and Anchor Tavern in the Strand. Yet the London Tavern was no less important as a place for good music, especially among such as lay east of Temple Bar. Indeed, in terms of dimensions and capacity it bears comparison with the more fashionable and more regularly used concert rooms in the West End.

On 7 November 1765 a great conflagration damaged an extensive area along and around Bishopsgate Street, affecting parts of Cornhill, Leadenhall Street and Gracechurch Street.[2] One of the buildings destroyed was the ancient White Lyon Tavern, no. 3 on the west side of Bishopsgate.[3] It was on this site that the London Tavern was erected in 1767–8,[4] to the designs of two architects.[5] William Jupp (*d* 1788) was responsible for the exterior and probably the lower floors, while William Newton (1735–90) completed the upper floor, which included the ballroom that was used for concerts. The façade of the London Tavern is illustrated in a water-colour drawing by Thomas Hosmer Shepherd (Pl. 16)[6] about 1848, showing that although the entrance may have been remodelled, Jupp's fine proportions remained unchanged for 80 years.

Besides mayoral banquets and other festivities held on political, social and

16 The London Tavern. Water-colour drawing by Thomas Hosmer Shepherd. *c* 1848. 260 × 185 mm.

historic occasions, the multifarious uses of the tavern included meetings of city companies and charitable committees. If additional space for banquets was required, the ballroom was pressed into service. In his book *Club Life of London*, John Timbs[7] records that the ballroom could seat 300 at tables, with 150 ladies in the galleries. Timbs also gives some of the dimensions of the ballroom, 33 feet deep and 30 high, and mentions that it had an organ, which can be seen in pictures in the *Illustrated London News*.[8] This gives us some idea of the elegance of the interior of the room, which is borne out by details on Newton's scale drawings, from which also the length can be computed at rather more than 90 feet. These have fortunately been preserved[9] and corroborate Timbs's figures.* They show that the style was neo-classical, distinctly in the manner of Adam, with elaborate decorations throughout, especially between the five tall windows. This room, which ran the full width of the tavern, was ventilated by openings over the cornice, a fortunate piece of design which would have mitigated the stuffiness then commonly complained of in West End concert rooms.[10]

	LENGTH	WIDTH	HEIGHT	SEATING
Almack's larger room	90–100	40	30	900[11]
Almack's smaller room	65	40	20[12]	?
Argyll Rooms	c 65	c 35	c 25	c 800[13]
Freemasons' Hall	90	43	60	?[14]
Hanover Square Rooms	90	30	?	800–900[15]
King's Theatre	95	46	35	c 1000[16]
London Tavern	c 95	33	30	?c 900 (excluding galleries)[17]

It is instructive to study the dimensions of the London Tavern's room and its probable capacity in relation to those of other contemporary buildings used for concerts. (All figures are in feet.) It seems that the dimensions of the concert room were roughly the same as those of the other principal rooms, with good natural proportions which would have given a satisfactory acoustic of the kind then traditional in London. The only documentary evidence

---

* Sotheby's sale of 22 May 1986 included, as lot 226, another set of drawings (apparently unrecorded) for the London Tavern, made in 1767 by Jupp and Newton. Besides some general plans, they show plans of the ballroom and dining-room. These drawings were acquired by the Guildhall Library.

that the London Tavern was used for concerts in the eighteenth century is its inclusion in the list of London halls referred to in note 17, though no programmes can be traced. But concerts certainly took place early in the nineteenth century and continued well into the 1850s. The evidence is sparse throughout this period, especially up to the mid-1830s, mainly because those newspapers and journals which reviewed performances generally dealt with opera and concerts in the West End. The critics of those days seem to have considered that most of the concerts given east of Temple Bar hardly deserved mention. But the following outline, from various sources, suggests that there was at least an intermittent flow of good music in Newton's spacious room.

Four brief advertisements in *The Times*[18] between 1806 and 1813 record benefit concerts, mostly of vocal music, though one, on 24 May 1810, included a cello concerto by 'Powell' (presumably Thomas Powell) and a piano concerto by Pleyel. In addition, the Harmonic Society (not to be confused with the Philharmonic) gave Beethoven symphonies in 1807 and 1809. Sir George Smart noted[19] that he conducted two seasons of London Subscription Concerts at the London Tavern, in 1818 and 1819. Though no programmes are known, the *English Musical Gazette* recorded that in January of the second season the singers were Eliza Salmon, Maria Dickons, Miss Stevens, Thomas Vaughan and Ambrogetti. Smart says that Mr Scotcher, the Secretary of the London Tavern concerts, paid him £40. 4s. for conducting the seven concerts of the first season.

It was perhaps in connection with these concerts that on 31 January 1819 the directors of the Philharmonic Society received – and refused – a request from the same Mr Scotcher for 'occasional loans' of music.[20] An anonymous article in *The Harmonicon* for 1830 (p. 175), probably written by Ayrton, mentions two different series of concerts, then 'flourishingly conducted and numerously attended' at the London Tavern. One such, led by Joseph Dando and directed by Weippert, included in an enterprising programme two overtures, Spohr's to his opera *Pietro von Albano* and Weber's *Beherrscher der Geister*, and Mozart's concert aria with piano obbligato *Ch'io mi scordi di te*. While this article also says 'bills' were available, none can now be traced. But the collection of playbills in the Department of Printed Books, British Library, includes a few later ones from the London Tavern. On 23 May 1833 Sir George Smart was in charge of a long concert of vocal music.[21] 1834 saw two notable concerts, both again conducted by Smart: the first on 2 April, under the Lord Mayor's patronage, included Beethoven's Pastoral Symphony and Mendelssohn's *Midsummer Night's Dream* overture, and the second, on 15 December, with the same Mendelssohn overture and those to *Fidelio* and Weber's *Jubilee*.[22] The new work was Neukomm's concertante for seven instruments. (All this was for the benefit of Thomas Harper, the trumpeter.)

In 1836 the Choral Harmonists, conducted by Charles Neate, made their first recorded appearance[23] at the tavern, which they used for all their concerts until their dissolution in 1851. Carse[24] says that in 1837 the tavern was the venue for six concerts, but gives no details. We find an example of the tavern's occasional use by foreign musicians at a concert of dance music which Johann Strauss and his orchestra gave there on 7 May 1838,[25] very soon after their first appearance in London. Later in 1838, the Choral Harmonists appeared again[26] in a concert that included Beethoven's *Mount of Olives* and Haydn's 'Mass in F': they had a large audience for a choir of 80, with full orchestra and organ. In 1839 they gave the first public performance of Beethoven's Mass in D, which was repeated in 1844.[27] It was perhaps in 1842 that the London Tavern reached its apogee as a musical centre, when it shared a series of six classical subscription concerts with the Hanover Square Rooms.[28] The full-column announcement specifies simply 'The Queen's Concert Rooms, Hanover Square' and 'the Great Concert Room, London Tavern' – the latter being by then so well known that 'Bishopsgate' was deemed superfluous. The announcement, which named a dozen concerto soloists including Sterndale Bennett, also said the band and chorus 'will amount to 150 performers'. (Some 60 orchestral players, all drawn from the West End orchestras, are named; the conductor was G F Harris.) This provides conclusive evidence that the tavern's ballroom could accommodate the largest forces needed in London during the first half of the nineteenth century. Of the three concerts allotted to the tavern, one was cancelled, and only one was noticed in the *Musical World*, which referred to 'these grand affairs'. It included the overtures to *La gazza ladra* and *Die Zauberflöte*, Beethoven's 'Calm of the Sea' and Bériot's Violin Concerto in B minor.

By the 1850s concert rooms of the size and proportions listed above fell into disuse. Larger, totally different halls (such as Exeter Hall, 1831) had already been built, and more were to come, notably St James's Hall in 1856. It is likely that the London Tavern had been little used for concerts for some years before it was demolished in 1876. As far as we know, most of its concerts were single events: the short joint series of 1842 was probably an exception. But as the activities of the Choral Harmonists showed, the tavern could attract and keep the loyalty of a single organization for quite a long time. Another one was undoubtedly the above-mentioned Harmonic Society during the early years of the century. We know that their regular seasons included performances of at least two Beethoven symphonies[29] – the third and the fourth – which were certainly the first in England, and, in the case of the latter, possibly the first anywhere outside Vienna. As the society and its organizers, John Sterland and Anton Schick, have fallen into undeserved obscurity, they and their activities warrant separate discussion at some length.

[1986]

Notes

1 Percy Young: 'Orchestral Music', *Music in Britain: the Romantic Age 1800–1914*, ed. Nicholas Temperley (London, 1981), 359. The London Tavern is mentioned briefly in Temperley's article 'Beethoven in London Concert Life, 1800–1850', *Music Review*, XXI (1961), p. 209.
2 There are three engraved plans of the fire area in the BL, Map Library, Crace VIII 58–60.
3 The London Tavern is clearly marked on Richard Horwood's *Plan of the Cities of London and Westminster...*, 1792–9, BL Maps 148.e.7. In the twentieth century, the site was occupied by the Royal Bank of Scotland until the 1970s, and in 1985 was again under redevelopment. It lies next to the Toronto and Dominion Bank and opposite the Banque Belge.
4 The London Tavern should not be confused with the City of London Tavern, 1807–c 1840, sometimes called the New London Tavern and also sometimes used for concerts. It stood at no. 17, on the east side of Bishopsgate Street. This distinction is set out by Bryant Lillywhite: *London Coffee Houses* (London, 1963), p. 711, no. 1807. BM, Prints and Drawings, Crace XXIV sheet 21, no. 43, illustrates the City of London Tavern, engraved by Samuel Rawle after George Shepherd (1809).
5 H M Colvin: *A Biographical Dictionary of British Architects* (London, 2/1978), p. 479.
6 BM, Prints & Drawings, Crace XXIV sheet 21, no. 42 (dated 1848 in the catalogue)
7 Vol. II (London, 1866), pp. 274–8; Timbs bases his account on an anonymous pamphlet, *The London Tavern, past and present* (London, 1852); copy in the Guildhall Library, A 2.2. no. 10.
8 April 1845 and Jan 1850, both showing the organ; see Guildhall Library C23.1 p. 18. This sheet has another illustration (? also from *Illustrated London News*), showing a gallery.
9 Dated April 1768: Royal Institute of British Architects, K9/14 (1) (2).
10 The ventilation is described in *The London Tavern* (note 7 above).
11 Elkin, 75–7; Carse: *The Orchestra from Beethoven to Berlioz* (Cambridge, 1948), p. 162.
12 Elkin, p. 77.
13 Elkin, 116, quoting *The Harmonicon*, gives the seating capacity as 800 but no dimensions. No plan of any part of Nash's building now seems to exist, but approximate figures for the rooms can be deduced from measurements given in a groundplan of the new leases granted after the fire of 1830 (PRO, L.R.1 272 attached to f.190r), combined with proportionate details seen in the engraving by William Wallis after Thomas Hosmer Shepherd in James Elmes's *Metropolitan Improvements* (London, 1827 [1828]), pl. [8], and other contemporary views. The large columniated semi-circular bay was perhaps used as an ante-chamber to the concert room. See also Carse, 211.
14 Carse, p. 162.
15 Elkin, pp. 93 (and 109, mention of the organ); Carse, p. 162.

16 Elkin, p. 113.
17 Slightly differing dimensions are given for the London Tavern, the King's Theatre, Almack's and Hanover Square Rooms (and, in addition, for the Crown and Anchor Tavern, and the Upper Room, Bath) in an anonymous list printed in the London *General Evening Post* (25 Feb 1794), reproduced in Michael Forsyth: *Buildings for Music* (Cambridge, 1985), p. 39. The purpose of this list (which also includes area measurements in square feet) and the brief accompanying text was to emphasize that the King's Theatre Concert Room was then the largest in England. It also shows, incidentally, that the London Tavern, at 3,200 square feet, was the fourth largest in London.
18 I owe this information to Professor Nicholas Temperley.
19 Smart Papers, BL Add.42225, ff.15*v*, 17r.
20 Minutes, BL Dept of Manuscripts, Loan 48.2/1.
21 BL Playbills 320.
22 BL Playbills 320.
23 *Musical World* (Nov 1836), 217, and George Grove: *Dictinary of Music*, i (London, 1878), s.v. 'Choral Harmonic Society' (Charles Mackeson).
24 p. 228, n. 1.
25 BL Playbills 323.
26 *Musical World*, p. 150.
27 Grove, 'Choral Harmonic Society'. An entire, private, performance of the Mass had been given by Thomas Alsager in 1832; see P J Willetts: *Beethoven in England* (London, 1970), pp. 53–4.
28 *Musical World* (1842), p. 288.
29 BL Dept of Manuscripts, Loan 4, RPS 7 and 5.

12

The Quest for Sterland – 2
Sterland, the Harmonic Society and Beethoven's fourth symphony

During the whole of its 11-year life, from 1823 to 1833, *The Harmonicon* was notable for the great range of its coverage. Besides current news and reports of musical events at home and abroad, it carried many articles on historical topics, the wide variety of which reflected the keen mind of its editor William Ayrton.[1] From time to time it included contributions on relatively recent aspects of music in London, among them a series of nine articles, each entitled 'Memoirs of the Metropolitan Concerts'. The first appeared in January 1831 and was prefaced by an undated letter from the writer of the series, 'S.D.' His last article was published in January 1833: the one that concerns us here is the eighth, printed in November 1832.[2] He makes clear at the outset that he is describing two distinct series of concerts – 'The HARMONIC, which was held for several seasons in the London Tavern, and the AMATEUR CONCERTS established in 1818 at the City of London Tavern'. Historically, the 'Harmonic' series is the more significant, because it includes the early performance of certain Beethoven symphonies.

The second paragraph of S.D.'s article must be quoted at some length:

The first of these concerts owed its establishment to the musical zeal and activity of a German merchant, residing in London, of the name of Schick, and of Mr Sterland, also an amateur, who filled the office of secretary as long as the concert endured, and whose collection of manuscript scores of the symphonies of Mozart, Haydn, and Beethoven, written from the detached parts by himself, long before any such thing was printed, while they are a proof of indefatigable industry and patience, form as complete a specimen of musical calligraphy as exists: they are now, by the gift of the copier, in the library of the Philharmonic. At this concert, Beethoven's Pastoral Symphony, and selections from the Don Giovanni of Mozart,[3] were performed for the first time in England. Spagnoletti was the leader, and all the principal parts were sustained by professors, while the ripieni violins and second wind instruments were confided to amateurs. The performances were chiefly instrumental, the funds not being calculated on a scale to admit, except on extraordinary occasions, the expense attending the engagement of a vocal corps. For several seasons this concert continued to flourish and admission to its meetings was eagerly sought after. But the seeds of decay exist in all things . . .

– in this case, the dance that concluded each concert, and ultimately exceeded it in extent and popularity. S.D. went on to praise the Harmonic Society for 'having promoted and kept alive the love and practice of the higher order of instrumental music in London'.

The nature, significance and location of the London Tavern was discussed in the first of these articles. A number of other questions now readily suggest themselves. Who were Sterland and Schick, and what were their professions? are any of the scores written by Sterland extant, and what chronological evidence do they offer? is the statement about the first performances accurate? Let us begin with what little seems now to be ascertainable about 'Schick'. The sole clue to his musicality lies in the invaluable index to Landon's *Haydn: Chronicle and Works: the Years of The Creation 1796–1800* (1977). Here the reference from his name leads to Haydn's own list (p. 630) of the subscribers to the vocal score of *The Creation*, in which the composer wrote that 'Anton Schökh aus London' (the spelling was corrected to 'Schick' in the first edition of 1800) had paid for two copies. He is likely to be identical with the Anton Schick who first appears in the directories in 1798, living at 32 Camomile Street, Bishopsgate. He was then, and remained for the next two decades, the only one of his name. By 1801 he had become 'Anthony Schick, Merchant' and by 1807 was at 3 Devonshire Square, Bishopsgate Street. Next year the entry reads 'Anthony Schick & Co. merchants, at St Martin's Lane, Cannon Street', and from 1815 onwards the firm is described as 'Schick & Co., Merchants and Patent Coffee Warehouse', its last address being 25 Gracechurch Street. After 1822 Schick's name disappears from the directories, and in default of any will right through to the 1860s it seems likely that he returned to the continent at some unknown date. It is worth noting that, for most of his time in London, Schick lived within a short distance of the London Tavern.

As a preliminary to the scanty facts about Sterland's life, we may turn to the minutes of the meetings and other papers of the Philharmonic Society (founded in 1813), now deposited on loan in the British Library, Department of Manuscripts. The references to Sterland are these:

Loan 48.3/1 General Meeting, 8 Feb 1814: 'Mr Sterland presented a valuable collection of music'.
Loan 48.2/1 Directors' Meeting, 16 Feb 1817: 'Mr Sterland's letter [now lost] read. Resolved that he be admitted on the free list'.
Loan 48.2/1 Directors' Meeting, 1 Dec 1818: 'Mr Sterland's letter [now lost] read, requesting the loan of music for the Amateur City Concerts... Acceded to'
[*ie* those at the City of London Tavern].
Loan 48.3/1 General Meeting, 7 Feb 1819: 'Ayrton to write to Mr Sterland of his admission as usual'.

Loan 48.6/1 Letter Books. Letter to Sterland from the secretary, W Watts, undated (but must be Jan. or Feb. 1840), confirming his admission to rehearsals and to concerts 'as usual on the free list'.
Loan 48.2/4 Directors' Meeting, 10 Nov 1848: 'Mr Sterland presented through Mr Collard' a MS containing 'a Beethoven quartet and the overture to Prometheus'.
Loan 48/6 Letter Books. Letter dated 23 Nov 1848 from the secretary, G W Budd, to Sterland, thanking him for the gift – a MS volume entitled 'Bibliothèque musicale' – 'the library already enriched by several of your very beautiful manuscripts'.

Sparse though these extracts are, they provide a pointer to Sterland's musical position. The obvious respect in which the Philharmonic held him for so long, and his earlier connection with the Harmonic, suggest that he must surely have known other important musicians besides Ayrton and, later, one of the Collard brothers. (It is strange that there is no mention of him in the two large collections of Ayrton papers in the British Library.) One might also expect him to have been a resident in or near London. But his name is not to be found in any dictionary of English biography, any lists of livery companies, or in any of the numerous directories covering the capital and the home counties in the first half of the 19th century. A fortunate clue came from the examination of six pamphlets on financial matters, all dating from the 1840s, entered under the heading 'J. Sterland' in the *General Catalogue of Printed Books* of the British Library. All were published for him, or issued privately by him, at Margate, where he lived at 6 Prospect Row, Dane Hill. The title of one of them, *Novel Computations to find the Commission – half-year's Interest – and value of Stock, within one Penny*, which he inscribed to the British Museum in 1846, includes the statement 'aetat.77'.

His death, which occurred in Margate on 23 March 1854, was reported in the *Gentleman's Magazine* ('for many years a resident') but passed unnoticed in both *The Musical World* and *The Musical Times*. As the latter omitted to mention Ayrton's death, this may not be very significant: Sterland had long been a forgotten man.

One might expect some information about Sterland's domestic life from the census return of April 1851,[4] made under an Act – the first of its kind – which required the head of the household to state the age and place of birth of both himself and the other occupants and their relation to him. Though it lifts the veil a little, it proves to be yet another tantalizing document. Sterland, who describes himself as 'fund holder, aged 81', did not know where he was born. There were two other occupants, both nieces – Elizabeth Bunn, aged 40, born in Middlesex, and Francis [sic] Kirby, aged 29, place of birth unknown! His short will,[5] drawn up on 15 October 1851, is also tantalizing but it is informative. It describes him as 'formerly of Clifton Street, Finsbury Square, then of Mark Lane'. Apart from a few small bequests, he left the rest of his estate, nearly £6,000, to his housekeeper, Elizabeth Bunn. The bequest to one of his executors, Nicholas Mason, 'gentleman', of 118 Wood Street, Cheapside, reads thus: 'my gold watch, sixteen volumes of Russia-bound books entitled "Bibliothèque musicale" written by myself, the silver inkstand with an inscription presented to me'.

The earliest Margate directory[6] to include Sterland's name appeared in 1832, which suggests that he moved there a year before,[7] having perhaps retired from business of some kind when he turned 60. His books and pamphlets suggests that he had financial acumen: they are written in a curiously whimsical style. The title-page of that cited above is headed: 'Figures are good for the mind', and further states, 'These tables have all been constructed purely for amusement'. They all deal with income tax, calculation of interest rates and the like. One would like to know where he lived in London, and where he was educated. But, as stated above, his name does not occur in the directories for the two streets mentioned in his will, and most of those in them seem to have been small firms. Again, Sterland's name does not appear in the lists of the public schools or universities of his day, nor in those of the legal profession. The French title used for his collection suggests that he might have had contacts abroad, but the extent of his musical education remains unknown. His musical handwriting is firm, clear and quite professional.

So it is to the scores themselves that we must turn, as the only tangible evidence of his activity. And this evidence is indeed, as 'S.D.' wrote in *The Harmonicon*, in the library of the (now Royal) Philharmonic Society – not in that portion of its scores deposited on loan in the British Museum in 1914, but in its 'secondary' collection of manuscripts which, having been stored for many years in the Royal Academy of Music, was transferred to the British Library in 1982, to join the earlier deposit (Loan 4) in the Department of Manuscripts.

There are now five scores written by Sterland in the Royal Philharmonic Society's library, Beethoven's Symphonies nos. 3 and 4 and his overture to *Prometheus*, and Mozart's Haffner Symphony and overture to *Così fan tutte* (RPS 7, 5, 514, 316 and 791).[8] The two Beethoven symphonies and the Mozart overture bear Sterland's signature: the other two manuscripts can be identified as his from a study of the hands, borne out by comparison with the inscription in the book he gave to the British Museum. Sterland clearly attached great importance to the two Beethoven symphonies, each of which has a full title within a ruled frame, reading respectively thus:

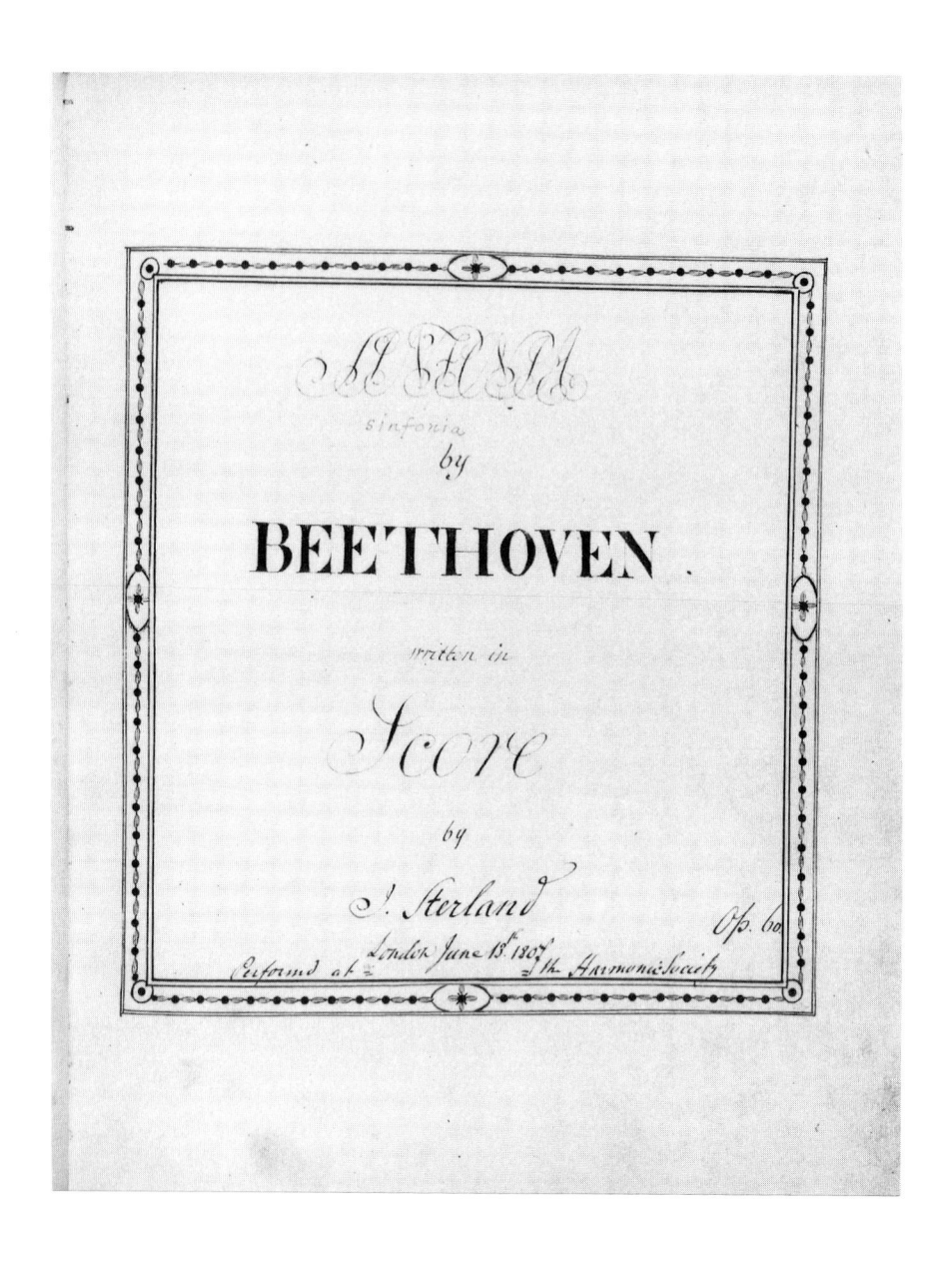

17 Title page of a score of Beethoven's fourth symphony, in the hand of John Sterland. 1807. 287 × 230 mm.

Sinfonia Eroica e Marcia funebre composta per festeggiare il souvenire di un grand uomo da Luigi van Beethoven Op. 55. Vol 22nd[9] written in score by J. Sterland. Performed at the Harmonic Society Dec.23.1807.

Sinfonia by Beethoven written in Score by J Sterland Op. 60. London June 13th 1807. Performed at the Harmonic Society. (Pl. 17)

    The above dates for the history of first and early performances of Beethoven in London were the subject of an article by Nicholas Temperley.[10] He left blank the date for the first performance of Beethoven's Fourth Symphony and gave '1806?' for the Eroica, basing his conjecture as to the identity of the work on advertisements of two concerts, 14 February and 2 May, each of which included a 'new' Beethoven symphony 'for a full band'. These identifications may be correct, but the Harmonic Society's is the earliest performance to name the symphony and give a definite date. As to Sterland's source for the Eroica, his wording suggests that he used a set of parts published in October 1806 'Nel contor delle arti e d'industria' in Vienna. His score of the Fourth Symphony is of much greater historical and chronological interest.

    Beethoven finished the work in the autumn of 1806, and the first performance took place in Vienna in March 1807. Its earliest appearance in print was the parts issued by the Bureau des Arts et d'Industrie in 1808 (the exact date is unknown). Now though Sterland did not state the date of the Harmonic Society's performance, it must have taken place fairly soon after he wrote out the score, and so antedates, by 13 years or more, the Philharmonic's performance of 1821, the earliest hitherto recorded in London. It also fills the blank in Temperley's table. All this leads to a cardinal question – how, while war was raging in northern Europe, could Sterland possibly have procured performing material of the Fourth Symphony and completed *his* score, some ten to eleven weeks after the first performance in Vienna?

    The question may be less difficult to answer if we recall that at this very time, the spring of 1807, this symphony was one of the group of Beethoven's recent compositions about which Clementi was personally negotiating with the composer in Vienna. The contract,[11] which comprised also the Op. 59 quartets, the Fourth Piano Concerto, the overture to *Coriolanus* and the Violin Concerto, was dated 20 April, and was the main topic of the excited letter which Clementi wrote two days later to his partner William Collard in London. The relevant phrase in Clause 4 of the contract reads: 'pour le concert pour le violon et pour la symphonie et l'ouverture, qui viennent de partir pour l'Angleterre'. But the passage in Clementi's letter runs thus: 'Today sets off a courier for London thro' Russia, and he will bring over to you 2 or 3 of the mentioned articles... The symphony and the overture are wonderfully fine'.[12] There is clearly some ambiguity here, and an obvious contradiction between the contract and the letter, for the phrase 'qui viennent de partir' can only mean 'which have just left'. Even allowing for this, and for the possibility that in his excitement Clementi wrote 'today sets off' instead of 'there set off two days ago', the discrepancy has worried the two writers, Alan Tyson and Leon Plantinga,[13] who have discussed the documents and their general implications. Both emphasized the fact that the Fourth Symphony was one of the works which, despite his enthusiasm, Clementi failed to publish.

While Tyson wrote that 'there may have been some difficulty in despatching the music to England owing to the troubled state of Europe', Plantinga had graver doubts:

Did that courier for some reason leave belatedly with two compositions rather than the three specified by the contract? And did he fulfil his mission? Napoleon's 'Continental System' (an embargo on trade with England) was at the time vigorously enforced; hence the long detour through Russia. But such an expedition might in any case have run foul of the fierce fighting that summer in East Prussia and Poland. It is not impossible that these were the two *actually* sent by courier – and that they never arrived. Nor can we be entirely sure that manuscripts for any of this music, other than the orchestral parts of the violin concerto, ever reached London.[14]

But the fact remains that Sterland had written his score by 13 June, and for this there are only two possible explanations. Either he and Schick had procured their material independently from Vienna; or, the music conveyed successfully by Clementi's first courier[15] included Beethoven's Fourth Symphony, and Sterland, hearing about its arrival, was quickly given access to it for his concerts. Though it is not totally impossible that he and Schick had contacts in Vienna, it does seem extremely unlikely that there were two couriers conveying Beethoven works to London at this same time. The fact that Sterland was highly regarded by the Philharmonic Society so soon after its inception suggests that, even earlier, when running the Harmonic Society's concerts, he enjoyed a considerable acquaintance among London musicians, perhaps including the Collard family (one of whom certainly knew him later). By June 1807 Clementi was far away in Rome and stayed there till November, and William Collard could hardly have consulted him quickly if he had received a request from Sterland.

It is perhaps worth emphasizing that Plantinga's doubts about the feasibility of a courier's then reaching London are unfounded. Clementi, a practical and much travelled man, with good contracts in the Baltic, chose the route 'thro' Russia' because he knew it *was* feasible. Some French route maps of the period[16] show that the roads led from Vienna north-east, via Breslau,

Warsaw, Bialystok, Grodno, Vilna and Drounia. Moreover, the roads were exceptionally dry that spring.[17] It is a fair conjecture that the courier made for Riga which, unlike St Petersburg, was an ice-free port and could have completed the journey of some 700 miles in ten days or so. Finding a ship, perhaps with the help of Clementi's business acquaintance,[18] would not have taken long, and the voyage to Lübeck is some 620 miles. By going overland the 60-odd miles to Hamburg in order to avoid the 600 miles sailing round the north of Denmark, the courier would have saved much time. A sea journey of 427 miles, to reach London by early June, would not have presented much difficulty. Clementi chose this route, or something like it, because it lay far to the east of the theatre of war. The battle of Eylau (7–8 February) was past; that of Friedland yet to come (14 June); and the operations on the Vistula between March and May could hardly have affected the courier. Indeed, Plantinga misjudged the extent to which he might have been impeded either by military action or by the Continental System.[19]

It is tantalizing that we know so little of the duration and content of the Harmonic Society's concerts. An unsigned article in *The Harmonicon* for 1830,[20] headed 'City of London Amateur Concerts', perhaps by Ayrton himself, mentions the establishment of the 'Harmonic' concerts as 'thirty years ago'. S.D. refers to 'several years' and 'several seasons' in a context pointing to the first decade of the nineteenth century, and this is borne out by the dates on Sterland's two Beethoven scores. S.D.'s emphatic statement about the first performance of the Pastoral Symphony cannot, in the absence of any score, be verified. His assertion that these were 'private [*ie* subscription only] concerts' is borne out by the lack of press notices. But their quality is confirmed by Bishop,[21] who wrote thus: 'the symphonies of Beethoven have just been made known to England through the zealous and praiseworthy exertions of a society of private gentlemen, at whose concerts many other classical pieces were admirably executed'. In the context of a period well before the Philharmonic's foundation in 1813, this can only refer to the Harmonic. (The fact that Sterland made his gift to the former soon after its inception suggests that the latter had ceased some years before.) But Bishop's tone points at least to some continuity, and the range is borne out by Sterland's two Mozart scores mentioned above.

Finally, who was S.D., the source of such seminal, detailed information? He was without doubt a man with a good sense of musical history, for besides the 'Memoirs of the Metropolitan Concerts', Ayrton published in *The Harmonicon* another, equally notable series by him, 'Chronicles of the Italian Opera in England', five long articles, all issued in 1830. They are prefaced by a letter, headed 'London October 30, 1829', in which S.D. says he had been going to the opera regularly for 30 years, and had kept a full record of all performances at the King's Theatre. He also mentions songs preserved by Hawkins and Burney, as evidence of the style of past singers. Besides these 'Chronicles', S.D. sent Ayrton an 'Index to Biographical Articles' covering all issues of *The Harmonicon* from 1823 to 1831, which appeared in May 1832. All three of S.D.'s prefatory letters reveal a strong personality, convinced of his own rightness. Now by the time he was writing in such detail of Sterland's gift to the Philharmonic, 17 years had passed since its acceptance was briefly minuted, and few if any of the original or subsequent directors are likely to have remembered the matter or even heard of it. Moreover, none of them, and no recorded musician of the time or anyone known to have been connected with music, has the initials S.D. Who, then, was this writer with such a long memory? Was it possibly Sterland himself? The theory is attractive because it would at least account for the detailed, accurate knowledge of the gift to the Philharmonic Society. But why did he only use the first and last letters of his surname instead of the initial letters of both his names? Perhaps the explanation can be found within the pages of *The Harmonicon*.[22]

Following the general practice of its time, this journal seldom named any of its contributors, but often gave their initials. Among those who have been revealed to posterity was J.R.S., who contributed five articles on Beethoven to *The Harmonicon*, between January 1824 and May 1829 (Alan Tyson has shown that he was J R Schultz).[23] Another contributor was James Satchell, who seems to have been a regular correspondent of Ayrton's. Under his initials, J.S. he contributed two pieces of music to *The Harmonicon*, in 1826 and 1830, and two letters – 'On the characters of keys' – in 1829. If Sterland's contributions, dating from almost the same period, had been published under his initials, J.S., the readership, while realizing that J.R.S. and J.S. were not the same, might well have thought that all contributions signed J.S. were by the same writer. Perhaps, therefore, S.D. was suggested to Sterland by Ayrton himself.

One further point is that, like Satchell, Sterland contributed a little music to *The Harmonicon*. Under the heading 'D., S.' the British Library's *Catalogue of Printed Music* has two entries, both for pieces printed in that journal (vol. IX, 1831, part 2). Both are arrangements, one of a number in Pacini's *L'Ultimo giorno di Pompei*, the other of the air 'Un ultimo addio' from Bellini's *Las straniera*. The words of the latter, 'The Parting', were by 'F Townsend'.[24] If S.D. was Sterland, may this song not be taken as his whimsical farewell to London and its musical life? For we know that by 1831 he had settled in Margate, and if the three historical contributions to *The Harmonicon* are his, it looks as if they were deliberately prepared in the later 1820s, in order to leave in print, before his retirement, some record of his musical life and knowledge.[25] Of course, all this may be mere coincidence, and in the last resort there is no proof of the identity of S.D. and John Sterland. But the writings of the former, and the remarkable though shadowy achievements of the latter, notably his London Tavern concerts, surely deserve a small place in the musical history of their time.

[1986]

Notes

1. The most detailed and authoritative account of Ayrton is given by Leanne Langley, *The English Musical Journal in the Early Nineteenth Century* (diss., U. of North Carolina, Chapel Hill, 1983), pp. 284–318.
2. pp. 246–8: this passage in *The Harmonicon* was first pointed out by Nicholas Temperley in *Instrumental Music in England, 1800–1850* (diss., U. of Cambridge, 1959), p. 21.
3. discussed in the third of these articles.
4. Census Office, 40. 107. 1629 (Margate sheet 10–443).
5. PRO, Grant of Probate S.T.2 1854, 337; will on Film Prob.11, 2190, 1–257.
6. Pigot's *National, London and Provincial Directory* (1832–64), p. 850.
7. His name does not, however, occur in the Margate rate books 1827–32 (now in the Kent County Record Office, Canterbury). I am grateful to Professor Frank Harrison for having verified this fact, which, coupled with Sterland's absence from the London directories and the relevant rate books, suggests that he preferred not to own property. Sterland's will records that he had shares in the Margate Pier Company and in the West India Dock. Such interests suggest that whenever, from 1840 onwards, he came to London for the Philharmonic concerts, he travelled to and from Margate by steamer, at least before the railway arrived in 1846.
8. This MS is now bound in a style used by the Philharmonic Society in the mid- to later nineteenth century. There is no trace of any Beethoven quartet in MS score, nor of his Seventh Symphony.
9. presumably of his 'Bibliothèque musicale'.
10. 'Beethoven in London Concert Life, 1800–1850', *Music Review*, xxi (1960), pp. 207–11. Temperley knew of the Harmonic Society from the article in *The Harmonicon*, but the Beethoven scores in Sterland's hand were then undiscovered. When identifying the 'new' Beethoven symphony with the Eroica, he seems to have assumed a very swift delivery of MS parts to London, as the work was not published till October 1806.
11. *The Letters of Beethoven*, ed. Emily Anderson (London, 1962), iii, pp. 1419–20, where this 'draft contract' is given in the original French.
12. quoted by Leon Plantinga: *Clementi: his Life and Works* (London, 1977), p. 197.
13. *Authentic English Editions of Beethoven* (London, 1963), pp. 18, 51, 52; Plantinga, 196–99.
14. Plantinga, p. 198.
15. Plantinga, 199, points out that in 1808 Beethoven reminded Clementi that the six works contracted for in 1807 had been sent to Collard 'by two expeditions'.
16. eg. *Carte des routes de poste de la Russie européene* (Paris, 1812), BL, Map Library, Maps 35830 (158).
17. F Loraine Petre: *Napoleon's Campaigns in Poland 1806–7* (London, 1907) also states (p. 55) that from 2 May to 14 June the weather in that area was fine and warm.
18. Plantinga, p. 192, mentions that Clementi had been in Riga in 1803 and 1805.

19 François Crouzot: *L'économie britannique et le blocus continental (1806–1813)* (Paris, 1958), points out, *inter alia* (pp. 209, 221, 253), that many officials at north German ports were corrupt, so that the blockade had little effect in the first half of 1807 and that there was regular trade from Riga to England.
20 p. 175.
21 quoted by Richard Northcott: *The Life of Sir Henry Bishop* (London, 1920), p. 13; cf. Percy Young, 'Orchestral Music', *Music in Britain: the Romantic Age 1800–1914*, ed. Nicholas Temperley (London, 1981), p. 359.
22 see Langley, op cit, pp. 358–9, 512; I am grateful to Dr Langley for suggesting the possible reason for Sterland's name being abridged to S.D.
23 *MT*, CXIII (1972), p. 450.
24 Dr Langley has pointed out that S.D.'s 'The Parting' was republished in 1835 in the *Musical Library* (which was also edited by Ayrton), the author of the words being given as 'the late F Townsend Esq.'; she suggests that this may be Francis Townsend, Rouge Dragon Pursuivant at Arms and editor of Debrett's Peerage, who died 14 April 1833 (*Gentleman's Magazine*, 378).
25 The tone of mild self-congratulation, and the manner of writing in the third person, are found elsewhere in *The Harmonicon*, notably in some articles definitely attributable to Ayrton.

13

The Quest for Sterland – 3
Don Giovanni in London before 1817

It has long been known that the first London staging of Mozart's *Don Giovanni* was at the King's Theatre, Haymarket, on 12 April 1817.[1] That most of the music had been heard some nine years earlier in a concert version was first revealed by Alfred Loewenberg in an important, authoritative article which appeared in 1943.[2] While lacking the impact of a true operatic première, this was a memorable event in English musical history, but Loewenberg's account was circumscribed and rather selective, partly no doubt because of the difficulties of research in wartime London. He was unable to relate his discovery to a fuller musical and chronological context because he was unaware of a parallel performance at the London Tavern and the relation of that venue to the Harmonic Society.

The essence of what Loewenberg wrote can be summarized under four heads. First, he showed that a few separate pieces from *Don Giovanni* had been heard in London in the 1790s as interpolation pieces, one at least used anonymously. Secondly, he quoted the following passages from the series of articles in *The Harmonicon*, 'Chronicles of the Italian Opera in England':

> Of every private circle they [Mozart's operas] had, in the mean time been the delight; and hopeless of hearing them, accompanied with all the pomp and circumstance of theatrical representation, amateurs had performed three of the greatest in orchestra or concert. Don Juan was the first. The parts were copied out, and most of them, instrumental as well as vocal, performed by amateurs. Spagnoletti led, and Miss Griglietti was the Donna Anna.[3]

Thirdly – and by far the most significant matter – was Loewenberg's fortunate acquisition of a copy of a previously unknown libretto[4] printed for a concert performance of *Don Giovanni* at the Hanover Square Rooms in 1809. In his article he gave the title-page in full, and this must be repeated here:

> Mozart's / Grand Opera / Don Juan. / The Principal Parts Performed at / Mr. Griffin's Concert, / Hanover Square, / April 20, 1809, / by Mrs. Billington, Miss Hughes / Miss Griglietti / Mrs. Bland / Signor Miarteni, / Mr. Bellamy / Mr. C. Horn, / Signor G. Lanza / and Mr. Braham. / London. / Printed by P. da Ponte, / 15 Poland Street, Oxford Street / 1809. / Price Two Shillings. / (111 pages. Italian and English.)[5] (Pl. 18)

18 Title page of the libretto for the Hanover Square Rooms performance of Mozart's *Don Giovanni*. 1809. 173 × 100 mm.

Loewenberg discovered an announcement in *The Times* of that same day, 20 April 1809, which stated that, 'In consequence of an event of the most melancholy nature having occurred in Mr Griffin's family', the performance had to be postponed. The delay lasted until 23 May, for which Loewenberg found another announcement, which is remarkable for giving the distribution of the 'twenty numbers' among the singers and from this he reconstructed the cast. (Details of this are given below.) By way of preface to these fascinating discoveries, Loewenberg discussed briefly two articles in *The Harmonicon*,[6] entitled 'Autobiography of an Amateur Singer', which includes a very curious account of another upstaged performance of *Don Giovanni* given a little earlier than 1809. This too, which is the fourth component of Loewenberg's article, will be dealt with below.

★

What Loewenberg wrote can now be amplified in various ways from both *The Harmonicon* and *The Times*. His quotation from 'Chronicles of the Italian Opera in England' omitted the immediately preceding sentence: 'Eighteen years had now elapsed since the death of that wonderful composer [Mozart]'. This is important, because it shows that even after 20 years S.D.'s recollection was quite precise although Loewenberg criticized him for inaccuracy. He also overlooked S.D.'s important letter published by Ayrton as the introduction to his other articles, 'Memoirs of the Metropolitan Concerts'. The salient sentence reads: 'the Harmonic, which was held for several years in the city, and at which Beethoven's Pastoral Symphony and parts of *Don Juan* were first publicly performed' – and this is repeated and confirmed in the full passage quoted above.[7]

So it is abundantly clear that there were two concert performances of *Don Giovanni* at about the same time – one, as outlined by Loewenberg, at Hanover Square Rooms, the other, unknown to him but faithfully recorded by S.D., at the London Tavern. Now having regard to the fact that in 1809 Mozart's music was still generally unfamiliar to London musicians and, as S.D. emphasizes, was considered very difficult, it is *prima facie* improbable that these two performances were wholly unrelated. Indeed, a little more research in *The Times* reveals a strong connection between them. The full sequence of the announcements in 1809 is as follows:

4 April:

New Room, Hanover Square. Mr Griffin[8] respectfully begs leave to acquaint the Nobility, Gentry and his friends in general, that his BENEFIT CONCERT is fixed for Thursday the 20th April, at the above Rooms. The first part will consist of the most beautiful compositions from Mozart's celebrated opera 'Don Juan'. This undertaking never having been before attempted in England, every exertion will be made on the present occasion to render the performance adequate to the uncommon excellence of the Music. Mrs Billington,[9] Miss Hughes,[10] Mrs Bland,[11] Signor Miarteni,[12] and Mr Braham[13] have already promised their assistance. The names of several other vocal Performers will shortly be announced. The instrumental department will be sustained by Professors of the first eminence, Leader Mr Spagnoletti.[14] The second part will be a Miscellaneous Selection to open with Mozart's Grand Symphony in E [sic]. A new concerto for the pianoforte by Mr Griffin will be performed for the first time in public. Books containing the entire opera of 'Don Juan', in Italian, with an English translation, will be printed for the occasion. Tickets 10s. 6d. each, to be had at the principal Music Shops.

6 April: full repeat of the above.
8 April, with one addition to the female singers 'Mrs Billington, Miss Hughes, Mrs Bland, Miss Lyon'. Also on 8 April, [immediately following the repeated Hanover Square Rooms announcement]:

By permission of the Right Hon. the Lord Mayor – Signor Spagnoletti has the honour to announce to the Nobility, Gentry and his friends in general, that his Benefit Concert will take place on Monday, April 17 at the Old London Tavern, Bishopsgate Street; when will be performed the Grand Opera of Don Juan by Mozart, never performed in public in this country. The vocal parts by Mrs Dickons,[15] Miss Hughes, Mr Horn,[16] Mr Bellamy,[17] Signor Miarteni and Signor Siboni.[18] Signor Spagnoletti will also play a new concerto on the violin. Tickets 10s. 6d. each, to be had of Signor Spagnoletti, Charles-Street, Middlesex Hospital: Messrs Clementi & Co., Cheapside; Monzani & Hill, no. 3 Old Bond Street, and at the London Tavern.

10 April, there was a repeat of the Hanover Square Rooms announcement of 8 April, but no London Tavern announcement.
11 April: repeat of the London Tavern announcement of 8 April; no Hanover Square Rooms announcement.
12 April: exactly as 11 April.
17 April (on front page):

New Rooms Hanover Square. Mr Griffin's Concert. Thursday next, April 20. Act 1. Overture Don Juan, Mozart. Solo Signor Miarteni, Trio Miss Hughes, Mr Bellamy, and Sig Miarteni. Trio Mr Bellamy, Sig Miarteni and Mr Horn. Duet Miss Hughes and Mr Braham. Song Miss Griglietti. Song Sig Miarteni, Song Mrs Bland. Quartett: Miss Hughes, Miss Griglietti,[19] Mr Bellamy and Mr Braham. Duet Mrs Bland and Mr Bellamy. Song Mrs Billington. Finale, by all the performers. The whole of this Act from Mozart's Grand opera Don Juan. Act 2. New concerto, pianoforte Mr Griffin. Song Mrs Billington (miscellaneous). Duet Mr Bellamy and Sig Miarteni (Don Juan). Song Mr Bellamy (ditto). Duet

Mrs Billington and Mr Braham (miscellaneous). Song Mrs Bland (Don Juan). Song Mr Braham (ditto). Finale, by all the performers (ditto). The orchestra will be on the grandest possible scale... Books... ready for delivery at the music shops, on Tuesday next.

17 April (p. 2):

Signor Spagnoletti's concert. By permission of the Right Hon. the Lord Mayor. Signor Spagnoletti has the honour to announce to the Nobility, Gentry and his Friends in general that his BENEFIT CONCERT will take place this evening, April 17, at the Old London Tavern, Bishopsgate Street; when will be performed the Grand Opera of Don Juan, by Mozart, never performed in public in this Country. The vocal parts by Mrs Dickons, Miss Hughes, Mrs Bland, Mr Horn, Mr Bellamy, Signor Miarteni, and Signor Siboni. [The remainder exactly as on 8 April.]

18 April: Hanover Square Rooms, exact repeat of 17 April.
19 April (p. 2): as 18 April.
20 April: the announcement of the postponement at Hanover Square Rooms ('tickets issued for this evening will then be available'), with another of Siboni's benefit concert at the Opera House that evening.
8 May: Griffin announces the date, 23 May, for his postponed concert.
15 May: Hanover Square Rooms, a partial repeat of Griffin's announcement of 17 April, but with some important differences:

Act 1 Trio. Miss Hughes, Mr Horn and Sig Miarteni. Recit and scene. Madame Dusseck [sic].[20] Duet Mrs Bland and Mr Horn. Quartett. Miss Hughes, Madame Dusseck, Mr Horn and Mr Braham. Act 2. Duet Mr Horn and Mr Bellamy. Song Mr Horn. Sestetto. Miss Hughes, Madame Dusseck, Mrs Bland, Sig Miarteni, Mr Bellamy, Mr Lanza.[21]

Here, too, the interpolated arias are specified: Mrs Billington sang one by Cimarosa, and her duet with Braham was by Nicolini.
19, 20, 22 and 23 May: repeats of the announcement of 15 May, but all without details of the sestetto.

Griffin's announcements are especially important because they name the singers for the quartet in Act 1, 'Non ti fidar',[22] and for the sextet in Act 2, 'Sola, sola in buio loco', so enabling the entire cast to be deduced with fair certainty. It also seems a reasonable assumption that, when any of these names are also found in the list for Spagnoletti's concert, the singers took the same roles there. The triple list, for the London Tavern on 17 April, and for Hanover Square, as intended on 20 April and as ultimately achieved on 23 May, is as follows:

	17 APRIL	20 APRIL	23 MAY
Donna Anna	Hughes	Hughes	Hughes
Donna Elvira	Dickons	Griglietti	Dussek
Zerlina	Bland	Bland	Bland
Il Commendatore	Bellamy	Bellamy	Bellamy
Leporello	Miarteni	Miarteni	Miarteni
Don Ottavio	Siboni	Braham	Braham
Don Giovanni	Horn	Horn	Horn
Masetto	—	Lanza	Lanza

Thus five singers sang both at the London Tavern and at the Hanover Square Rooms. Clearly, it was not easy at the outset to find complete, stable casts. Bland's name does not occur at the Tavern before 17 April, and Elisabeth Sarah Lyon, a lesser artist, appears in only two lists, for Hanover Square Rooms on 8 and 10 April. Perhaps she withdrew because she became too busy with preparations for her marriage to Henry Bishop, which took place on 30 April. Her replacement was presumably Griglietti, who was intended to sing on 20 April but, as Loewenberg noted and as the notice of 15 May confirms, was in turn replaced by Dussek, whose name the owner of the libretto only wrote in on the day of the performance. The reason is unknown, as is also that for the replacement of Siboni by Braham. The lack of a Masetto on 17 April may be due either to economy or to the difficulty of finding the right man. In any case, at this period, even in staged performances, the same bass sometimes sang both Masetto and the Commendatore.[23] It is perhaps worth mentioning that of all the ten singers who sang or were engaged to sing in the two concert performances in 1809, only Hughes went on to appear in the King's Theatre performances of 1817, but in a different part: as Elvira. Lastly, Griffin did not conduct, as Loewenberg said: he was the soloist and beneficiary of that evening, and Spagnoletti, the other soloist and beneficiary, led on both occasions.

Loewenberg observed that only two of the big arias were not given on 23 May – 'Madamina' and 'Finch' han dal vino' – and surmised that no recitatives were sung. This must surely have been the case because, apart from any dramatic considerations, substantial reduction was needed in order to allow, during a long evening with only one interval, enough time for a concerto and, at Griffin's benefit, the interpolated songs. Though no supporting counterpart to Mrs Billington is recorded at Spagnoletti's evening, it is likely that similar cuts were made there also.[24]

★

We can now bring together some remarkable facts about these two concert performances of *Don Giovanni*. Although the first London Tavern announcement appeared four days later than the first for the Hanover Square Rooms, there is nothing to suggest that the two enterprises were in competition. Indeed, the fact that Spagnoletti led for both, and that five noted singers ultimately sang twice, not to mention the wasteful effort of producing two separate sets of parts, point strongly to cooperation and continuity. Even allowing for some hyperbole, the tone of the sequence of announcements in *The Times* suggests that the organizers knew that these performances were historic. The musical attractions were considerable, including two top professionals as the beneficiaries and half a dozen or so of the best-known singers of the day among the ten who ultimately sang on both occasions. We have seen that there were 15 announcements (including repeats) in *The Times* of these two benefit concerts. No others of this period enjoyed such repetition. Spagnoletti and Griffin, or someone working on their behalf, probably planned to derive the greatest benefit possible from their well-publicized double association with Mozart, first in the City, then in the West End.[25]

One wonders whether the libretto was available only for the latter. As the translation and schedule for publication must have been put in hand some time before 4 April, it is possible that another issue, differing only in respect of the cast and venue given on the title-page, was prepared for the London Tavern, but if so, no copy has survived. The relevant announcements all emphasize that permission for the use of this building was given by the Lord Mayor, and it is a thousand pities that the records of licences issued by his office at this period are not extant. Otherwise we would certainly know the name of at least one of the organizers. Because S.D. thrice mentions the Harmonic Society's performance of *Don Giovanni*, and was also passionately devoted to Italian opera, he may well have had something to do with it all. In any event it was, as he emphasized, at the London Tavern and not, as Loewenberg believed, at the Hanover Square Rooms, that the music of this opera was first heard in England, substantially complete and in public.

★

By way of a long, but no means irrelevant, coda, something must be said about the slightly earlier attempt to perform *Don Giovanni* privately, as described in the second[26] of the two articles already mentioned, 'Autobiography of an Amateur Singer'. This article described only one performance of *Don Giovanni*, though Loewenberg wrote 'performances' and said 'they were extended and lost their amateurish character'. He went on to quote the passage from S.D.'s 'Chronicles', quoted above, which ends: 'Spagnoletti led, and Miss Griglietti was the Donna Anna', and took this to refer to the

1809 concert performance. But this cannot be so, because she did not sing, nor was intended to sing, this part then. S.D. was clearly referring to the events recorded by the 'Amateur Singer' who states that Griglietti did sing Donna Anna. This source includes other indications of musical reality which Loewenberg largely disregarded because he considered the two articles 'the despair of historians trying to bring some sequence into the events told in them'. What matters, however, is not so much the sequence as the names and the mention of other Mozart operas besides *Don Giovanni*, as in fact S.D. also emphasized.

The 'Amateur Singer's' style is repetitive, digressive and verbose, tinged with laboured anonymity and mock humility. (One wonders how Ayrton, as a skilled editor, found this contribution acceptable.) Nevertheless, what he wrote is not totally impenetrable, and it is fair to assume that the names recorded are given in good faith and the period of time indicated is reasonably accurate. The *terminus post quem* is set, as Loewenberg realized, by the mention of the first staged performance of *La clemenza di Tito* (27 March 1806) as a past event. A passage at the end of the article reads thus: 'For three years we kept up these friendly meetings and performed, besides our essay piece, the *Clemenza di Tito, Figaro, Don Juan*, and the *Così fan tutte*. At the end of this period the Opera people had begun to honour Mozart by their tardy patronage'. The writer also says that the idea of these 'meetings' was born of a long, late-night talk between Griffin and himself, but nowhere mentions the concert performance given for the former's benefit. This must surely place the events between the late spring or summer of 1806 and the late winter of 1808–9, and the phrase 'the Opera people' must allude to the performances of *Die Zauberflöte* and *Così fan tutte* staged at the King's Theatre in 1811.

Moreover, the 'Amateur Singer' had a vivid recollection of the place where some – perhaps all – of this activity took place:

An amateur, whose name shall be rescued from oblivion if these lines can do it – Mr Hayward – lent us his floor-cloth manufactory to perform in; and, with the exception of the *Clemenza di Tito*, brought out by Mrs Billington for her benefit in 1806, the first opera of Mozart's ever heard in this country was got up by a party of amateurs, and performed, oratorio fashion, without action, amidst the mingled effluvia of canvas, oil and turpentine.

Now the London directories record 'Thomas Hayward & Co. Floor-cloth manufacturer. 195 Whitechapel Road'. So this 'amateur' was a real person, and the place and its atmosphere are wholly genuine. Is it just coincidence that these meetings were held only a few minutes eastwards from the London Tavern?

The writer also names a number of singers and players, and though his style here reaches an apogee of absurdity, they deserve to be considered in rather more detail than Loewenberg thought fit. 'The parts of Donna Anna and Zerlina', the Singer says, 'were supported by Miss Griglietti', and goes on to remark that Elvira 'was enacted by Mr C. E. Horn (let his name be enrolled among the original singers of *Don Juan* in England)'. This is clearly grotesque,[27] unless he meant that Horn mimed the part during the rehearsals. The Amateur Singer further records that he himself sang 'the Commendatore, in Act I only', and took the part of a 'choral demon' in the finale of Act 2. Whatever the writer's own merits as a singer, Griglietti was one of considerable distinction, and made 28 appearances at the King's Theatre from 1806 to 1815.[28] As Loewenberg noted, she sang Servilia in *La clemenza di Tito*, in 1806 and again in 1812, and took the Queen of Night in 1811. Her other roles were in operas by Cimarosa, Mayr, Paisiello, Winter, Fioravanti and similar composers of the day. Griglietti was also heard at a Philharmonic Concert in 1815,[29] when, with Mrs Dickons and other notables, she sang in 'A la bella Despinetta'.

In addition, this article mentions more musicians whom Loewenberg did not discuss. One of them, a young German merchant, remains cloaked in obscurity as 'Mr G.' We learn, however, that he was a native of Hamburg where he had been a pupil of 'Schwenke' – presumably Christian Friedrich Gottlob (1767–1822) – and under his tutelage had arranged the whole of *Don Giovanni* for wind band. Mr G. himself played oboe, piano and clarinet. A later passage in the article reads thus:

> The names of the amateurs who joined us I have no right to communicate, while I conceal, nor should I have a right even if I subscribed, my own. But with those whom public applause have made public property, I may take a greater freedom, and adorn my little narrative by recording that among our vocal assistants we numbered Miss Griglietti, already mentioned; the two Misses Bolton (the elegant and high-mannered Mary, afterwards Lady Thurlow, and now alas! no more; with her livelier, and, though unadorned by a coronet, no less happy sister Eliza), Charles Horn; with the younger Rovedino and his sister. In the orchestral department we had for leader Mr Watts, whom I have always found readiest of the ready to lend his hand and talent to the furthering any scheme which had the advancement of the art for its object. Among our violins the veteran Dance condescended to assist; and Eley to whose admirable school (the band of the East India Company's Volunteers) we owe a Willman, a Harper, and an Ireland, was our original violoncello a cembalo.

The Bolton sisters seem to have been amateurs of nearly professional class. Mary Katherine was born about 1790 and on 13 November 1813 married Edward, second Baron Thurlow. A pupil of Lanza, and a contralto, she made her first appearance on the stage at Covent Garden in 1806 in the role of Polly Peachum and remained 'a popular singer during the seven years of her stage life'.[30] In the Philharmonic's first season, on 15 March 1813, she took part with Maria Hughes and others in the sextet 'Sola, sola' from *Don Giovanni*.[31] She died in 1830, 'aged 40'. 'Eliza' may well be the Frances Elizabeth Bolton who married John Braham, as his second wife, in 1816.[32] Both sisters sang at the Oxford Music Room concerts in 1809 and 1810.[33] Something of their considerable standing in London can perhaps be deduced from an announcement in *The Times* of 1 May 1809 (repeated on 4 May), headed 'Miss Bolton's Concerts, Willis' Rooms'. The singers included Mrs Dickons, Miss Hughes, Miss Lyon, Mary Bolton and Eliza Bolton ('her first and last appearance prior to the opening of the English opera', *ie* at the Lyceum), Bellamy, Miarteni, Gesualdo Lanza and Horn. (It is worth comparing these names with those listed above.)

'The younger Rovedino' is presumably G Rovedino[34] son of Carlo:[35] he appeared in the 1816 King's Theatre performances of *La clemenza di Tito* and *Le nozze di Figaro*, respectively as Publius and Bartolo. His sister is likely to have been Stefania, recorded by Smith[36] as having been heard 45 times at the King's Theatre from 1798 to 1804. Though she sang no Mozart, she took roles in operas by Gluck, and by Sarti, Cimarosa, Salieri and other Italian favourites.

Among the instrumentalists, Spagnoletti is by far the best known, and as mentioned earlier needs no detail. 'Mr Watts' is probably William Watts who played both violin and viola,[37] published a large quantity of arrangements of the music of his times, and was active in the Philharmonic Society, serving as its secretary from 1815 to 1847. The 'veteran Dance' is probably the William of that family (1755–1840), violinist,[38] pianist and composer, and like Watts was associated with the Philharmonic, which Society was formed from a meeting held at his house; later he served it as a director and as treasurer. 'Eley' is less easily identifiable for certain.★

Besides those names in the article, there must have been other musicians to fill all the parts in the performances of the Mozart operas, and they were probably friends (including competent amateurs) or colleagues of those discussed above. The records of the orchestras engaged in London at this time, in concerts and opera houses, suggest that the total of the players did not exceed 200 or so. Similarly, the number of singers was small. Though some of those who came from Italy stayed only for a few seasons, many – like Griglietti – remained longer, while the same English names recur regularly.

★Almost certainly R T Eley, a German bandmaster. (Cf. Scott Sorensen and John Webb. 'The Harpers and the Trumpet', *Galpin Society Journal*, XXXIX, Sept. 1986, p. 35 and p. 52, n. 3.

Many must have known each other socially and professionally, some as close friends. For instance, we learn from Kelly[39] that in 1808 Siboni and Spagnoletti went to Ireland on a concert tour together, with other musicians.

It was, then, from this kind of musical club that there came the musicians who assembled in Mr Hayward's manufactory to perform Mozart's operas, of which *Don Giovanni* seems to have been the first.[40] Since these performers included a good many professionals, with a fair sprinkling of amateurs such as Eliza Bolton, they must have taken the music seriously even though it was all done for their private enjoyment. So it is hard to imagine that there can have been many occasions when they would have tolerated such an absurdity as Horn 'singing' Elvira. Behind all the meiosis, verbosity and facetious banter of the Amateur Singer's writing there seems to lie a significant historical fact, namely that, within the period 1806 to 1809, London musicians of standing explored privately four Mozart operas, including *Don Giovanni*, and so created a climate of enthusiasm in which the two public concert performances of 1809 could be mounted. These in turn formed a stepping-stone towards the staging of *Die Zauberflöte* and *Le nozze di Figaro* in 1811 with the epochal *Don Giovanni* of 1817 as the climax. Throughout these 11 years the regular recurrence of the names of such musicians as Horn, Hughes and Spagnoletti suggests a strong element of cohesiveness and continuity born of the vital, magnetic attraction of Mozart's operas.

★

It remains to consider what possible bearing the operatic events at Mr Hayward's premises and the London Tavern performances of *Don Giovanni* may have on 'the quest for Sterland'. We know that Sterland wrote out the overture to *Così fan tutte* in score: this can hardly have been a purely academic exercise. We know also that Sterland's scores of Beethoven's Third and Fourth symphonies were used in 1807 at the London Tavern by the Harmonic Society. Spagnoletti, who led at Thomas Hayward's premises and again for the two *Don Giovanni* performances of 1809, also led for the Society's concerts. Sterland must have known him, and would, therefore, at the very least, have heard of the meetings housed by Hayward and, as they both worked in the City, perhaps knew him too.

Whether or not Sterland was S.D., it is a remarkable fact that the latter's 'Chronicles' appeared in the same journal, *The Harmonicon*, at almost the same time as the 'Autobiography of an Amateur Singer'. The two authors, each of whose identity was certainly known to Ayrton, must have read each other's work. It is a curious coincidence that both writers – one in great, if perhaps intentionally confusing, detail, the other only incidentally – refer to the same private operatic events, at Hayward's premises, over two decades after they took place. Sterland's partner in his orchestral ventures was a German merchant, Anton Schick. Another, unnamed merchant of the same expatriate business community was involved with the Amateur Singer in the nearly contemporary exploration of Mozart's operas... There are many other obvious common threads in this web, some factual, some shadowy, and the range of permissible speculation is extensive. Nevertheless, until more facts and – dare one hope? – more documents about John Sterland and his circle come to light, the quest for his true musical identity and significance must remain unfulfilled. If such historical sources are discovered, much new light will surely be shed on the cultivation of music in London during the first decade of the nineteenth century.

[1986]

Notes

1 The fine editions issued by Goulding, D'Almaine, Potter & Co., London, to mark this production and other premières of Mozart operas in London, are described above, pp. 80 ff.
2 'Some stray Notes on Mozart, V: Don Giovanni in London', *ML*, XXIV, pp. 164–8; see also Loewenberg's *Annals of Opera* (London, 1978), p. 455.
3 The last sentences form a footnote in the original, (1830), p. 113; Loewenberg brought them into the text. He failed to mention S.D. as the author.
4 Now in the BL, Hirsch IV. 1377.b.(3), and bound with three other London librettos of this period. Hirsch's pencil note of acquisition, 'L. L. A. Dr' (the first 'L' stands for London, followed, as was his practice, by the seller's initials in reverse), shows that he bought the whole volume from Loewenberg. No other copy of this *Don Giovanni* libretto has since come to light. This volume has armorial bookplate of John Waldie (d 1826). Burke's *Landed Gentry* (1868) shows that he was the owner of Heldersyde Park, Kelso, and a connoisseur of the fine arts (catalogues in BL). He and his sister Charlotte Ann Waldie, author of the famous *Waterloo Days* (1817), seem to have been staying in London at the time of the *Don Giovanni* performance (see DNB). The MS correction on the title-page of the libretto is almost certainly his.
5 This libretto, like all the others in this volume, was printed by Paolo da Ponte, the poet's half-brother. He seems to have come to London in about 1800, and worked first in a piano manufactory: see *Memoirs of Lorenzo da Ponte*, trans. Elizabeth Abbott, ed. Arthur Livingston (Philadelphia, 1929), p. 329 n. 1.
6 *The Harmonicon* (1831), pp. 106–8, 135–7. Loewenberg gave the first word of the title, erroneously, as 'Recollections'. The continuation promised at the end of the second article never appeared.
7 *Musical Times*, CXXVII (1986), p. 434.
8 George Eugene Griffin (1781–1863), composer and pianist; perhaps he was the 'Mr Griffin' who subscribed to Haydn's *Creation*: see Landon, op cit, p. 625.

9 Elizabeth Billington (?1765–1818), one of the greatest sopranos of her day, as famous in Italy as in London.
10 Maria Hughes is referred to in *The Times* notice of *Le nozze di Figaro*, quoted by William C Smith: *The Italian Opera and Contemporary Ballet in London, 1789–1820* (London, 1955), p. 164, as 'Madame Gatti (late Miss Hughes)'. Her last recorded appearance at the King's Theatre was in 1820, as Rosina in *Tancredi*. She sang six times for the Philharmonic Society, from 1813 to 1817, always in ensemble numbers from Mozart – 'Andro, ramingo' and 'Placido e il mar'. Clearly she was not an amateur, as Loewenberg believed.
11 Maria Theresa Bland (1769–1838), née Romanzini, was popular until 1824, both as a ballad singer and in opera.
12 Nothing seems to be known about this bass. Smith (op. cit.) records ten operatic performances in London, from 1802 to 1812, the last in *Le nozze di Figaro*.
13 John Braham (1774–1856) was as a child a pupil of Leoni, and sang in London and abroad; returning to London in 1801, he became one of the best-known tenors of his time.
14 Paolo Spagnoletti (1768–1834) spent most of his career in London where he was in continual demand. For details see *The New Grove* and its predecessors.
15 Maria Dickons (c 1770–1833), née Poole, was a pupil of Rauzzini at Bath and well known in London and elsewhere at concerts and in operas; she also sang in Paris and Venice.
16 Charles Edward Horn (1786–1849), a popular singer and composer; full details of his career are given in *The New Grove*.
17 Thomas Ludford Bellamy (1770–1843) was a chorister at Westminster Abbey and a pupil of Tasca; he had been a theatrical proprietor in the provinces and sang at Covent Garden in 1807–9.
18 Giuseppe Siboni (1780–1839) first appeared in London at the King's Theatre in 1806, and later sang in many European houses; Prince Christian of Denmark took him in 1819 to Copenhagen where he founded the Royal Conservatory in 1821.
19 Nothing seems to be known about Griglietti's life.
20 Sophia Dussek (1775–1847), daughter of Domenico Corri and wife of Jan Ladislav Dussek; she was also known as composer, pianist and harpist.
21 Gesualdo Lanza (1779–1859), composer and teacher of singing, left three treatises on the subject.
22 In the Hanover Square Rooms announcement of 17 April the names of those due to sing 'Non ti fidar' suggests that Bellamy was first intended to take Don Giovanni; in the cast given on 15 May Horn is listed for this part, from which it may be inferred that Bellamy was to be the Commendatore.
23 *The Times* (12 April 1817), quoted by Smith, op cit, 144, remarked that Angrisani sang both these roles.
24 Even at the first staged London performance of *Die Zauberflöte* considerable cuts were made and arias from non-Mozart works were included: see William C Smith, *The Italian opera and Contemporary Ballet in London, 1789–1870* (London, 1955), p. 109
25 One wonders if, even in 1809, there was some link between the London Tavern and the Hanover Square Rooms. There certainly was later on: see p. 123.
26 *The Harmonicon* (1831), pp. 135–7; the first of these articles contains little of relevance to *Don Giovanni*.
27 Or did Horn sing falsetto? *The New Grove* says 'his voice was a poor one, its chief merit being a wide compass covering both the tenor and the baritone ranges'. Horn

was among the first Associates of the Philharmonic Society, but never sang for it, nor at the King's Theatre.
28 Smith, op cit, pp. 79, 84, 96, 115, 127, 131 and the references there cited.
29 Myles B Foster: *History of the Philharmonic Society of London, 1813–1912* (London, 1912), pp. 18, 19.
30 G E C[okayne], *The Complete Peerage*, ed. G H White (London, 1953), xii/1, p. 732.
31 Foster, op cit, p. 9; this was just before her marriage.
32 *The New Grove*, s.v. Braham.
33 J H Mee: *The Oldest Music Room in Europe* (London, 1911), pp. 160–61.
34 Smith, op cit, p. 136 refers to G Rovedino's singing twice in 1816.
35 The first of his many London appearances, at the King's Theatre on 13 March 1777, is recorded in *The London Stage 1660–1800*, pt. 5, 1776–1800, ed. Charles Beecher Hogan (Carbondale, 1978), p. 65.
36 op cit, pp. 50, 55, 60, 63, 67, 71 and the references there cited.
37 Foster, op cit, p. 606.
38 J D Brown and S S Stratton: *British Musical Biography* (Birmingham, 1897), record that he led at the King's Theatre, 1775–93.
39 *Reminiscences* (London, 1826), vol. II, p. 242.
40 It is not clear from the Amateur Singer's narrative whether *La clemenza di Tito*, given 'in the ensuing Passion-week', preceded or followed *Don Giovanni* (but it undoubtedly took place after the King's Theatre première). Perhaps it was on this occasion that Watts led, while Spagnoletti, as S.D. recorded, was in charge for *Don Giovanni*.

14

The Library of the Royal Philharmonic Society

During the period from 1790 to the early 1830s, quite a number of organizations came into being in London to provide public musical entertainment of various kinds. The only one of them still active today is the Philharmonic Society, which was established in 1813 and received the title 'Royal' exactly one hundred years later. It owed much of its endurance and success to the fact that its founders were shrewd professional musicians wholly dedicated to giving regular seasons of orchestral concerts of the highest possible standard.

The history of this Society has many aspects. They are variously reflected in the concerts given during the last 172 years and their influence on English musical taste; in the Society's world-wide reputation; and in the names of the composers and executants actively associated with its work. Moreover, from its earliest years, the Society amassed and maintained a continually growing library and an important – indeed, unique – archive, which together can be said to represent another aspect of its history. The present article will be confined to the management and use of the library, based on information found mostly in the archive[1] – the minutes of meetings, a large collection of letters, and a wealth of other documents and papers now deposited on loan in the Department of Manuscripts in the British Library. This article will not deal with the contents of the surviving part of the Society's library, nor with the nature and extent of the archive. Essential details of both these topics are readily available elsewhere.[2]

The numerous discussions of matters relating to the library at the Directors' Meetings and at the General Meetings reveal a fascinating story of much historical interest. The documents show that while each successive generation of management took some pride in an ever-growing collection, the library also proved from time to time to be a cause of anxiety, occasionally indeed of embarrassment. For it was established primarily as a source for the music performed at the Society's concerts by its own orchestra. But as the Society's prestige grew, and as the library increased, it received many requests for loans, right up to the end of the nineteenth century. Like any other expanding collection, it needed storage space, staff, and catalogues. Thus there developed a complex web of demands and services which can perhaps be most conveniently described if it is divided into three main, partly

19 Samuel Chappell, first librarian of the Philharmonic Society, 1813 to 1819. From a miniature by Thomas Overton. 102 × 90 mm.

interwoven, strands: the location, control, and staffing of the library; the catalogues; and the loans.

The Library and its Librarians

After their inaugural meeting, held on 24 January 1813, the directors had much to do to bring the Society into active life, and clearly the library could not be given a high priority. But on 8 December 1813 they decided that 'the office of Librarian be offer'd to Mr Samuel Chappel [sic][3] (Pl. 19) at £50 per annum' (fig. 1), and at the same time they instructed the treasurer to affix his seal to the 'Music Closet', and the secretary to write to Mr Henry Dance, to whom Mr Jenkinson was to deliver the keys. Six days later, Chappell accepted office. In February 1814 a Mr Sterland 'presented a valuable collection of music' – he gave a little more in 1848 – and by November the library had grown sufficiently to warrant the decision that 150 copies of a catalogue should be printed and distributed to Members and Associates. At the same time some binding was undertaken.

In February 1815 the General Meeting modified its earlier intention slightly, and decided that a reduced number of catalogues (100) should be printed, and that the proof be submitted to Griffin,[4] Ayrton,[5] and Horsley.[6] That the Meeting could make this arrangement for the proof-reading suggests that Chappell must at least have made a start on the catalogue. All this, however, was rather premature, because nothing more happened for four years, during which time Chappell seems not to have over-exerted himself on what was, after all, not a very extensive task. When the catalogue was ultimately printed it contained only 189 thematic entries and just over 200 brief verbal, descriptive, or short-title entries. This might explain what happened at the General Meeting of 28 June 1819 when, on a proposal for Chappell's re-election, it was decided that a competition be held for the librarianship. Chappell received thirteen votes, Joseph Calkin fourteen, and the latter was elected on 2 August.

Calkin[7] was a member of the Society's orchestra: he played, according to various sources, either the violin or the cello,[8] and was undoubtedly a man of purpose and dedication. In 1826 he was a trustee and auditor. In October 1820 the directors ordered that a stamp be made for the library and that 'the catalogue be completed in the form in which it has been begun'. It seems likely that this was done and the volume issued to members in 1823, or at the very latest in 1824. For on 24 October 1825 the directors resolved that 'the members' catalogues be sent to Mr Calkin for the insertion of the new music'. This would hardly have happened unless enough time had elapsed for there to be a substantial quantity of accessions. A year after taking office, he made a report to the directors on the state of the library: unfortunately, this document has not survived. In November 1820 new bookcases were ordered, additional to the early 'closet', and were housed in the Argyll Rooms, the seat of the directors' meetings and the concerts for the next ten years. Calkin's duties presumably also included the supervision of the copyist whom the Society seems to have hired as early as 1814. That Calkin also had to act as an intermediary between the directors and a soloist is shown by a letter (Add. MS. 17838, fol. 23) written to the secretary, William Watts, on 24 January 1824, in which he explained that Dragonetti,[9] when contracted to play a familiar work, wished to be excused playing at a rehearsal. In September 1831 Calkin was asked to make a charge for his services as auditor and librarian, but it seems doubtful if he did so, because in June 1840 it was reported to a General Meeting that he worked gratuitously.

20 The Argyll Rooms, Regent Street (facing north). The rooms occupied the entire upper floor of the buildings, including the domed bay. Water-colour by William Westall, 1825. 125 × 190 mm.

His time of greatest responsibility came in the early morning of 6 February 1830, when a fire destroyed the Argyll Rooms (Pl. 20) and nearly consumed the library. The episode is graphically – though somewhat breathlessly – summarized in the directors' minutes: 'Sherrington[10] reported that he met D'Almaine, Beale and Ford who were contending with the police about the right of forcing the locks of the Philharmonic Library. That Mr Sherrington having satisfied them as to his being a proprietor, it was resolved to break open the doors, and that Mr Cocks[11] should be requested to take charge of the music, who most readily consented and who with the assistance of four of his men, and the above gentlemen, succeeded in saving the whole of the music.' Where Calkin was at this time is not stated, but on 15 February the books were removed from Cocks's care in Prince's Street to Calkin's house in Pall Mall where they stayed for nearly three years. In January 1833 the library was moved to the Hanover Square Rooms, which the Society had just leased for its concerts, after three unhappy seasons at the King's Theatre. The treasurer was 'instructed to have new closets made', and the old ones (presumably having survived the fire) were offered to Calkin. In November 1831 Calkin asked the directors for free admission tickets for the concerts, in recompense for his care of the library, the insurance on which had, he pointed out, cost them nearly 1 per cent less than when it was in the Argyll Rooms. But the directors refused. About the same time they paid £29 15s 9d to repair some minor damage which the library had suffered at the time of the fire, apparently because of its hasty removal to safety.

Calkin produced two more catalogues, the first, of vocal music, begun in 1833, and the second, of instrumental music, begun in 1835. His work must have increased in 1844 when the directors decided that all past and future letters should be deposited in Japan boxes in the library.[12] On 10 March 1844 it was 'resolved that Mr Calkin be written to calling his attention to a request made to him last season to fill up the catalogue placed in the library, and that the secretary send him his for the same purpose'. Calkin's twenty-seven years' term of office came to an end when he died on 30 December 1846. On 12 July 1847 his business partner Budd[13] was offered 'the joint situation of Secretary and Librarian', and was elected at the General Meeting of 10 July 1848. He held office until his death in August 1850 and thereafter the librarian, so designated, disappears from those elected to office at the General Meetings. Later references suggest that the secretary or a director exercised supervision.

Even before Budd's appointment there began the trouble in the library which was to last for some eight years. On 19 December 1847 the directors decided 'that the Secretary write to Mr Goodwin informing him that it was the intention of the Directors to meet at Hanover Square Rooms on Sunday January 16 for the purpose of inspecting the library, when, if the same was not found in order and the new catalogue completed, the Directors would be under the unpleasant necessity of dispensing with his services'. Their next minute, of 16 January 1848, reads: 'Mr Goodwin's letter applying for a fortnight more to complete the Library Catalogue was read. The Secretary was desired to say his request would be granted, but another failure in his engagement would forfeit his situation.'

Unfortunately, we do not know exactly what Goodwin's 'situation' then was. But from other documents we can deduce something of the events which led the directors to make these threats, and to continue to do so until 1854. At some time in Calkin's last years of office, they realized that the existing catalogues could not meet the needs of their ever-expanding library, and decided that something much more comprehensive was required. The earliest watermark in the paper of the new catalogue – now Loan 48.11/3, to be discussed later – is 1845. This suggests at least a *terminus ante quem* for their unminuted decision. But while we know who 'Mr Goodwin' was, we do not know when he entered the regular service of the Society. He was William Goodwin, who founded the firm of Goodwin & Tabb about 1826–7,[14] and worked also as a music seller and copyist to the Society of British Musicians. Later he was librarian at the Royal Academy of Music, and a billhead describes him as 'Music Copyist. Music Seller and Publisher. 4 Upper Wellington Street, Covent Garden'. He died in 1876.

A minute of 2 November 1829 records payment to Goodwin 'for laying out the books &c', and there exists his bill[15] for copying paid by Calkin on 12 June 1837. But when he was appointed 'assistant librarian' – his later designation – is not known. It is also unclear whether he was engaged primarily to work on the new catalogue; for his normal duties were to ensure that all the parts were correctly made and laid out at each concert and then returned to the library. On 24 November 1850 he was reminded that he should submit his account punctually to the treasurer, and on 15 December he was warned that he should not make copies of parts (perhaps intended for hire) without the secretary's written authority. But the main object of the directors' concern was the completion of the catalogue, which is mentioned thirteen times in their minutes from December 1847 to February 1854. The Society's letter books (Loan 48.6/1) contain numerous letters – threatening, cajoling, pleading – written by Budd to Goodwin from 1847 to 1850. If Goodwin was dilatory, the directors were vacillating to an extraordinary degree. He continually asked for more time, and produced his work unfinished. In the early autumn of 1850 the directors dismissed Goodwin, only to reinstate him in November. In the winter of 1853/4, they lost patience and ceased to trust his promises. They recorded their 'high displeasure' on 5 February and dismissed him again a fortnight later, this time for good.

Fortunately, however – at least for the story of the Society's library – that was not the end of the matter. Throughout the winter of 1854 and the spring of 1855, Goodwin submitted accounts for work done but not paid for. By 1 July the various sums were agreed, including £52 10s for services in connection with the catalogue. He was determined to have the last word, and on 7 July he sent to all members a printed circular letter[16] which stated his side of the case. There is no reason to doubt the veracity of this fascinating though rather rambling document. It suggests, incidentally, that Budd himself was not very competent, for he took home 'Spohr's Historical Symphony, with a variety of other music, to have it bound'. One would have expected him to take it to the binders, and not surprisingly at his death it was all lost. On 16 August 1853, however, Mrs Budd told Goodwin that 'the long missing Philharmonic Society's music was found'. At her request, he went to Puttick & Simpson's and retrieved the missing items, including the Historical Symphony.

Regarding the catalogue, Goodwin wrote thus: 'This new catalogue was planned by the late Mr Joseph Calkin, who had the paper ruled and headings printed, which I received from him a short time before his last illness [presumably in the autumn of 1846]. I commenced it in accordance with his written instructions, but I soon found it unnecessarily complicated... I also collected a variety of matter to be inserted under the head of Observations... Both vocal catalogues were planned and written by me.' Goodwin went on to remark that he had been connected with the Society for twenty-five years, which squares with the minute of 1829 mentioned above. Goodwin referred to 'the relabelling and numbering of the whole library, of which upwards of 15,000 copies were done when I left'. This gives some indication of the size of the collection. Procrastinator though he was, he deserved better of the directors, at least in respect of the library's maintenance: his judgement of the unnecessary complexity of the catalogue can be tested against its layout as described below (pp. 167–9). In defence of the directors, it may be said that they were all exceedingly busy professional men, who gave much time and energy to their primary task – the planning and management of eight concerts a year. But as will be seen, the directors of Goodwin's time were not the only ones to have difficult relations with their librarian. As a final point from this troubled period, it may be noted that the second Joseph Calkin[17] produced in 1854 (when he was a director) a manuscript classified list of all the vocal music given in the Society's first forty-one seasons.

Concerning J Horton, appointed to succeed Goodwin on 19 February 1854, the day the latter was dismissed, nothing seems to be known. The minutes record Horton's terms of employment – £10 p.a. as deputy librarian for having the music ready and laid out at the concerts; £5 gratuity at the end of the season, and further payment for all the necessary copying of the music; extra remuneration for putting the library in order, according to the catalogue. Horton reported as missing various items which were apparently in Goodwin's possession, though the latter maintained there were 'many things in the hands of the binder'. They seem to have been recovered in due course. Horton's term of office was uneventful. On 31 March 1860 he received an unusual instruction – 'to put the names of the violoncellos on their desks'. He must have had a good deal of extra work in October 1861, when, under the supervision of Stanley Lucas, the then secretary, the entire library was temporarily removed to the premises of Addison & Co while the Hanover Square Rooms were being redecorated. In 1863 the directors expressed their dissatisfaction at the loss of the score of a Beethoven symphony, and in May 1867 deemed him careless when he put out the wrong parts for a concert.

The minutes do not state when or why Horton ceased to be deputy librarian, but some inference is possible. On 8 November 1870: 'attention having been called to the state of the library, it was proposed that Mr

A Mapleson be asked if he would undertake the duties of deputy librarian and copyist.' Mapleson's appointment was confirmed on 7 January 1871. Horton's name is last found on 17 June 1871 when 'the Secretary reported that he had made an application to Mr J Horton for some wind parts of the overture Tannhauser [sic] which were missing from the library and threatening legal proceedings unless they were returned'. With this, another uneasy chapter in the library's history came to an end. Less turbulent though it had been than Goodwin's tenure, it clearly left much to be desired. Perhaps the office of librarian as it had been up to 1850 was allowed to lapse.

What is certain is that as early as 2 November 1868 the Society was unhappy with the space it had in the Hanover Square Rooms. For at their meeting held on this day the directors discussed the possibility of moving the library to St James's Hall, having agreed a week before that the concerts should be given there. On 12 December the availability of a room was confirmed, and on 6 February 1869 a letter from Robert Cocks (the manager of the old Rooms) was read, consenting to the removal of the library. The exact date of the move is not recorded, but presumably it took place without much delay; one wonders if the strain and consequent disorder had anything to do with Horton's departure.

Mapleson enjoyed a more varied career than any of his predecessors. He was a viola player and a member of the Queen's private band from 1883 onwards,[18] and in 1885 he is also listed as librarian to the band. In 1895 he was still playing the viola, and is described as 'Secretary to the Band and Librarian to H.M. the Queen'. On a billhead of 1905 in the Philharmonic Society's papers,[19] Mapleson printed the royal warrant which he held as 'Music Librarian & Copyist to H.M. the King'. The same billhead gives the name of his firm: 'Alfred Mapleson's Music Library (established 1790) Albion Chambers 60 Haymarket W.' He was presumably a relation of 'Colonel' J H Mapleson, the operatic impresario, but this, and the history of his old-established firm, has yet to be investigated. As the Philharmonic Society's deputy librarian, Mapleson was a fortunate appointment. For he was always diligent, and never was this quality needed more than during his term of office which lasted for thirty-nine years, a period of prolonged difficulty in the library's affairs, when the directors were often faced with conflicting needs and awkward decisions.

The relevant minutes of their meetings are sometimes all too brief, and unclear in detail. Plans were apparently made but not put into effect; proposals were met by counter-proposals. One of the fundamental problems was that a good deal of the performing material was becoming obsolete, and its bulk took up a lot of valuable space. Difficulties arose after barely two years in St James's Hall. A minute of 4 March 1871 reads: 'The question of demanding from the Government a room for keeping the Society's records, the [Beethoven] bust &c. &c. at Burlington House considered.' On 18 November: 'With regard to the old parts and useless music in the library, the Secretary was instructed to keep them in some place of security.' Burlington House came up again on 15 February 1873: 'Mr Cusins having mentioned the disgraceful state of the room in which the Library was at St James's Hall, the Secretary was instructed to consult Sir Thomas Gladstone[20] as to the best means of obtaining rooms in Burlington House from the Government.' Another attempt is recorded on 17 May 1884, but on 4 October it was minuted that the Board of Works had refused the request. The difficulties in St James's Hall continued. On 13 September 1885 Mapleson wrote to the secretary, Francesco Berger,[21] and complained that, because of ill-controlled workmen, the library was (literally) cut off: 'the staircase has been taken away entirely'.

In January 1886 it was reported that a lot of old parts which were 'knocking about in St James's Hall' were to be examined 'prior to disposal as waste paper' and in May it was ordered that a parcel of old music should be given away to the Hall keeper. In the next few years, there were several discussions about bringing together in the Hall various groups of the Society's property, which had apparently become scattered. Two directors, Stephens[22] and Gardner,[23] were responsible for making alterations to the library in February 1890, and it appears from a minute of a General Meeting of 12 July 1890 that Stephens, with Goldschmidt[24] and Cummings,[25] already constituted a library sub-committee. At the same time Henry Richard Tedder, the secretary and librarian of the Athenaeum, was asked to make a report about its condition. Tedder sent his report to Goldschmidt, on 24 May 1890, in the form of a long letter from which only excerpts need be quoted: 'No provisions for heating ... roof shows evident signs of dampness ... exposed to dust and dirt ... spots of mould ... librarian deeply distressed ... dirty attic ... should be properly arranged in glazed bookcases ... no accommodation for consulting a score ... proper catalogue should be drawn up ... autographs and rareties placed under lock and key.' Consequently, by the summer of 1891, the library seems to have been moved to a different room, hired from the Society of Architects; and the programme for the concert given on 10 March 1892 included a six-page report on the library.[26] All this, however, produced no lasting benefit, for by the end of 1894 the library was removed to a room in Queen's Hall.

Over the next few years, Alfred Gilbert,[27] the Society's orchestral manager, was very active in improving the accommodation and security of the books. But towards the end of 1900 things began to go wrong again. In mid-October Robert Newman, the manager of Queen's Hall, requested that two of the music cases be moved from the library into the conservatory, due to some unexplained difficulty. On 2 November the crisis suddenly worsened. Gilbert reported that one case had already been displaced, and that the whole library would have to leave Queen's Hall. This threw the directors into a panic, though in the event the removal was delayed for a year. The minutes do not reveal whether Newman granted them more time. Various directors examined rooms in St Martin's Lane, at the London Academy of Music, at Chappell's in New Bond Street, at Boosey's in Regent Street, and at the Polytechnic Institute in Regent Street. None proved suitable. A letter received from Newman on 6 July 1901 prompted more searching, but without result until 21 November, when Gilbert reported success at the premises of Rudall & Carte, 23 Berners Street, for a yearly rental of £25. By 24 March 1902 the library was in its new home.

It seems, however, that security there was poor, for the directors decided to deposit all the valuable manuscripts in the London & County Bank, Hanover Square. Two years later, the early minute books, the Beethoven relics, and other valuables were added to the deposit. But the Society's other property was still scattered: in 1906, for instance, there were four tin boxes of letters in Berger's house and another box, with contents unspecified, in that of Charles Gardner. Long before this time, such material had already assumed an archival quality, for there was no other active musical society in London of comparable longevity and repute. Moreover, with the growth of orchestral hire libraries, it seems pretty certain that the Society now seldom used its own parts at the concerts. The dust of the present began to settle quickly over the historic past. On 16 October 1908 Stanley Hawley, a director and later secretary, 'called attention to the condition of the library'. A week later, Hawley and Myles Birket Foster,[28] another director (and the Society's second remembrancer), put in a graphic report which has fortunately been preserved.[29] Parts deserve quotation, if only to show how little things had changed in eighteen years: 'The Library of the Philharmonic Society is housed at 23 Berners Street, in a small back room, used by a lady secretary of Messrs Rudall, Carte & Co. The lady's hat and cloak hang from nails driven into our cupboard. We would suggest that there is, in view of the Society's fame and its Library's history and contents, a lack of dignity about the present habitat.' Then follows an account of unsuccessful attempts to find a new home in the Queen's Hall, at Messrs Boosey's, and at Trinity College of Music. The reporting officers therefore urged better housing in the existing room, and went on, referring to the old parts: 'the dust is about half an inch thick. The books are out of order, and in some cases missing, and the brown-paper covers not sufficiently protective. In dust that would grow mustard and cress, are letters of much historic value from the Royal Family

& all the great artists, in similar soil rest the receipts (with 1840 and other postage stamps) for engagements...'. After noting some missing items, and pointing out that some bound parts of Franck's Variations for Piano and Orchestra belonged in fact to Pugno and should be returned to him, Hawley and Foster recommended that the obsolete material be disposed of.

At about the same time Frederick Corder[30] made a similar report,[31] which is not mentioned in the minutes. Corder emphasized the quantity of obsolete material, including over 500 vocal pieces by old Italian composers, never likely to be used again. He made the same judgement about the symphonies of Spohr, Cherubini, Potter, Gounod, Pleyel, and Romberg, but remarked that the Pleyel works were autographs. Corder suggested that they be hired out or sold to the Royal Academy or Royal College. Apart from the autographs whose value he described as 'unassessable' (including, one imagines, those in the bank), Corder thought that 'the intrinsic value of the library is quite fully represented by the £800 for which it is insured'. This was presumably the purpose of his report.

Some positive actions followed the report by Hawley and Foster. On 8 March 1909 the directors decided to move the library to a room at 19 Berners Street, where the Incorporated Society of Musicians had its office, and where the annual rent would be £15, a saving of £10. They also appointed a new librarian, one S O Goldsmith (recommended by Hawley), to take office at the end of the season. It seems rather sad that Mapleson, dilatory as he may have been in his last years – Hawley and Foster had suggested this – should have received no word of thanks for his long service. The following autumn, it was decided to get rid of a mass of old band parts, excepting what had been scored for the Society, or was unpublished and rare. Sundry old parts were offered to the Royal Academy, in the hope that they might be 'of a certain educational value' to students, and were accepted. Berger still had the Beethoven relics and a lot of letters.

In November the directors ordered that the relics should go to the bank, but in May 1910 Berger reported that the relics, and his twenty-six years' accumulation of letters had been added to the library in Berners Street. Foster undertook to index all the letters. At the end of May 1910 W P Rivers (who held an appointment in the library at the Royal Academy of Music) replaced Goldsmith as librarian. The latter was duly thanked for his services which had lasted barely a year. Rivers set about the parcelling and labelling of the parts in the library. Early in 1912 he asked for an advance of his salary, 'owing to domestic affairs'; in October he retired, and he too was thanked for his services. John Pointer was appointed honorary librarian and orchestral manager. Berger, then seventy-nine, announced that he was not coming to any more meetings. He died in 1934, only two months before his hundredth birthday. The directors continued to be exercised by the safety of the letters, which were stored in packets in pigeon holes, and, perhaps concerned at the way Berger had accumulated them for so long, sought legal advice about their custody.

The year 1913 marked the Society's centenary, in recognition of which, as already mentioned, it had been permitted to add the word 'Royal' to its name. The following year saw the beginning of a new approach to the conservation of its library. For on 16 April 1914 the directors 'resolved that the Honorary Secretary be authorised to communicate with the authorities of the British & South Kensington Museums respectively with a view to depositing therein on loan the Beethoven and other manuscripts and the Beethoven bust'. On 21 July the secretary reported that the autograph scores had been deposited with the authorities of the British Museum on permanent loan, and 'the MSS letters had been valued by Messrs Quaritch with a view to their sale on condition that they be presented to the nation & deposited in the British Museum'. In the event only one of these desiderata was put into effect, the deposit of the autographs, as Loan 4, in the Department of Manuscripts at the British Museum. Some binding and repairs, after deposit, cost £13 2s 0d, and the Society duly reimbursed the Trustees for this expense within a year. The letters joined the Beethoven relics at 19 Berners Street, and the Beethoven bust was deposited at the Royal Society of Musicians.[32]

What induced the directors to take these steps is not recorded. Pointer ceased to be librarian in May 1914[33] and Goodwin & Tabb, doubtless unaware of their founder's relations with the Society, then became librarians and orchestral managers. Eight years elapsed before the library is heard of again. In April 1923 the directors decided to ask 'Mr Goodwin' (presumably Felix Goodwin) to be librarian, 'his firm continuing its offices as before'. But he declined, and the minutes for 23 August record that Frederick Laurence became librarian, while Goodwin & Tabb continued as librarians for the concerts. In November it was reported that there were ninety sets of bandparts at the Royal Academy, placed there about 1910, and in due course the scores were joined to them. By April 1924 Goodwin & Tabb had given up the orchestral management of the concerts, and Laurence had become both librarian and orchestral manager. It is not recorded how long he exercised this dual function. Another mysterious minute, of 25 September 1924, says that 'due to changes in the building during the war period' Laurence and William Wallace,[34] a director, were to prepare a new list of the Society's property, but it seems doubtful if this was ever carried out. There is, however, mention of an inspection of the property at the bank, including the Wagner letters.

The year 1925 saw the penultimate phase of the whole affair, which began in February with yet another proposal about the library. The secretary, J Mewburn Levien,[35] reported that he had spoken to Felix Goodwin, who had suggested that Mr Tabb might revise and complete the catalogue of the Society's library. Nothing more was heard of this. But in March and April there were active discussions about removing most of the library to the Royal Academy, 'due to changes at 19 Berners Street', and by 3 July this was done. Some more books were added to those in the bank. In February 1926 Wallace wrote a letter, which cannot now be traced, about the disposition of the library. Next July Wallace was allowed to withdraw the Wagner letters to inspect them for possible binding. Thereafter, no more is heard of the library for some thirteen years.

In the programme of the concert of 23 November 1939 the name of D Ritson Smith (an Associate since 1925, and then honorary secretary of the Philharmonic Choir) appears among the officers as honorary librarian. The minutes do not record the date of his appointment as librarian, but at a General Meeting of 12 April 1940, it was reported that Ritson Smith 'undertook to catalogue, and to investigate the catalogues already made, of the possessions in the Society's library, as soon as the war was over'. During the war the Society's records had been sent away by Keith Douglas, the then honorary secretary, to Yorskhire, whence their safe return was reported in 1947. Ritson Smith's intention went unfulfilled, and at his resignation in the summer of 1948 he was succeeded by C B Oldman, Principal Keeper of Printed Books in the British Museum, who had been a Fellow of the Society since 1927.

During Oldman's tenure of office the first significant event was an exhibition of the most important autograph scores from the library, held at the Royal College of Music in September 1951. The second event marked the final stage of the safe keeping of the Society's archives. In the summer of 1960 the committee of management proposed, on Oldman's recommendation, to deposit in the Department of Manuscripts at the British Museum most of the minute books, all the old catalogues and early papers, the Beethoven relics, and the large collection of letters, over 6,000 in all, the preservation of which had been begun in principle by the decision taken by the directors in 1844. The proposal was accepted by the Museum Trustees at their meeting of 14 October 1960. It was not the least of Oldman's many services to the Society that in 1964 he was largely instrumental in securing from the Pilgrim Trust a grant of £1,000 to meet the cost of repairing and binding these letters. The negotiation of this deposit, which constitutes Loan 48, meant that the complete archive of the Society was available for scholarly study. After Oldman died, on 7 October 1969, it was only fitting that the programme of the concert given a week later should have contained a brief tribute to him.

The present writer was elected honorary librarian in December 1969, and he in turn was succeeded in September 1982 by Arthur Searle, Assistant Keeper in the Department of Manuscripts in the British Library. Early in 1983 the residue of the Society's music stored in the Royal Academy was deposited on loan in the British Library: it comprised some 400 volumes in manuscript, and a similar quantity of printed scores.

It is amply clear from the foregoing that the successive directors of the Society became more conscious of the historical importance of their heritage, which expanded whenever new works were performed. Such continual growth posed great problems of storage and management. Whatever the premises occupied, they were never adequate and they had also to be used for meetings. The Society never had enough money to acquire a permanent home. In terms of security, the directors did the best they could, and nothing of significance seems to have been lost. Their unending difficulty lay in finding the staff who could combine the duty of conserving and cataloguing the music with that of providing from it the performing material needed for the concerts. Here they faced an almost insoluble paradox. Use entailed deterioration, and much expense. Moreover, professional standards in this specialized field hardly existed in the nineteenth century outside such institutions as the British Museum; it is curious that when advice was sought in 1890 the directors applied to the Athenaeum rather than to the Museum. Consequently, the skill of the Society's staff was limited in each generation to what the work itself could teach them, or what, in Mapleson's case, the librarian could bring to it from the practice of hire libraries.

The Catalogues

The various systems of cataloguing and shelving developed slowly and became very cumbersome. But the catalogues and other types of list were the basis of much of the Society's work, and remained essential to its continuity for the best part of a century. Ten volumes have been preserved, and now form part of Loan 48 in the Department of Manuscripts in the British Library. All are of historical or documentary significance, and all save the first two are in manuscript. The list, in order of compilation, as far as this can be ascertained, is as follows:

No. 1. Loan 48.11/1. *A Catalogue of the Library belonging to the Philharmonic Society, London. Instituted 1813. Joseph Calkin, Librarian.* Undated. Watermark date 1817. Published in the early 1820s (see p. 0 above). Pp. 92, ff. 49 (Pl. 21). At the foot of the engraved title-page is a manuscript note: 'To 1828. Afterwards W Goodwin.' (Presumably given by Calkin, for Goodwin's use

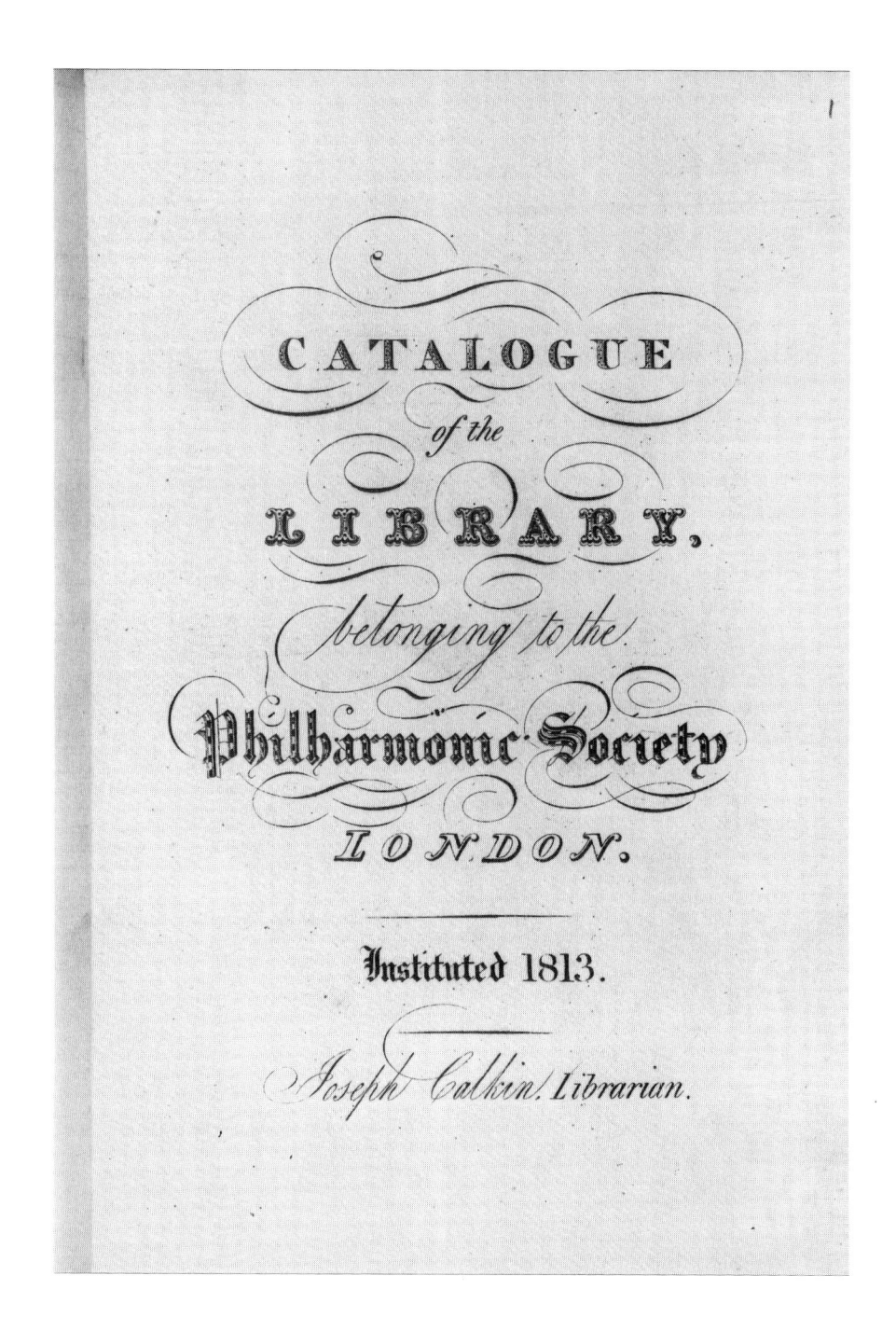

21 The first catalogue of the Philharmonic Society's library, printed c 1823. Title page. 255 × 165 mm.

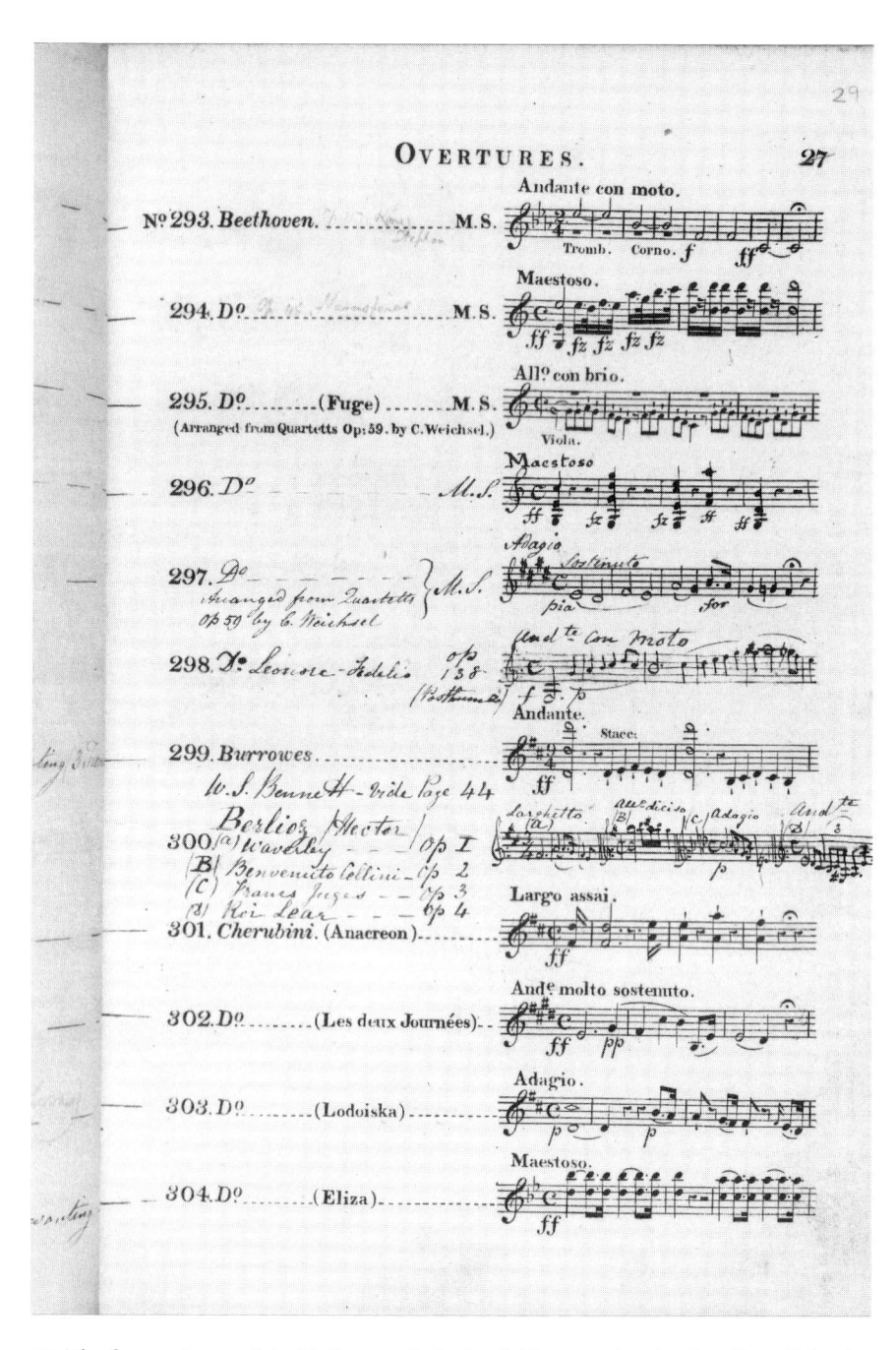

166 The Library of the Royal Philharmonic Society

22 The first catalogue of the Philharmonic Society's library, printed c 1823. P. 27 (fol. 29) showing some manuscript additions including the score of Berlioz's overture *Le roi Léar* published in 1843 (see p. 167). 265 × 165 mm.

when employed as a copyist.) Opposite, pasted on a sheet of later paper, is an engraved label: 'With Messrs Goodwin and Tabb's compliments' and a manuscript note 'Recd. 9.v.13 [i.e. 1913]'. Engraved throughout, with engraved thematic incipits for symphonies and overtures and some incipits added on staves left blank. These works occupy nos. 1–508. No. 509 onwards, vocal works, have no incipits.

No. 2. Loan 48.11/2. A duplicate of the preceding, with a manuscript label on the front cover reading: 'Director's Catalogue. Corrected to 1831.' In fact, at least to 1843, the publication date of Berlioz's *Le roi Léar* overture (Pl. 22), entered in manuscript. Interleaved with sheets watermarked 1822 and headed 'observations'. Pp. 49, ff. i + 92. With five additional leaves at the end, paginated 94–100, bearing additional titles (non-thematic) in manuscript.

No. 3. Loan 48.11/6. *Theme Catalogue of the Vocal Music belonging to the Philharmonic Society London. Instituted 1813. Joseph Calkin Librarian.* 1833. Watermark date 1831. Ff. i + 186. This title-page is apparently printed with a stamp. The verso of the title-page has a note signed 'Alfred Mapleson 1899', recording the removal of 'obsolete music' to 'another cupboard'. Another note states that in 1891 the Society allowed Mapleson to purchase three items: 2138 Mendelssohn, *Athalie*, including seventy-eight chorus parts; 2149 Weber, *Preciosa*, vocal score and 177 chorus parts; 2161 Liszt, *Christus*, full score, vocal score, and chorus parts. Many of the 2163 numbers are blank. There are two sections in the catalogue – Italian, and English, respectively subdivided 'Arie', 'Duetti', etc., and 'Airs', 'Duetts', etc., and ending with ensemble numbers from operas, oratorios, etc.

No. 4. Loan 48.11/3. Without title. Watermark dates, 1845 in the early folios, 1851 and 1852 in the later ones. The second flyleaf has the watermark date 1861, which perhaps indicates a date of rebinding. Ff. 167. The front cover has a label reading: 'Philharmonic Society. Symphonies, Overtures etc.' The catalogue numbers run from 1 to 1997, and within this sequence blocks are allocated to different categories of music: 1 to 500, symphonies; 501 to 1004, overtures, and so on. There is a second sequence, 1 to 684, for operas and other vocal works with orchestra. Most of the catalogue is planned on an open-page layout, with five columns on the left-hand page (Pl. 23). On this page there is one column for the numbers, a second for the composers' names, a third for the works with thematic incipits, a fourth, 'Remarks', denoting, with the fifth column, the number of parts and scores. The right-hand page is headed 'Memorandums' [*sic*]. The thematic incipits, some in a fine script, are written on staves stamped on the sheet. The space

23 The principal later catalogue of the Philharmonic Society's library, in manuscript, begun *c* 1846. Fol. 15ᵛ includes the entries, nos. 137 and 138, for the autograph scores of Haydn's symphonies no. 95 in C minor and no. 96 in D major, respectively. 255 × 315 mm.

headed 'Remarks' is mostly used for a series of single numbers which record the completeness, or otherwise, of sets of parts, and their issue and return. 'Memorandums' are most informative. They include notes of dates of purchase or presentation, of performance, and sometimes of issue on loan. In concept, this catalogue is an extension of the first, engraved, catalogue of *c* 1823 (Loan 48.11/1, no. 1 above), but greatly enlarged as a general catalogue, and excluding only the vocal works found in No. 3 (Loan 48.11/6). Despite its inflexible nature and some overcrowded, rather confused portions, this was the most important of all the Society's catalogues; it is a unique document spanning at least sixty years. It was in constant use certainly until the early 1900s, and probably up to the time of the First World War. Two notes by Mapleson, about temporarily displaced music, are dated 1900 and 1902. Mapleson also noted music missing in 1895, when the library moved to Queen's Hall, and again in 1902, on its removal to Berners Street. There are notes of verification of certain manuscripts by 'A.G.' (Alfred Gilbert), dated

1899, 1900, and 1901, and of most of the autographs by Goldschmidt and Cummings, dated July 1891.

No. 5. Loan 48.11/10. Manuscript title: 'A classification of all the Vocal Music that has been performed at the first forty-one Seasons of the Philharmonic Society. Showing the number of the Concerts of the Season, and the Year, with the number of times each piece has been performed. With the names of the performers. Arranged and dedicated to the present and future directors by Joseph Calkin (Director for 1854).' Watermark date 1853. Ff. 33. Classified by types of music, with a scheme similar to that in No. 3 above.

No. 6. Loan 48.11/4. No title. Label on front cover reads: 'Symphonies & overtures.' Watermark date 1865. Ff. 108. Unnumbered. A fair copy of part of No. 4 above (Loan 48.11/3). It is in four columns, of which the last, headed 'When performed', is unused throughout. At the end of the volume, folded on guards, are two upright bifolia, each with watermark date 1827. The first leaf is headed: 'Sinfonia's & overtures. Philharmonic. 5 years. 1826–30.' Ruled in columns for each year, and marked 'x' for performance. The third leaf is headed: '1831–1834', and is similarly ruled, but is unused. The fourth leaf is headed: 'List of leaders and conductors. 1826–1829.'

No. 7. Loan 48.11/5. No title. Watermark date 1865. Ff. 93. A partly thematic catalogue of operatic arias, concertos, and miscellanea.

No. 8. Loan 48.11/7. Without title or watermark date. The front cover bears a label lettered: 'Philharmonic Society. Instrumental works performed from 1813 to   ' Ff. 77. The flyleaf bears a note (? in the hand of W H Cummings): 'Anyone finding this book is requested to send it to F Berger at 6 York Street, Portman Square who will reward Messenger suitably.' This catalogue was apparently in use up to the early 1900s. The last date is 1915 on fol. 50^v.

No. 9. Loan 48.11/8. Without title or watermark date. Of late nineteenth-century appearance. The front cover bears a label lettered: 'Philharmonic Society. Vocal works performed from 1813 to (apparently 1873). Parts in the library.' Ff. 114. The numbers run from 1 to 2200, with many blank pages. Apparently a fair copy made from an earlier volume by an uninstructed copyist (cf. no. 1467: 'Miseri Cordias Domini'), perhaps in the 1870s.

No. 10. Loan 48.11/9. Without title or watermark date. Of late nineteenth-century appearance. The front cover bears a label: 'Philharmonic Society. Vocal works performed from 1813 to (apparently 1873). Parts not in the Library.' Ff. 51.

Loans

Such were the catalogues maintained primarily to control the Society's stock of music and record its use. It should perhaps be pointed out that their above designation 'Loan 48.11/1', etc., refers to the numerical sequence of collections 'placed on long-term loan' in the Department of Manuscripts. This designation should not be confused with the term 'loans' in the sense of music borrowed from the Society's library, which is the subject of the remainder of this article.

While a number of entries in the main catalogue record loans (generally under the heading 'Observations'), by far the most copious record of them is in the minutes of the Directors' Meetings, supplemented by those of the General Meetings. Together, they show that the requests began in the Society's first decade and continued until the early years of the twentieth century. The earliest discussion of loans was at a General Meeting on 28 December 1814, when it was agreed that 'in future the Librarian do not lend any music', which suggests that there had already been difficulties. Later meetings, on 5 November 1827 and 29 June 1831, decided that loans should be restricted to members, for such private use as their benefit concerts. But meanwhile, on 16 June 1817, some unspecified loans had been sanctioned, and the first detailed loan in September 1819 caused trouble. John Braham[36] borrowed Méhul's opera *Le jeune Henri*, but despite several applications over the next three years he failed to return it. The year 1820 saw the first loan to an institution: the Amateur Concerts borrowed unspecified music 'for the season'. On 21 May 1826 a Mr Heath was allowed 'to have the use of Beethoven's Pastoral Symphony', and Weber 'to have the use of such music as may be required for his concert'. In 1830 Charles Neate[37] and Sir George Smart,[38] both borrowed Beethoven's Ninth Symphony (presumably the dedication copy) for concert use, and in 1831 Bishop[39] had the scores of Spohr's *Berggeist* and *Jessonda*. But loans had already caused concern, for on 1 April 1827 it was 'resolved that it be recommended to the next General Meeting that the Directors shall not have the power to lend the music, except to a member of the Society, without the sanction of the said General Meeting'.

Beethoven's Ninth Symphony was lent yet again, in 1841, to Moscheles, but after this no loans are recorded until the 1860s. This may have been due to the prolonged trouble with Goodwin and the catalogue. In 1863 the directors refused to lend the autograph score of the Cherubini symphony to the Frankfurt Museum Concerts, but sent a copy of the parts, and dealt with the identical request from Leipzig in the same way. In the same year, a Mr Hecht of Manchester was allowed to borrow the score of Schumann's ever popular *Das Paradies und die Peri*. In 1869 the directors changed their policy and lent the autograph of the Cherubini symphony to the Musical Society at Bonn. Such foreign loans were unusual but show how well known the Society was. No other is recorded until 1906, when Breitkopf & Härtel requested that the autograph scores of Haydn's symphonies Nos. 95 and 96 should be lent to Weingartner for editorial purposes. This was agreed to, subject to the manuscripts being insured for £100.

At home, Grove[40] was by far the most frequent borrower. The first of his many requests came in 1864, when he was allowed to borrow the score and parts of Berlioz's *Romeo and Juliet*, which, the Society was told, the composer himself could not lend. The last item lent to Grove was Chaikovsky's Sixth Symphony, in 1894. At one time, there seems to have been a temporary awkwardness, for when, in 1867, Grove asked for Schumann's *Das Paradies und die Peri* overture, the directors noted that it was 'contrary to the rules', but in the end they gave way.

Among many other borrowers were W T Best[41] (1872 – printed scores of Haydn's symphonies); the Bach Choir (1880 – parts of the Brahms *Requiem*); Manns[42] (1894 – Dvořák's 'American' Symphony); Sullivan (1883 – the parts of *Marmion* overture), and Carl Rosa[43] (1885 – Goetz's overture, *The Taming of the Shrew*). On occasion some directors took advantage of their personal position. Walter Macfarren[44] had the overture to *Tannhäuser* in the 1880s,[45] in 1899 Mackenzie[46] borrowed an unspecified work by Bruch, and some time earlier Gilbert borrowed an overture by Ludwig Schloesser.[47] None of these was returned. As a body, the directors found this constant use of their library tiresome and sometimes an embarrassment. In January 1870, when Hallé[48] asked for Schumann's *Das paradies und die Peri* overture, they had to tell him it could not then be traced. Later in that year, the Revd H Cooper-Key of Hereford made the same request. Perhaps Grove had failed to return the score. Loans were undoubtedly a time-consuming and unremunerative business. In 1893 the directors agreed to Mapleson's suggestion that he be paid a fee of 10s 6d per loan. In 1896 they decided that 'permission to borrow music from the Society's library be but very rarely accorded and only by consent of the Board'. In 1900 they raised the borrowing fee to one guinea. Sometimes they enforced their rules strictly. In 1876 they refused to lend the parts of the Brahms *Requiem* to the Amateur Musical Society of Cambridge, and in 1878 the minutes briefly state 'loan of parts of Symph. Beethoven &c to Mr Campbell of the Normal College declined'. In 1896 they also declined to lend unspecified music to Sir Henry Irving, and in 1900 a minute records 'Liverpool Philharmonic Society refused hire of scores and parts from Philharmonic Society's library – no discourtesy to Cowen intended'. On the other hand, in 1910 they approved a loan of some

Beethoven relics and documents, including the Ninth Symphony, to Sir Beerbohm Tree for René Fauchois's play *Beethoven*, in which Tree played the title-role. The loan was displayed in the foyer of Her Majesty's Theatre. In return for this loan the then chairman and directors were given a box and fourteen stalls at the first night.

From all this it appears that the directors never had a clear policy on loans. But they must have known they were acting inconsistently, which caused them worry. To judge by Mapleson's complaints,[49] there may well have been more loans than are recorded in the minutes and the catalogue. By the end of the century, the growth of orchestral hire libraries (including Mapleson's own) meant that this part of the Society's work, sporadic and irregular as it was, had really become superfluous. Indeed, it was probably only the historical importance of the collection which caused the borrowing to go on as long as it did.

Generally speaking, this borrowing was time-consuming and often involved tiresome or arbitrary decisions. But such matters can now be seen as marginal to the principal purpose of maintaining the library. As circumstances changed in the course of the nineteenth century, the directors gradually developed a pragmatic approach to the burden of its maintenance. Clearly the quality of the library contributed to the Society's repute and sometimes enabled it to be of service to music far beyond its headquarters in London. It is no exaggeration to say that this collection of music, and the voluminous archive from which its history can be reconstructed, played a long and important role in the Society's activity.

A Note on the Calkins

The Calkin family was active in music throughout the nineteenth century, and is of interest here because at least eight of them were connected with the Philharmonic Society. Several bore the same Christian name, or very similar ones, sometimes obscured in the archives by their restriction to initials. Consequently they present a rather confusing picture which can be clarified to some extent by the following genealogical tables. (These, and the details which follow, are based on information in G Hogarth, *The Philharmonic Society of London* (London, 1862); J D Brown and S S Stratton, *British Musical Biography* (Birmingham, 1897); M B Foster, *The History of the Philharmonic Society of London* (London, 1912); P A Scholes, *Concise Oxford Dictionary of Music* (London, 1964); *Catalogue of Printed Music in the British Library to 1980* (CPM) (London, 1981–1987); and on the Society's archive.)

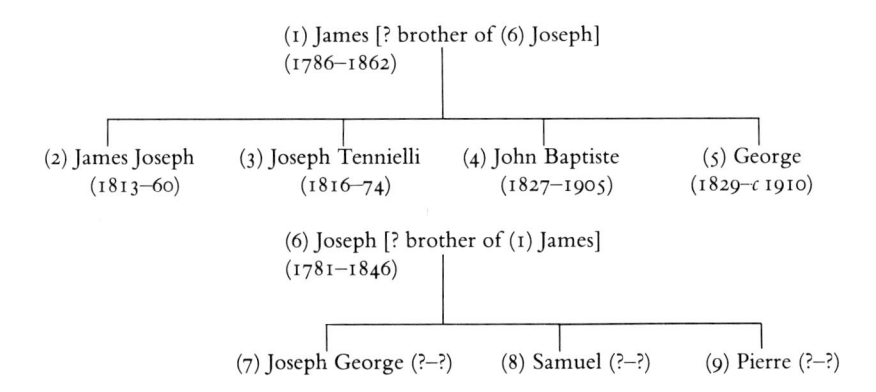

```
                    (1) James [? brother of (6) Joseph]
                        (1786–1862)
    ┌───────────────────┬───────────────────┬───────────────────┐
(2) James Joseph   (3) Joseph Tennielli  (4) John Baptiste   (5) George
   (1813–60)          (1816–74)            (1827–1905)        (1829–c 1910)

                    (6) Joseph [? brother of (1) James]
                        (1781–1846)
              ┌───────────────────┬───────────────────┐
       (7) Joseph George (?–?)  (8) Samuel (?–?)   (9) Pierre (?–?)
```

Those connected with the Philharmonic Society were:

(1) James – Associate, 1823, proposed by Joseph Calkin and Charles Neate. On 3 January 1819 the directors ordered a symphony by James Calkin 'to be listed for rehearsal'; nothing more was heard of it.

(2) James Joseph – violinist (Foster, p. 26, says 'violist'), from 1839 in the Society's orchestra. He had previously played at Drury Lane.

(3) Joseph Tennielli (Scholes says his mother was a Tenniel; a sister of Sir John?) – a tenor who sang at a concert in 1846; a director from 1854 to 1868 (see the catalogue No. 5, p. 17 above, and Loan 48.15/4). Co-treasurer in 1872 and a minor composer, works published between 1860 and 1871. Generally referred to as 'Joseph', but his notepaper bears his monogram 'JTC'. A circular ivory ticket of admission now in the collection of such tickets comprising Loan 48.15/6) bears the legend 'Mr Jos^{ph} Calkin'. This was almost certainly his, and did not belong to Joseph (6): see pp. 3–5 above.

(4) John Baptiste – Member: a minor, prolific composer, works published between 1855 and 1895, one reprinted 1963. He served as a director in 1867 and 1868 but on 22 July 1872 failed to be re-elected.

(5) George – cellist in the Society's orchestra: composer and arranger, active from 1866 to 1895.

(6) Joseph – violinist in the Society's orchestra; the first librarian; later a partner in the firm of Calkin & Budd, 'Booksellers to Her Majesty' which dealt in old music, and issued an important catalogue, in 1840 and 1844, with a supplement in 1849. The firm's collection was sold in three parts, in 1852 (copies of the catalogues in the Drexel collection NYPL).

(8) Samuel – recommended by Joseph, in a letter of 1819 for a vacancy as viola player in the Society's orchestra.

(9) Pierre – recommended by Samuel in a letter of 1854 to deputize for him. He published a few pieces in London between 1858 and 1873.

Besides those in the above table, there were three other Calkins active during the same period in London, in New York, and beyond. Since Calkin is a relatively uncommon name, it seems possible that they were all related. CPM records two Calkins: William, who published two songs c 1830 and C Calkin, one song by whom appeared in New York c 1840. *The National Union Catalog of America* records Milo Calkin (1810–72), as a joint-editor of *Hawaian Collection of Church Music* (Honolulu, 1840).

Hogarth (1862) records a Miss Calkin as a 'Female Associate'. The list of 'Elections' (Loan 48/7) names Miss Annie Calkin as an Associate in 1895.

Librarians

1814–19	Samuel Chappell
1819–46	Joseph Calkin
1847–50	George William Budd
18?–54	William Goodwin
1854–70	J Horton
1871–1909	Alfred Mapleson
1909–10	S O Goldsmith
1910–12	W P Rivers
1912–15	John Pointer
1915–23	Goodwin & Tabb (orchestral librarians)
1923–?	Frederick Laurence (orchestral manager and librarian)
1939–48	D Ritson Smith
1948–69	Cecil Bernard Oldman
1969–82	Alec Hyatt King
1983–	Arthur Searle

Location of the Library

1813–20: Old Argyll Rooms, corner of the present Oxford Circus and Argyll Street.
1820–5 February 1830: New Argyll Rooms, Regent Street.
5–15 February 1830: Robert Cocks's house, Prince's Street, Hanover Square.
15 February 1830–33: Joseph Calkin's house, 118 Pall Mall.
1833–69: Hanover Square Rooms (temporarily to Addison & Co.'s premises, 210 Regent Street, in 1861).
1869–94: St James's Hall, Piccadilly.
1894–1902: Queen's Hall, Langham Place.
1902–9: 23 Berners Street.

1909–25: 19 Berners Street (selected manuscripts to the British Museum in 1914).
1925–39: Royal Academy of Music, Marylebone Road.
1939–47: Wartime removal to Yorkshire home of Keith Douglas, secretary of the Society.
1947–82: Royal Academy of Music (Letters, minute-books, catalogues, and all other early papers to the British Museum, 1962).
1983: All remaining manuscripts and printed music from the Royal Academy of Music to the British Library.

[1985]

Notes

1 For the first few decades of the Society's work, the minutes of the Directors' Meetings (Loan 48.2/1–14) and of the General Meetings (Loan 48.3/1–4) are complementary, although the former give rather more information about the library than do the latter. After about 1840, the information from the Directors' Meetings preponderates, but even in the 1890s and later the General Meetings discussed some library matters not touched on at all by the directors. It would have been impracticable and cumbrous to give, for every event mentioned, a reference to either, or sometimes to both, of these long series of minutes. But I have usually given the date, from which any reference can easily be made to the originals. For important information from other papers in the archive and from British Library manuscripts, I have given the full reference. I must thank the Honorary Committee of Management of the Royal Philharmonic Society for permission to quote from its archive.

2 In the article 'music libraries' in all editions of Grove; in the *Catalogue of the Musical Manuscripts Deposited on Loan in the British Museum by the Royal Philharmonic Society* (London, 1914); and in Pamela Willetts, *Handlist of Music Manuscripts acquired 1908–67* (London, 1970), pp. 76–9 (Loan 4) and pp. 81–2 (Loan 48). Subsequent additions to both loans have been recorded in the register of manuscripts on loan maintained in the Students' Room of the Department of Manuscripts in the British Library. The Society's Beethoven manuscripts and other papers and relics are fully described by Pamela Willetts in her book *Beethoven and England* (London, 1970), pp. 43–50, 67–8. The autograph scores of two of Haydn's London symphonies (nos. 95 and 96), and the important contemporary manuscripts of the other ten, are mentioned in two articles by Arthur Searle, 'Haydn Autographs and "Authentic" Manuscript Copies in the British Library', *Early Music*, x, no. 4 (1982), pp. 495–504, and 'The Royal Philharmonic Society Scores of Haydn's "London" Symphonies', *The Haydn Year Book*, xiv (1983), pp. 173–86.

3 Samuel Chappell (1776–1834) went into partnership with J B Cramer and F T Latour to found the firm of Chappell & Co in 1811.

4 George Eugene Griffin (1781–1863), a founder member of the Society, music teacher, and a prolific composer.

5 William Ayrton (1777–1858), a founder member of the Society, and noted music critic, editor, and musical director of the King's Theatre.

6 William Horsley (1774–1858), a founder member of the Society, composer of popular glees and a friend of Mendelssohn.
7 Joseph Calkin (1781–1846), a member of a large family of musicians, a number of whom were associated with the Society throughout the nineteenth century. Details are given on pp. 173.
8 The latter seems more likely, for in 1825 the directors remunerated him 'for repairs to his violoncello'.
9 Domenico Dragonetti (1763–1846), a famous double-bass virtuoso.
10 William Sherrington was a founder member of the Society and a violist in the orchestra. D'Almaine and Beale were music publishers. But for his part in this episode, Sherrington would have had as little claim to mention as many other musicians associated in various ways with the Society, many of whom were otherwise quite unknown. In the subsequent footnotes, only those who were of some repute in a wider musical context are briefly described.
11 Robert Cocks founded a highly successful music publishing firm which lasted from 1823 to 1858.
12 This decision must be due to an episode mentioned in a letter written by Calkin on 13 January 1844, in which he stated that lot 108 of an unnamed auction comprised '71 letters of musicians of note relating to the Philharmonic Society, and addressed to Watts'. These seem to have included some Clementi letters. There had apparently been a similar sale a little earlier. Calkin wrote: 'our Secretary [Watts] is in the habit of making a profit of his official correspondence.'
13 George William Budd (1806–50), also the founder of the Western Madrigal Society, and an editor for the Musical Antiquarian Society.
14 Sotheby's Sale Catalogue, 21 November 1878, lot 320.
15 Loan 48.5/1, fol. 22.
16 Copy in Loan 48.13/13, with many letters in Goodwin's hand.
17 i.e. Joseph Tennielli Calkin, probably a nephew of the earlier librarian, see p. 173.
18 In *Reeves' Musical Directory* his name is found up to 1894.
19 Loan 48.13/22.
20 The elder brother of the Prime Minister.
21 Francesco Berger (1834–1933), the Society's secretary from 1884 to 1911, was also a popular pianist.
22 Charles Edward Stephens (1821–92), treasurer of the Society from 1881 to 1892, composer, pianist, and examiner. He was a founding member of the (Royal) Musical Association in 1874. Nephew of the soprano Kitty Stephens, afterwards Countess of Essex.
23 Charles Gardner (1836–19?), pianist and composer, and author of educational works.
24 Otto Goldschmidt (1829–1907), pupil of Mendelssohn and husband of Jenny Lind, founded the Bach Choir.
25 William Hayman Cummings (1831–1915), the Society's treasurer from 1892 to 1915, and a noted tenor and musical antiquary, who served as Principal of the Guildhall School of Music from 1896 to 1910.
26 This included the incipits of the most important manuscripts in it, and was almost certainly the result of the verification undertaken by W H Cummings and Otto Goldschmidt in July 1891. It was probably about this time that the idea arose of preserving these manuscripts separately from the rest of the library.
27 Alfred Gilbert (1828–1902), pianist, composer, and a notable manager of other concerts in London. He was the father of the sculptor Sir Alfred Gilbert.
28 Myles Birket Foster (1851–1922), son of the water-colourist, and a pupil of Sullivan. Foster's card index of the Society's papers forms Loan 48/16.

29 Loan 48.5/1, fols. 54, 55.
30 Frederick Corder (1852–1932) was a prolific composer and curator of the Royal Academy of Music from 1909 to 1923. With his wife, Henrietta, Corder made the first English translation, published in 1887, of Wagner's *Ring*.
31 Loan 48.5/1, fol. 53. Undated, but before 1910, being written on paper headed 'Royal Academy of Music, Tenterden Street, Hanover Square W. London, 190 '.
32 After many vicissitudes the bust was ultimately accepted on deposit by the Royal Festival Hall in London, on 23 March 1977, and is displayed there on Level 5.
33 Pointer later served the Society as a director on its Committee of Management from 1922 to 1925.
34 William Wallace (1860–1940), the Society's secretary from 1911 to 1913, was also noted as a composer and author.
35 John Mewburn Levien (1863–1953), the Society's secretary from 1918 to 1928 and its treasurer from 1915 to 1918, was a noted singing teacher, trained by Manuel Garcia (1805–1906).
36 John Braham (1774–1856), a famous tenor, composer of popular songs, and a theatre manager.
37 Charles Neate (1784–1877), a founder member of the Society, pianist and friend of Beethoven.
38 Sir George Thomas Smart (1776–1867), a founder member of the Society and a distinguished conductor.
39 Sir Henry Rowley Bishop (1786–1855), a founder member of the Society and a prolific composer, who became musical director at Covent Garden and held the chair of music successively at Edinburgh and Oxford.
40 Sir George Grove (1820–1900), builder of lighthouses, editor of the famous *Dictionary of Music*, author, and director of the Royal College of Music. He founded the Palestine Exploration Fund, and was secretary to the Crystal Palace Concerts from 1854 to 1873.
41 William Thomas Best (1826–97), an organist of wide reputation, and an occasional conductor.
42 Sir August Manns (1825–1907), conductor of the Crystal Palace Concerts from 1855 to 1901.
43 Carl Rosa (1842–89) founded in 1874 the Carl Rosa Opera company which toured British provincial centres until 1958.
44 Walter Cecil Macfarren (1826–1905), treasurer of the Society from 1877 to 1880, and active as conductor, pianist, composer, and editor.
45 Noted in Loan 48.11/3, against no. 999.
46 Sir Alexander Campbell Mackenzie (1847–1935), composer, conductor, and Principal of the Royal Academy of Music.
47 The borrowings of Mackenzie and Gilbert are mentioned in the Hawley–Foster memorandum, Loan 48.5/1, fols. 54, 55.
48 Sir Charles Hallé (1819–95), founder and conductor of the Hallé concerts in Manchester.
49 Voiced in his letters written from 1871 to 1910, and now preserved in Loan 48.13/22.

15

The Wandering Minstrels and their archive

At the Castle Hotel, Windsor, in the county of Berkshire, there took place on 14 November 1860 a very unusual gathering of musicians, who had just finished a short, informal concert including the overtures to *Zampa* and *Oberon*. In the chair was Captain the Hon Seymour John Grey Egerton of the First Life Guards, the son of the Earl of Wilton, and a well known amateur. Under his guidance those present passed a resolution: 'to meet on the first Thursday in each month throughout the year.' Egerton was elected president and conductor. The treasurer and librarian was the Hon the Lord Gerald Fitzgerald (who also played the cello), second son of the 3rd Duke of Leinster, and the secretary was Algernon Bertram Mitford (afterwards Freeman-Mitford), later the first Baron Redesdale (who played the cornet). He was succeeded by Val Morris in May 1861. The honorary members included Sir Frederick Gore Ouseley, the Duke of Leinster, Lady Katherine Coke, and the Earl of Wilton. Among the ordinary members were Lord Grey de Wilton (timpani), Colonel P L C Paget (cello), and other holders of very distinguished names. The society which they formed adopted the title 'The Wandering Minstrels'. Besides the aristocracy, it took into its ranks skilled players of a lower social rank (such as the famous lithographers Michael and Nicholas Hanhart who played horn and violoncello respectively) but never employed professionals. For the next thirty-eight years, all these performers played an active and useful part in English musical life, and became widely known. Yet though the name of the 'Wandering Minstrels' is found in the first and second editions of Grove's *Dictionary of Music and Musicians* the short, and rather inaccurate article was omitted from the third and subsequent editions. After its activity ceased in 1898, this remarkable body seems to have been almost entirely forgotten. The following account of it is based upon documents in its archive[1], which was presented entire to the British Museum in the mid-1920s.

The earliest concert took the form of interludes in a programme of theatricals given at the Theatre Royal, Windsor, in November 1860. It was followed on 31 January 1861 by a concert at the Corn Exchange in Melton Mowbray, one of the great centres of the aristocratic hunt, in Leicestershire. The Wandering Minstrels met for the thousandth time on 14 December 1893 at Grosvenor Hall, in Buckingham Palace Road, London, and their final concert took place in the same hall on 24 March 1898. In the intervening years, they had given 138 concerts for charity, and raised what was then the huge sum of £16,657, worth over 400 times as much in modern money values. These concerts were given mostly all over the southern part of England, particularly in London and its surrounding counties. The money was raised for hospitals, schools and church repairs, and to relieve distress of all kinds. The Minstrels regularly adorned such famous social occasions as the Canterbury Cricket Week, and their wide social connections ensured everywhere the unfailing support of wealthy patrons. Indeed, the printed lists of those who gave their patronage read like a roll-call from the pages of Debrett.

Apart from their charity concerts, the Wandering Minstrels made music mostly to entertain themselves and their friends. Many of their gatherings were held at the London home of Lord Gerald Fitzgerald who built a hall at the back of his house at 47 Sloane Street specially for the purpose. These social gatherings became famous as 'smoking concerts', and at them the collection of musical prints and other curiosities seems to have been regularly on display. Such activities as these soon helped to define the body's character and establish its traditions. Having their roots in the upper classes, the Minstrels were clearly in the line of the Noblemen and Gentlemen's Catch Club, founded in 1761, and the Concerts of Ancient Music, which lasted from 1776 to 1848. In their own time, the Minstrels' music-making ran roughly parallel to the Magpie Minstrels, which was founded in 1885, and gave concerts generally for charitable purposes. (These concerts specialised in Italian madrigals and other music of the sixteenth and seventeenth centuries.) The Wandering Minstrels claimed to be 'the only complete orchestra formed exclusively of amateurs in Europe' (*Morning Post* 10 July 1873). How far this was true in such wide terms is difficult now to establish, but it was certainly correct for the United Kingdom.

Their repertoire was largely of music composed in the first half of the nineteenth century, with an occasional nod towards an established classic such as *Messiah*. (The Minstrels had no difficulty in finding vocal forces as required by music beyond their normal orchestral range.) They once (20 June 1861) gave a performance of Mendelssohn's *Elijah*. It is difficult now to ascertain what standard of musicianship the Minstrels attained. Their archive contains many press-cuttings of their concerts, usually unsigned and generally enthusiastic rather than critical. Much of the space is often devoted to the notabilities in the audience. Egerton was, like his father, the second Earl of Wilton, a composer – the archives included the full score of an overture in his hand – and as he was also a violinist, one imagines he had at least a competent command of his forces. A work such as *Elijah* in public performance would offer too many hazards to be undertaken by the totally inept. On one occasion the Minstrels made musical history in London, when on the afternoon of 25 February 1871 they gave the first concert ever heard in the Albert Hall. According to the programme, the audience comprised only 'Messrs Lucas Brothers' workmen', but it was nevertheless a historical affair. For the result was to prove for the first time how bad was the echo in the Hall: the archives of the Minstrels contain a note that 'in consequence of this, the acoustics were modified by a velarium under the roof'.

One interesting feature of the Wandering Minstrels is that quite early in their existence they seem to have developed an historical, corporate sense. They preserved their programmes, press-cuttings and other records of performance. They collected photographs of themselves, singly and in groups, and of the places where they performed. (Many of these are fine examples of Victorian art.) They collected also rare prints and other records of musical interest, and preserved the menus of their own supper parties. They also developed an engaging habit of laughing at themselves by cultivating what Robert Louis Stevenson called 'a little judicious levity'. This took the form of humorous drawings of members made by other members. It is perhaps surprising to find, in a musical fraternity, artists gifted also with pen and pencil. One such was Lord Gerald Fitzgerald, revealed as a very talented draughtsman, by his beautiful pencil designs for the Wandering Minstrels' badge, which appears, framed within their motto 'fidibus et flatu' on all their programmes.

It seems a reasonable conjecture that the original moving spirit behind all this was Lord Gerald, for as already mentioned, it was he who displayed these treasures to members at the smoking concerts. The result of this continued assiduity is now to be found in the three huge guard-books, bound in full morocco and preserved in leather carrying cases. The first of them is particularly fine, being covered in brown morocco with the Minstrels' device inlaid in various colours at the corners. Throughout these books, hand-drawn decorations and coloured borders are of a quality that matches the fine printing of the programmes. Lord Gerald's continued interest in linking the visual and fine arts with the Minstrels' musical activity was mentioned in a concert notice that appeared in the *Whitehall Review* on 29 April 1880: 'Lord Gerald showed his splendid collections of old prints and engravings to the guests.' If it was he who urged his fellow Minstrels to look out for musical rarities while travelling abroad, some of them, notably perhaps A B Mitford, certainly followed his advice. It is hard otherwise to explain how the collection was enriched by such treasures as autograph leaves in the hand of Mozart and of Auber, and the very rare Russian programme of 1864.

In the Wandering Minstrels' second decade changes began to take place in the management of the Society. The Hon Seymour Egerton retired as president and conductor in 1873, for reasons that are not quite clear. (He did not succeed his father as third Earl until 1882.) HIs successor was Lord Gerald Fitzgerald who served, it seems, as president, conductor and librarian until 1881. In that year his Lordship was replaced as conductor by Lionel Benson, a captain in the third battalion of the Gloucestershire Regiment, and Colonel H P de Bathe, who played the drums in the orchestra, became president. It is worth mentioning that a press-cutting of 1881[2] records that Benson married Miss Marion Fotheringham of Forfar in Perthshire, an event of some significance for the destiny of the Minstrels' archive. (Benson, a close friend of J A Fuller Maitland, later music critic of *The Times*, was also active as conductor of the Magpie Minstrels, mentioned above.) Another change occurred in 1881 when H D Curtis assumed the duties of honorary secretary and librarian, but between this time and 1898, when the Minstrels disbanded, there were no notable alterations in their management.

It is curious that throughout their existence the Wandering Minstrels had a connection, however tenuous, with the British Museum. For the first bassoon, recruited in 1861, was Charles John Evans, who was a member of the staff of the Music Room, and was in charge of its collections from 1870 until his premature death in 1884. He was thus a 'Minstrel' for twenty-three years. In 1887 his successor in office, William Barclay Squire, made his first appearance among the Wandering Minstrels, as a tenor. Unlike Evans, who was his social inferior, Squire, the son of a well-to-do business man who lived at Feltham Hill in Middlesex, was never elected a member of the society. The programmes show that Squire sang at their concerts fairly regularly up till 1897.

One of the most revealing occasions was on 15 May 1890, when Squire's name appears among the tenors at a concert given jointly by the Wandering Minstrels and the Magpie Madrigal Society (as those Minstrels later called themselves) with Lionel Benson as conductor. (Squire had most probably been introduced to this circle by Benson's close friend J A Fuller Maitland[3], who was Squire's brother-in-law.) The choir included many ladies and gentlemen from the aristocracy, and with two of the ladies Squire was to have some connection in the future. One was Viscountess Folkestone, who later became Helena Countess of Radnor. Squire collaborated with her, in 1909, in a *Catalogue of the Pictures in the Earl of Radnor's Collection*. The other was Countess Valda Gleichen, well known in society as a singer, and at the Court. It is recorded[4] that it was she who smoothed Squire's path in his efforts to have the Royal Music Library deposited on loan in the British Museum.

Moreover, it seems almost certain that it was through Squire's association with the Wandering Minstrels that its archive was ultimately given to the Museum. For the evidence, though only circumstantial, points to him. The first link in the chain is the way in which the three large volumes were stamped when they came into the collection. Nearly every leaf bears the yellow stamp then used for gifts, but the impressions are – in technical language – 'blind', *ie* without a date. At this period, stamps without a date were only used if the gift had not been reported to the Trustees. It is incredible that such an important gift was received without any such report, but there is none, either in the minutes of Trustees' meetings in the 1920s, or in the records of the Department of Printed Books.

The gift must therefore have been made privately, and the clue is provided by the manuscript catalogue of the Wandering Minstrels' library, which came to the Museum later than the main collection. From its date stamp, 12 July 1930, reference is easily made to records of donations kept in the Department of Printed Books. The acknowledgement for this catalogue was sent to 'Miss Fotheringham Fotheringham, Forfar, Scotland'. If we recall that in 1881 Lionel Benson, who later became a friend of Squire's, married Miss Marion Fotheringham, the link becomes clear. For the donor was undoubtedly a descendant of Benson's wife, and the original gift must have been offered to Squire personally and accepted for the Museum by him. This explains the lack of a date stamp, and why the collection, though containing very little music, was placed in a case in the Music Room, and not in the General Library, where, strictly speaking, it belonged. The most probable date is 1925 or 1926, for during this time Squire, who had retired in 1920, was still working in the King's Music Library. He was then in uncertain health, and is reputed to have become rather arbitrary in his last years. He died in January 1927, which is therefore the *terminus ante quem* of the gift, and the circumstances explain the irregular way in which it was added to the collection. But it was the last service of this kind which he rendered to the institution that he had served so well for over forty years.

In the 1870s and 1880s, the Wandering Minstrels must have been one of the best known groups of performers in the southern part of England. Their work for charity took them among a wide audience, at many levels of society. In fact, despite their aristocratic connections, the name of the Wandering Minstrels surely became a part of the general musical consciousness of their time. At the opening of the first Act of *The Mikado*, the tenor Nanki-Poo ('disguised as a wandering minstrel') sings one of the most famous songs in all the Gilbert and Sullivan operas –

A wandering minstrel I,
A thing of shreds and patches.

The phrase must have struck a chord in the minds of many both in the fashionable first night audience on 14 March 1885 and among the many thousands who heard the work in the next ten years or so. Was Gilbert's use of the phrase deliberate, or was it just a co-incidence?

[1984]

Since this was written, a fourth folio volume, complementary to those above, has come to light. Smaller in bulk and bound in a more modest style, it contains some identical prints and musical drawings by some of the same artists, and other related matter. It must have been owned either by a member of the Wandering Minstrels or by someone connected with them, and is now in the possession of Mr Christopher Fifield who found it in a junk-shop in Cape Town.

Notes

1 Pressmark K. 6. e. 1–7: now in the Music Library of the British Library.
2 K. 6. e. 3, f. 11r.
3 Together, Benson and Fuller Maitland wrote and published a witty parody of the typical concert programme of their own day, written for St James's Hall, Piccadilly. Headed 'Salle de St. Jacques, 43 Hyde Park Gate' (the home of the composer Jacob Blumenthal and his wife), 27 April 1894, it contains every cliché used by programme-note writers, then and later. Copy in Music Library, pressmark: d. 480. a. See Fuller Maitland, *A Door-Keeper of Music* (London, 1929), pp. 240–4.
4 See below, p. 191.

Select Inventory of the Wandering Minstrels' Archive

(Names marked with an asterisk are those of members and associates who will be found in Ulrich Thieme and Felix Becker, *Allgemeines Lexikon der Bildenden Künstler* Leipzig, 1907–50.)

Volume 1 (K. 6. e. 1)

f. 16r.	programme of concert given at the Corn Exchange, Melton Mowbray, 31 January 1861, including the finale from Rossini's *Barber of Seville*.
f. 18s.	programme of concert given at the Corn Exchange, Melton Mowbray, 4 February, 1861, consisting of Handel's *Messiah*.
f. 24r.	sheet of pencil sketches for the Wandering Minstrels' badge and monogram by Lord Gerald Fitzgerald.*
f. 33r.	programme of a concert given at the Freemasons' Hall, London, 20 June 1861, consisting of Mendelssohn's *Elijah*.

f. 39,40.   programmes of concerts given during the Canterbury Cricket Week, beginning 15 August 1861.
f. 46r.   programme of concert at Heaton House, Manchester, in aid of the Windsor Dispensary and Infirmary. The Minstrels' first charitable concert.
f. 48r.   photograph of Nicolas Hanhart, cellist.
f. 55   humorous pen and ink drawing of instruments by Lord Gerald Fitzgerald.★
f. 84v.   lithograph of Domenico Dragonetti, by F Salabert. 1845.
f. 85v.   lithograph of Charles de Beriot, by M Gauci after G Krusemann.
f. 90v.   satirical etching by J Geyn [= probably Jacques II de Gheyn], showing players of bellows and grid-iron.
f. 90v.   'The Laughing Audience'. A ticket engraved by Hogarth in 1733, for subscription to his *Rake's Progress*.
f. 92r.   unsigned photographs of Rossini, Meyerbeer, Auber, Verdi and Gounod.
f. 98r.   unsigned lithograph of Michael Hanhart (horn).
f. 100r.   pen and ink drawing, signed 'ADC' [*ie* Alexander Davis Cooper★], 1862 of A B Mitford (cornet) and Edward A Breedon (cornet).
f. 102r.   pen and ink drawing by Alexander Davis Cooper★, 1862, of A D Cooper and W L Turner (violas). (Partly a self-portrait).
f. 119r.   programme in Russian, with English translation added in MS, of a concert given at 13 February (old style) 1864, 'before their Majesties the Emperor and Empress of all the Russias'. 'Brought from S. Petersburgh by A. B. Mitford W.M.'
f. 120v.   unsigned lithograph of Dover Harbour and Castle, *c* 1860.
f. 123r.   'Trahit sua quemque voluptas', etching of fiddler with peasants by Cornelius Vischer after A Brouwer.
f. 142v.   lithograph of Paganini by Kriehuber. Published by Artaria, Vienna, 1828.
f. 148r.   chromolithograph 'Market Place, Nottingham', by W F Gibson, *c* 1865.
f. 170r.   chromolithograph poster of concert given by the Wandering Minstrels 3 July 1867, at Hanover Square Rooms, for the Royal Caledonian Asylum. 'M & N Hanhart lith'.

Volume 2 (K. 6. e. 2)

f. 2r.   pen and ink humorous titlepage, probably in the hand of Lord Gerald Fitzgerald.★
f. 6v.   lithograph,? after D. Maclise, of Paganini with an orchestra, trimmed to an octagon.
f. 10v.   'Le joueur de violin hollandais', etching by (Jean Baptiste) Fosseyeux after Dietricy (C W E Dietrich).
f. 14v.   unsigned lithograph of Paganini.
f. 14r. & f. 15r.   two watercolour drawings, signed T. G. C. [*ie* Thomas George Cooper★] and entitled 'Fact' and 'Fiction', excuses for Wandering Minstrels' non-attendance.

f. 15v. lithograph by Gavarni of a cornemuse player.
f. 17r. leaf in Mozart's autograph, containing sketches for the opening of the finale of the piano quartet in E flat, K. 493, and eight canons K. 508a.
f. 18r. unsigned etching of animal concert,? c 1600.
f. 19v. lithograph of Sir Michael Costa, by C Baugniet, 1853.
f. 24r. trimmed photographs of Verdi, Auber, Gounod, Meyerbeer, Rossini and Offenbach.
f. 26r. pen and ink drawing of Colonel H P de Bathe (drummer), by A Davis Cooper*, 1867.
f. 31v. 'Playing in parts', etching, coloured by hand, by William Broods junior. Published by J Sidebotham, 88 Burlington Arcade.
f. 35r. 'A Monster-Concert', conducted by a pterodactyl, chalk drawing by Lord Gerald Fitzgerald.*
f. 40v. 'Concert d'amateurs' (a cat's concert), lithograph c 1850. p. 197 of *Souvenirs d'artistes*.
f. 41v. 'Tartini's dream', lithograph.
f. 42v. Leopold Mozart with his children. Lithograph by A Schieferdecker after L C de Carmontelle, c 1860.
f. 44.   'A smoking concert by the Wandering Minstrels', woodcut by Hubert Herkomer, *The Graphic*, 25 June 1870.
f. 50r. programme of the Wandering Minstrels' concert in the Albert Hall, 25 February 1871, the first ever given there.
f. 55v. A lace-bordered, coloured Christmas card. 1871.
f. 60r. 'Minstrels of the Carpathian Mountains'. Two photographs by N Boyd.
f. 72v. 'Design for a 'Sgrafito' panel for a Cole-Hole or National cave of Harmony, South Kensington', by T Villiers Lister.
f. 79r. etching, signed J [Lucas van Leyden], of a man playing the lute and an old woman playing the fiddle, 1524. (Holstein p. 174.)
f. 80r. Autograph three-part textless Allegro by Auber. July 1852.
f. 82v. Japanese drawing on mulberry paper by Sukenobu of a court musician playing a *ryuteki* (transverse flute). Pre-1875. Presented by A B Mitford.
f. 90r. pen and ink drawing of L W Beddome (clarinet) by Thomas Williamson*.
f. 95r. lithograph of Nicholas Hanhart by A Ring. 1877.
f. 95v. lithograph of pen and ink caricature of Wagner ('The Flying Dutchman') by Thomas Williamson*.? 1877.
f. 101v. & Venetian Carnival Scene. Engraving by Pieter de Jode I after
f. 102r. Ludovicus Pozzorato (Toeput), printed by the widow of Gerard de Jode. Masked lutenist, with six musicians in a portico – two lutes, regal, viol, cornet and singer – with other masked figures on a terrace.
f. 102v. etching of musicians. MS note reads 'A Tempesta 1700'.
f. 116v. pen and ink drawing of T Ramsay Dow (flautist) by Thomas Williamson*.
f. 117. pen and ink sketches of George Mount (conductor) and the Rev E Ker Gray (percussion) by Thomas Williamson*.

Volume 3. (K. 6. e. 3)

f. 3v.	lithograph of Robert Lindley by M Gauci after F Rosenberg.
f. 4v.	lithograph of Dragonetti by M Gauci after W F Rosenberg.
f. 5v.	lithograph of Maurice Hanhart by A Ring. 1881.
f. 54r.	programme of concert given at Holborn Town Hall, 15 May 1890, jointly with the Magpie Minstrels.
f. 56r.	photograph of the exterior of Grosvenor Hall, Buckingham Palace Road, London.
f. 58r.	photograph of Countess Valda Gleichen, signed 1891.
f. 65r.	programme of the thousandth meeting of the Wandering Minstrels, held 14 December 1893 at Grosvenor Hall, London.
f. 66r.–67r.	historical account of the Wandering Minstrels printed for its thousandth meeting, originally printed as a pamphlet, cut up into sheets and mounted.
f. 78r.	photograph of the interior of Grosvenor Hall, showing the Wandering Minstrels' orchestra at their final concert, 24 March 1898.
f. 78v.	menu of the final dinner 8 February 1899.

William Barclay Squire, 1855–1927: music librarian

So little has been written about William Barclay Squire (pl. 24) that it is not easy, after the lapse of a century, to discover many details of the upbringing and education which he received until about his twentieth year.[1] There is little here to foreshadow his later career of such distinguished public service, and such fertile intellectual energy. He was born on 16 October 1855, the second child and only son of William Squire of Coleman Street, E., and Feltham Hill, in Middlesex, some 14 miles from Hyde Park Corner and then in open country. His father, who was a manufacturer of drugs, married a Miss Elizabeth Ogden, of an old Lancashire family. She was a talented singer, who for many years inspired and organized the musical life of her family, and it was from her that the boy inherited his love of music. After study at home with a private tutor, the young Squire, who was not robust, was sent to an establishment at Isleworth sponsored by the Prince Consort.★

Later, there was some doubt as to his future, and his father sent him to Frankfurt to learn German, intending that he should enter the family business. There he developed religious interests, and decided to take Holy Orders. In 1875 he entered Pembroke College, Cambridge, where he read history, but after graduating with third-class honours in 1879, he felt he could not face the Thirty-Nine Articles. Being also disinclined to follow his father's career, he joined a firm of solicitors, in due course passing all the necessary examinations. During this time of uncertainty his passion for music had asserted itself more and more strongly, for it was in this field that he had made his name while an undergraduate.

Musical life at Cambridge had blossomed to a wonderful flowering in the late 1870's, principally owing to Charles Villiers Stanford, that volcanic and magnetic personality from Dublin, who was then organist of Trinity and conductor of the University Musical Society. Squire's friendship with Stanford found practical expression in 1881 when he provided the libretto for his opera *The Veiled Prophet*.[2] Another Trinity friend was J A Fuller-Maitland,

★This was the remarkable so-called 'International College'. See Cyril Bibby, 'A Victorian Experiment in international Education, the college at Spring Grove'. *British Journal of Educational Studies*, London, vol. v no. 1. November 1956, pp. 25–36. Its pupils in the generation immediately after Squire's included Frederick Delius.

24 William Barclay Squire. After the drawing by William Strang. 345 × 245 mm.

who married one of Squire's sisters in 1885 and subsequently became music critic of *The Times*. It was presumably through one of these two men that Squire was recommended to Sir George Grove* to examine the music in the Fitzwilliam Museum for the article on 'Libraries' in his great dictionary, which was then coming out in parts. The total of articles that Squire wrote for the first edition of *Grove* ultimately exceeded 130, of which nearly half were done by the time he was twenty-nine. These articles really founded his reputation as a scholar.

Had he been forced to continue his career as a solicitor, his talent for research could hardly have developed to the full, but in 1884 fate began to play the decisive cards. For in the autumn of that year there died one C J Evans, who had entered the British Museum in 1858. He had worked on the music catalogue from 1863 onwards, and was apparently still some way off the normal retiring age at the time of his death. The then Keeper of Printed Books, Mr George Bullen, proposed to fill the vacancy from departmental staff. He recommended to the Trustees 'that Mr Birch-Reynardson, Assistant, be entrusted with the duties formerly discharged by Mr Evans: the appointment of a specially qualified man from outside being, in his opinion, unnecessary'. But the Trustees' Minute of 17 January 1885 continues: 'Resolved, that it is preferable to apply for a specialist.'

Who Squire's competitors were cannot now be discovered. But his testimonials, from Grove, Stanford, A D Coleridge, Leslie Stephen, W H Husk, W S Rockstro, and J F Bridge, are still preserved and make most impressive reading. Squire's appointment dated from 4 November 1885: he was 'specially certified by the Civil Service Commission under Clause VIII of the Order in Council of 4 June 1870, as sanctioned by a Treasury letter of 30 July 1885, to take charge of the collections of music'.[3] How momentous this appointment was for the British Museum can best be judged from a brief glance at the history of its printed music.[4]

The various foundation collections which formed the basis of the Department of Printed Books contained a scanty amount of music, mainly because it was then too specialized to appeal to the collectors of books. What little had accumulated by the early nineteenth century came from gifts and the spasmodic working of the Act governing copyright deposit. Purchases were very few. In the mid-1820s no less a person than Vincent Novello realized how serious this was for the future of musical research, and very sensibly tried to persuade the Trustees to create a co-ordinated Music Department with himself at the head. He was rebuffed. In 1840 Thomas Oliphant was appointed to work on both printed and manuscript music. After ten years'

---

*Grove's letters to Squire, written from 1878–98, are now BL Add. MS 39679.

faithful toil he submitted to the Trustees a memorandum for the further improvement of the collections; its only immediate consequence was that his engagement was not renewed. Then came an interregnum in which the Music Room and its catalogue struggled into existence, while Oliphant's purchasing policy was at least not wholly abandoned. By the 1860s the quantity of acquisitions by purchase and copyright became so great that under Evans and others★ the cataloguing began to fall into arrears.

When Squire took office, things were in a bad way. With indomitable energy he worked off most of the arrears single-handed, though he apparently received little or no instruction in cataloguing in the General Library, and had had previous experience only as librarian to the Cambridge University Musical Society in 1878 – a very different matter. More important still, he gradually changed the attitude of those in authority towards music. It must have been an uphill task at first, for in 1885, as he said much later with heart-felt understatement, 'it was always understood that music was not to be encouraged'.[5] Before long, however, he was able to increase antiquarian purchasing substantially, for he realized how much great music of the past could thus be discovered. So much of this was acquired that by 1899 he was able to compile a special Accession Part of music printed before 1801, which was the forerunner of his catalogue of 1912. Long before then, the influx of copyright music again became so great that Squire's staff had to be increased in order to free him, after sixteen years, from the treadmill of routine and facilitate his concentration on new catalogues. But it never exceeded four, including himself and a stalwart pillar of the Music Room named Lister, who had been seconded from the Bindery some years before 1885. The latter became responsible for the sorting of music, for its parcelling, for pressmarking and filing of titles, and for the rearrangement and rebinding of the 370 volumes of the catalogue after the upheaval of 1912. In 1900 Mr William C Smith was transferred from the General Library to take over most of the current cataloguing, and in 1908 came Mr Charles Humphries to assist him, even as he has assisted me since Mr Smith's retirement in 1944.[6]

The 1912 catalogue, of which I shall say more later, was far from being the sole end of Squire's official life. He continued to devote his immense antiquarian knowledge to purchasing rarities on an ever-increasing scale. Such notable sales as the Kockx of 1886, the Borghese of 1892, the second Heredia sale of the same year, the second Marshall sale of 1904, the Taphouse sale of 1905, the Cummings of 1917, and the Aylesford of 1918 brought many additions to the Music Room. His interests were by no means confined to

---

★A fuller estimate of the work of this generation is given in my *Printed Music in the British Museum*, etc, (London, 1979), pp. 79–110.

printed music. The Treasury letter confirming his appointment had specified the charge of the 'collections of music', by which Squire understood manuscript as well as printed. In the event, he had officially nothing to do with manuscripts, though he doubtless kept in close contact with his colleague Augustus Hughes-Hughes, who was likewise at that time working on a monumental catalogue. Thus it was Squire who was instrumental in securing for the Department of Manuscripts one of its greatest musical treasures, the autographs of the last ten string quartets of Mozart. For he persuaded their owner, Miss Harriet Chichele-Plowden, to bequeath them to the Museum in her will. Squire must have been much relieved at the failure of the legal action subsequently taken by her heirs to upset the bequest.[7]

Outside the Museum, one of the most important collections of music in the country was that in the Royal Library, at Buckingham Palace. It was noted for its manuscripts, above all for the ninety volumes of Handel autographs, which constitute the largest collection in the world of a great composer's manuscripts preserved in a single library. The gradual growth of musicology had brought this collection into such continual demand that it was obvious that it could be consulted in the Museum far more conveniently than in a Royal residence. Squire first tried to negotiate the transfer during the reign of Edward VII but was unsuccessful.[8] But after the accession of George V the matter was brought to a happy consummation, probably through the good offices of Countess Gleichen,[9] and the transfer took place in 1911.

It might be thought that all these and similar affairs, coupled with the general supervision of the routine of the Music Room, would have absorbed all or most of Squire's energy, but this was not so. He still had ample to spare for a continuous stream of other work, which is made none the less remarkable by the fact that he led the life of a bachelor of means in the relatively stable world of pre-1914. In 1885, when barely thirty, he was awarded a silver medal for his notable services in connexion with the Historical Music Loan Exhibition held in the Albert Hall. He became honorary secretary of the Purcell Society in 1889 and seems to have been largely responsible for rescuing it from its hesitant beginnings. He held this office until 1922, and edited the keyboard works. In the early 1890s he began, with Fuller-Maitland, to edit the Fitzwilliam Virginal Book.

This internationally famous piece of scholarship merits a slight digression. It does not seem to have occurred to anyone to consider how it was possible for two busy men, working in London, to spend in Cambridge the long time needed for the laborious transcription and proof-checking of this lengthy manuscript, which runs to 938 folio pages in modern engraving. The answer is simple: practically all their work was done from photographs taken over a period of two years by Mr Charles F Bell, later Keeper of the Department of Fine Art at the Ashmolean. It was he who first suggested publication of the manuscript in a modern edition, and worked out a practicable plan.[10] This notable task, in which Squire had the larger share, was published, not in 1899, as is frequently stated, but from 1894 to 1899, in parts. The dedication of the edition to Queen Victoria is a curious one, as the manuscript had nothing at all to do with the Royal family. May it suggest that even in the 1890s Squire had his eye on the music in the Royal Library?

During this period Squire served as an active member of the Magpie Madrigal Society, for whose performance he edited from the original editions a large quantity of Italian madrigals. In 1898 he participated in the foundation of the Folk Song Society. He was one of those responsible for preparing for the press the huge and sumptuous catalogue of the exhibition of music and musical instruments held at Fishmongers' Hall in 1904 – an occasion unparalleled in the annals of English musicology. In 1911 occurred the London congress of the International Musicological Society. Here again his capacities as organizer were in demand: he served *inter alia* as chairman of the Lecture Subcommittee.[11] Perhaps Squire's most remarkable feat outside the Museum, even though he did not supply dates where necessary, was the cataloguing of the printed music in the Library of the Royal College of Music, whose librarian he became in 1894. The resultant volume of 368 pages was published in 1909. He did most of this work in the evenings after he left the Museum; he was elected an Honorary Fellow of the College in 1924, and at once began work on the catalogue of its manuscripts.

In 1903 he published a small but valuable catalogue of the printed and manuscript music in the library at Westminster Abbey.[12] He also studied and drew attention to two very important but then little-known collections of early English music – the Eton Manuscript,[13] and the Old Hall Manuscript.[14] One other book not his own must have made heavy demands on his leisure, because it was too intricate to have been covered entirely in official hours. This was Robert Eitner's *Quellen-Lexikon*, for which Squire seems to have supplied by correspondence – a staggering thought by modern standards – most of the information not only for the holdings of the Music Room, but also for many other British Libraries. (He also gave much information for the supplements compiled by Wolfheim and Springer from 1911 to 1913.) We may also presume that he had a good deal to do with Steele's *Earliest English Music Printing*, published by the Bibliographical Society in 1903. Squire's intensive study of the subject in its broadest aspects gave him a profound knowledge of the influence of continental printing in England.[15] In a very different field from all these scholarly activities, he found time to serve as music critic to four journals between 1890 and 1904 –

The Saturday Review, Westminster Gazette, The Globe, and *The Pilot.*★ Besides purely musical work, he was active as a connoisseur of fine art. In 1909 he collaborated with the Countess of Radnor in a sumptuous two-volume *Catalogue of the Pictures in the Collection of the Earl of Radnor.*

The rest of Squire's official career can be briefly told. In 1912 he was promoted to Assistant Keeper, the equivalent of the present grade of Deputy Keeper. Immediately after the completion of his catalogues he turned his energy to another field, the Museum's important but scattered collection of opera libretti. In order to locate them he read through the greater part of the General Catalogue, consisting even then of nearly four million entries, of which only those in some obviously irrelevant headings could be safely skipped. Thus he compiled, on some 10,000 slips, a catalogue of libretti which, through lack of staff, has unfortunately never been printed or kept up to date with accessions. When war came in 1914 he continued to supervise the work of the Music Room, but also served first in the Intelligence Department of the Admiralty and later in the Historical Section of the Foreign Office. In 1916 the Admiralty published his description of the tribes of Tunisia, which still makes fascinating reading. In his capacity as Assistant Keeper Squire organized the war-time loan of Museum books to the Admiralty for service requirements.

On 4 November 1920 he retired, a few weeks after his sixty-fifth birthday. In September 1921 he attended the International Fine Arts Congress at Paris, at which he read a paper urging the inception of an international catalogue of the portraits of musicians, a project which still has to be realized. Freedom from official cares gave fresh rein to his energy. He completed the arrangement of the King's Music Library in its special apartment within the Music Room and began work on the cataloguing of it. He finished the volume devoted entirely to the Handel manuscripts and did most of the printed music and musical literature. He was not able to complete the miscellaneous manuscripts before he died, but for his earlier work on the collection he was awarded the MVO in 1926. In that year he completed after seventeen years' intermittent toil the catalogue of the manuscripts in the Royal College of Music.[16] With Fuller-Maitland he prepared for publication the unknown Handel keyboard pieces in the Aylesford manuscripts, which he had purchased in 1918 and added, by special permission, to the Handel material in the Royal Music Library. In 1925 he was elected an Honorary Fellow of Pembroke College. One of the last things he wrote was a masterly summary

---

★For the huge collection of programmes which Squire amassed, with the help of fellow critics, and ultimately presented to the British Museum (now at press mark 7892 W.1) see my *Wealth of Music,* etc, (London, 1983), p. 47.

of the iconography of Beethoven for the centenary of 1927.[17] He died, at the age of seventy-two, on 13 January in that year.

A fair idea of both his greatness and his limitations as bibliographer and librarian can be deduced from the methods and principles underlying his catalogues, particularly that of 1912. The antecedents of these two volumes are of some relevance. Although a catalogue of the Museum's musical manuscripts had been printed in 1842, a catalogue of printed material was still a desideratum in 1885 when Squire took office. The authorities were aware of this. They had indeed received a reminder, unfortunately based on inaccurate facts, in 1877, from the Council of the Musical Association, then a stripling in its fourth Session and sixty-seven years away from enjoying the prefix 'Royal'. The reply sent by Winter Jones, then Principal Librarian, was remarkable for its masterly evasion of the issue. 'In regard to the proposal of the memorialists', he wrote, 'that a catalogue of music and musical literature should be printed, I am to acquaint you that the Trustees feel they must postpone consideration of this subject.'[18] This at least suggests that it was officially realized how urgently such printed catalogues were needed. We may be pretty sure that Squire realized this from the beginning of his official career. Fifteen years later, when he had been freed from burdensome routine work and had completed his trial volume of 1899, there was only one way of proceeding – to read through all the volumes of the music catalogue, numbering well over 360, and extract all the pre-1800 items that had come into the collections before 1885. The next stage was to examine and re-catalogue some 20,000 pieces, including several thousand of the late eighteenth and early nineteenth centuries, about the dating of which there was considerable uncertainty. He also scoured the General Library for all seventeenth- and eighteenth-century periodicals containing musical supplements.

It was, apparently, thought inevitable that the two volumes so produced should also serve, with their columns cut up and laid down on folio sheets, for departmental use. Thus the benefits of publication were purchased at a heavy price, for the split in the catalogue,* of which the vast post-1800 residue went entirely unrevised, had disastrous consequences. The reader in the Museum was now confronted with two totally different arrangements for composers such as Handel, Purcell, Palestrina, Haydn, or Mozart – one, the pre-1800, based on generic groupings, the other post-1800, purely alphabetical, by title. Entries for the earlier section were more elaborate than for the later. Gradually there grew up the ludicrous idea that in 1800 music

---

*The catalogues were unified 75 years later when the firm of K G Saur, London, Munich, etc, published *Catalogue of Music in the British Library to 1980*. This ran to 62 volumes, issued 1981–87, and included both the pre-1800 and post-1800 catalogues as well as all relevant music from the Hirsch and Royal libraries.

ceased to be 'old' and became 'modern'. It is interesting to speculate what public reaction would have been had a similar dichotomy been practised on the General Catalogue of Printed Books at, say, the year 1600. But for Squire, the end justified the means.

Accepting this, his two volumes of 1912 must be praised as a very fine single-handed achievement, unrivalled in scope and purposeful planning. Cross-references and title-indexes included, they contain well over 40,000 entries, representing music printed in practically every European country and in nearly a score of languages. Squire gave the printer or publisher, or both if necessary, for foreign publications for all periods, right down to the twentieth century and not merely for pre-1700 items, as was, and still is, the usage for foreign works in the General Catalogue of Printed Books. Considering the speed at which he must have worked, he was astonishingly accurate. He paid great attention to incunabula and gave short collations for all books printed up to 1520. On the other hand, his cataloguing also had its limitations, in matters of practice rather than detail. He did not keep up to date with the slowly changing methods and rising standards of the General Library. He ignored pagination altogether, even for scores and other works not issued in musical parts. His practice generally was based on principles derived from and analogous to the cataloguing of books. He does not seem to have considered devising new methods to meet some of the essential distinctions between books and music. For instance, he entirely burked the difficult but not insoluble problem of reconciling the difference between the number of musical parts and the number of bibliographical parts. He simply avoided it, by not stating the number of parts in either case.

The handling of a vast quantity of music gave Squire a rare knowledge of imprints. His dating of undated eighteenth-century pieces was, with few exceptions, uncannily accurate, and untrammelled by the flood of bibliographies and reference books which now makes the cataloguing of music so slow. The imprints which he supplied for imperfect copies were usually correct. This and his datings were put to the test during the cataloguing of the Hirsch Library in 1949–50, from which numerous variants and other issues of music had to be compared with the Museum copies. The dates in which Squire was out by a decade or so are very few. One group of instances is provided by the London firm of G Walker, who, though they commenced business *c.* 1795, issued little before 1800. Squire put almost all their numerous publications well before 1800. Had he examined the watermark dates in the paper, he could have avoided this error, and a few similar ones. But he ignored watermarks, though he took note of plate numbers, at least implicitly. He obviously used them as an aid to dating, but did not give them as part of a catalogue entry. In 1914[19] he wrote what is one of the first studies, perhaps the very first, of this intricate matter in any language. Shorn though the entries in his 1912 catalogue generally were of bibliographical detail, he could give this fully if he thought fit. The style of his catalogue of the music in Westminster Abbey Library is fully up to the most elaborate standards of bibliographical description as practised in 1903. But he had curious lapses as a bibliographer. For instance, he discovered in the Bagford fragments the title-page of John Bull's Gresham College *Oration* of 1597. Because no complete copy, or any other fragment, of the book is known, this leaf is of great bibliographical and historical interest. But Squire failed to notice that the blank verso bears an almost entirely legible offset of the first page of the very interesting text.

From this account of Squire's methods and principles certain inconsistencies which present parallels with different sides of his character are obvious. I can only attempt to exemplify and present these contradictions, because it would be presumptuous for one who never knew him to try to analyse them on personal grounds. His autocratic nature is detectable in his sudden decision to have burnt, during the 1914 war, the Museum's obsolete but still invaluable catalogue of the words of songs and their authors, in over fifty volumes. This arbitrary self-sufficiency is also revealed in his cataloguing, for he left practically no notes at all on his titles giving the source of any information. Yet he annotated all his reference books meticulously. Besides being arbitrary, he was fundamentally a shy man who often took refuge in extreme brusqueness. It was these qualities that tended to make him a formidable figure to some of his younger colleagues, especially if they took a more leisurely view of their duties than he thought proper. On the other hand, he was the embodiment of kindness and courtesy to all who sought to draw on his vast store of knowledge. This was especially appreciated by foreign visitors and correspondents: indeed his helpfulness and affability are even now vividly remembered by scholars and librarians abroad who met him in their youth. To his own staff Squire was loyal and considerate, sometimes in unexpected ways. For one of them, when on war service, he knitted a muffler and sent it to him.

His impatient and impetuous nature seems at variance with his meticulous scholarship – perhaps exemplified at its best in the catalogue of the Handel Manuscripts – and with his perseverance in a long grind, such as reading through the General Catalogue of Printed Books to extract the entries for his libretto slips. Yet, possibly because of his standards of scholarship, he tended to take an unequal view of his departmental responsibilities. While it was reasonable that he should have decided not to catalogue modern dance music, popular songs and band parts, to refer to them publicly as 'rubbish', as he did, was unpardonable.[20] He must have been aware of their importance as copyright material and social documents, even if he could not foresee the increased use of them that the concatenation of sound-film, radio, and television would bring. In other matters, however, his vision was amazing. He anticipated the idea of a British union catalogue of music by twenty-five years when he appealed[21] in 1919 for all uncatalogued collections to be temporarily deposited in the British Museum so that a centralized slip-catalogue could gradually be built up. He also anticipated by nearly thirty years the fundamental changes of principle that have recently taken place in the system of musical degrees at Oxford and Cambridge. For in 1919[22] he urged that university professors of music should themselves devote some of their energies to research and encourage it in others as part of the course for a degree.[23]

But these inconsistencies, whatever their explanation, are trifling compared with the true measure of Squire's achievement. In his own generation and circle, so full of famous names, he can now be seen as outstanding for several high qualities. His exceptional versatility of mind was enhanced by a prodigious range of learning. Although he never wrote a book, a collected edition of his miscellaneous essays[24] would reveal an unsuspected charm of style blended with widely cultivated tastes. In thoroughness of scholarship his best work has stood the test of time. Very many of his articles in *Grove* have gone through to the fifth edition, with the minimum of alteration, after three-quarters of a century. But what now stands out most is his concentrated and selfless singleness of purpose – something that a more diffuse generation should respect and, indeed, envy.

Squire devoted his life to making known and accessible the musical treasures hidden in English libraries. The best witnesses to this are his six great catalogues, which he compiled practically single-handed – an unsurpassed achievement in their own field. It was mainly through his work that the larger consciousness of the value and importance of music libraries in Great Britain has arisen. Although only twenty-eight years have passed since he died, the pace of thought and events in his world has become very quick. Consequently, the greatness of what he did as librarian, editor, and scholar has been brought into sharp focus sooner than might have been expected. In the early twentieth century there were a number of distinguished men who served the cause of music in libraries, such as O G Sonneck, at the Library of Congress; Alfred Wotquenne, at the Brussels Conservatory; J B T Weckerlin, at the Paris Conservatory; Rafael Mitjana, at the Royal Library of Stockholm, and others. William Barclay Squire of the British Museum does not suffer by comparison with any of these. His coat of arms, which adorns his bookplate, bears the motto *Maneo indefessus labore*. These words surely epitomize the enduring quality of his life and work.

[1955]

Notes

1 I am much indebted to the late Mrs Laura Nicholson,* Squire's younger sister, who, in 1949, furnished me with most of the information about this period of his life. The obituary notices in *The Times*, 14 January, 1927, and the *Daily Telegraph*, 15 January, 1927, cover broadly the same ground as the articles in the *DNB* and *Who's Who*. On 22 January, 1927 *The Times* printed an important article by Professor E J Dent (not noticed by Lawrence Haward in his check-list of Dent's writings, *Music Review*, November, 1946), entitled 'The Rewards of Scholarship'. It set Squire's work in perspective against the musical research of his day, but gave little biographical detail.
2 Squire later summarized his views on some aspects of libretti in 'The Libretto of the Future', an article reprinted from *The Musician*, in *Studies in Music*, ed. Robin Grey (London, 1901), pp. 311–23. Squire also wrote the libretto for J F Bridge's cantata *Callirrhoë* (1888).
3 This was presumably necessitated by the fact that he was thirty, some years past the normal age of entry. I have to thank the Trustees of the British Museum for permission to quote from their Minutes and to examine the papers relating to Squire's appointment. The *Times* obituary stated, erroneously, that Squire did not enter the Museum as a specialist.
4 This topic is dealt with more at length in my paper 'The Music Room of the British Museum. 1753–1953', in *Proceedings of the Royal Musical Association*, 79th session, 1952/3, pp. 65–79.
5 'Musical Libraries and Catalogues', in *Proceedings of the Musical Association*, 45th session, 1918/19, pp. 96–111.
6 I am indebted to both Mr Smith and Mr Humphries for much relevant information.
7 Edward Speyer, *My Life and Friends* (London, 1937), pp. 208–9. (I have given a fuller account of this affair in 'The Chichele Plowdens and the British Museum. Footnotes to a musical bequest', which is due to appear in a *Festschrift* for Carleton Sprague Smith, 1988.)
8 Information from the late Mrs Laura Nicholson.
9 Information also from Mrs Nicholson.
10 Information from Mr Bell, whose name was accidentally omitted from the preface. Cf. also J A Fuller-Maitland, *A Door-Keeper of Music* (London, 1929), p. 221.
11 A portrait group of all the participants is in *Musical Times*, July 1911. Squire is the eighth from the right in the second row.
12 Published in *Monatshefte für Musikgeschichte*, 1903, Beilage.
13 *Archaeologia*, 1898.
14 *Sammelbände der Internationalen Musikgesellschaft*, Bd. 2, 1901.
15 Cf. 'Notes on Early Music Printing', in *Bibliographica*, iii (1897), pp. 99–122.
16 This was issued in six typed copies in 1931, with some additions by Mr Rupert Erlebach.
17 Published posthumously in the Beethoven number of *Music & Letters* (vol. VIII, no. 2).
18 The full texts of the memorandum and of Jones's reply are printed in *Proceedings of the Musical Association*, 5th session, 1878/9, Report of the Council, pp. xiii, xiv. The paper which gave rise to the memorial was read in the preceding session by W H Cummings, 'On the Formation of a National Music Library'. It gives a good deal of information about the shortcomings of music in the British Museum.
19 'Publishers' Numbers', *Sammelbände der Internationalen Musikgesellschaft*, XV, pp. 421–4.

*Laura Nicholson's letters, as are also those of Charles Bell (cf. n. 10), are now preserved in BL Add. MS 62678.

20 'Musical Libraries and Catalogues', in *Proceedings of the Musical Association*, 45th session, 1918/19, pp. 96–111.
21 Ibid.
22 'On editing Old Music', *The Chesterian*, October 1919, pp. 40–44.
23 After his death, the Barclay Squire Prize for musical palaeography was established at Cambridge by his sisters.
24 The library of Pembroke College, Cambridge, contains six volumes of his offprints and extracts, bound in chronological order. A different aspect of Squire's erudition is to be found in the remarkable recipe for rum punch brewed under his personal superivision to sustain those present at the first private performance of Walton's *Façade*, in 1922. Cf. Sir Osbert Sitwell, *Laughter in the Next Room* (London, 1949), p. 191.

Index

Abbott, Elizabeth 148 n.5
Abel, Karl Friedrich 110
Abert, Hermann 58
Addison & Co, 157
Albert, Prince Consort 117 n.24, 187
Albert Hall, London 180
Allgemeine Musikalische Zeitung 65
Almack's Rooms 121
Alsager, Thomas 125 n.27
Amateur Concerts 126
Ambrogetti, Giuseppe 87, 122
Ambros, August Wilhelm 15
Ames, Joseph 34, 35, 37 n.11
Anderson, Dorothy 37 n.17
Anderson, Emily 135 n.11
Anderson, George F 115
André, Johann Anton 99
Andrews, Hilda 103 n.4, 107
Andrews, Hugh 73, 74
Anfossi, Pasquale 78
Anglo, Sydney 31 n.15
Angrisani, Carlo 149 n.23
Ansbach, Markgräfin of 57
Argyll Rooms 121, 153–5, 174
Arnold, Samuel 97 n.38
Arnold, Samuel James 89
L'art et instruction de bien danser 5
Asher, A & Co, 1
Attaingnant, Pierre 7, 11, 14, 15, 19, 29, 30, 33, 36
Auber, Daniel 101, 102, 180, 184, 185
Augusta, Princess 109
Aylesford sale 190
Ayrton, William 122, 126–8, 134, 139, 144, 148, 153, 175 n.5

Bach, John Christian 110
Bach Choir 176 n.24
Bagford, John 38
Ball, William 91, 92
Bämler, Johann 2
Banks, Sir Joseph 70 n.12
Bannister, John 40
Barclay Squire Prize 199 n.23
Barker, Nicolas 30 n.1, 31 n.21
Barrington, Hon. Daines 57, 60, 68, 70 n.12
Bath, Upper Room 125 n.27
Bathe, Col. H P de 181, 185
Battishill, Jonathan 58, 70 n.17
Bauer, Wilhelm A 69 n.1

Baugniet, C 185
Beale, T Frederick 154, 176 n.10
Beaumont and Fletcher 66
Beddome, L W 185
Bedford, Duchess of 78
Beethoven, Ludwig van 45, 122, 123, 126, 129–34, 193; bust 159, 162, 177 n.32; relics 162, 163, 172
Bell, Charles Francis 192, 198 n.10
Bellamy, John Ludford 137, 140, 142, 146, 149 n.17, 149 n.22
Bellini, Vincenzo 134
Bennett, Sir William Sterndale 123
Benson, Lionel 100, 103 n.3, 181–183 n.3
Bercula, Thomas 16
Berger, Francesco 159, 161, 162, 169, 176 n.21
Bériot, Charles Auguste de 123, 184
Berlioz, Hector 166, 167, 171
Berridge, Frederick 62, 71 n.18
Berry, James N 115
Best, William Thomas 171, 177 n.41
Betts, Miss (singer) 91, 93, 98 n.47
Betts, Arthur 98 n.47
Beyer, F E 117 n.7
Bibby, Cyril 187 n.*
Biblioteka Jagellióńska, Krakow 72 n.25
Billington, Elizabeth 137, 140, 141, 142, 146, 149 n.9
Birch, Rev. Thomas 58, 59
Birchall, Robert 73, 79
Birch-Reynardson, Herbert Frederick 189
Bishop, Sir Henry Rowley 80, 133, 170, 177 n.39
Bismarck, Count von 112, 116
Blades, William 38
Bland, Maria Theresa 137, 140, 149 n.11
Blom, Eric 92, 95 n.41
Blumenthal, Jacob 183
Bolt, Johann Friedrich 97 n.27
Bolton, Eliza *see* Bolton, Frances Elizabeth
Bolton, Frances Elizabeth 145–7
Bolton, Mary Katherine 145, 146
Bonn Musical Society 171
Boosey & Co 160
Borghese sale 190
Boyce, William 109, 111; sale 111
Braham, John 140–2, 146, 149 n.13, 170, 177 n.36
Brahms, Johannes 113, 117 n.19
Brayley, Edward A 184
Breedon, L A 101
Breitkopf & Härtel 171

200

Bridge, John Frederick 189, 198 n.2
Bristol Baptist College 18, 34, 37 n.14
Bristol Baptist Society 35
British Library: Garrick plays 66; manuscripts: Additional *4309* 58, *17838* 153, *37386.f.7* 117 n.6, *39679* 198 n.4, *42225* 125 n.19, *42981* 97 n.39, *61949* 71 n.24, *62678* 197 n.; Harleian *5414, 5419, 5892–5998* 38; opera libretti 193. *See also* British Museum
British Museum 52–70, 163; Old Royal Library 57, 107; Royal Music Library 107, Royal Music Library, 'Smith Collection' 15; Royal Philharmonic Society loans 162–4. *See also* Montagu House
British Stage and Literary Cabinet, The 97 n.35
Britton, John 95 n.7
Broods, William 185
Brown, James D 150 n.38, 172
Browne, Sir Thomas 29
Brunet, Jacques Charles 15
Buckingham Palace 107, 112, 115, 116, 191
Budd, Mrs 156
Budd, George W 128, 155, 156, 174, 176 n.13
Bull, John 39, 196
Bullen, George 189
Bunn, Elizabeth 128, 129
Burlington House 159
Burney, Charles 14, 110, 134
Burney, Fanny 110
Byrd, William 109

Cabot, Thomas 22
Calkin, Annie 174
Calkin, C 174
Calkin, George 173
Calkin, James 173
Calkin, James Joseph 173
Calkin, John Baptiste 173
Calkin, Joseph 153–7, 164, 169, 173, 174, 176 n.7
Calkin, Joseph George 173
Calkin, Joseph Tenielli 173, 176 n.17
Calkin, Milo 174
Calkin, Pierre 173
Calkin, Samuel 173
Calkin, William 174
Calkin & Budd 173
Cambridge, Duchess of 96 n.21
Cambridge Amateur Musical Society 171
Cambridge University Library 39
Campbell, Mr 171
Capell, Edward 32, 33
Canterbury Cricket Week 179, 184
Cardross, Lord 53
Carlisle, Lady 78
Carmontelle, Louis Carrogis de 61, 62, 71 n.23, 185
Caroline, Queen (as Princess of Wales) 80
Carraciolo, Marchese Domenico 58
Carse, Adam 123, 124 n.11, 124 n.14
Carter, Harry 14, 29, 30 n.1
Catalogue of Printed Music in the British Library to 1980 194 n.*

Cawse, Harriet 91, 93, 94, 98 n.48
Caxton, William 29
Chaikovsky, P I 171
Chalon, Alfred Edward 92–4, 98 n.54
Chalon sale 98 n.55
Chapel Royal, London 74
Chappell, Samuel 152, 153, 174, 175 n.3
Chappell & Co 160, 175 n.3
Charles V, Emperor 16
Charlotte, Queen Consort of George III 107, 109, 111
Cherubini, Luigi 161, 171
Choral Harmonists (Choral Harmonic Society) 123
Christie, John 109
Chrysander, Bertha 113
Chrysander, Friedrich ix, 107, 112–7
Chrysander, Rudolf 112, 116
Cimarosa, Domenico 141, 145, 146
City of London Tavern (or New London Tavern) 124 n.4
Clarence, Duchess of 96 n.21
Clementi, Muzio 131–3, 135 n.15, 176 n.12
Cockayne, G E 150 n.30
Cocks, Robert 154, 158, 174, 176 n.11
Coke, Gerald 109
Coke, Lady Katherine 178
Coleman, Roger 30 n.1
Coleridge, Arthur Duke 189
Collard, Mr 128
Collard, William 131, 132
Colvin, Howard M 95 n.6, 124 n.5
Concerts of Ancient Music 179
'Constance Gradual' x, 11
Cooke, Matthew 63–5, 71 n.21, 72 n.25
Cooper, Alexander Davis 184, 185
Cooper, Thomas George 184
Cooper-Key, H 171
Corbould, Henry 89, 90, 94, 97 n.34
Corder, Frederick 160, 177 n.30
Corder, Henrietta 177 n.30
Corfe, Joseph 70, 71 n.13
Cornish, William 22
Corri, Domenico 149 n.20
Costa, Sir Michael 185
Cosyn Virginal Book 111
Covent Garden Theatre 77
Cowper, Robert 22
Cowper, William 22
Cramer, John Baptist 175 n.3
Cream, P J 94 n.1
Croce, Giovanni 39
Crockford's Clerical Directory 71 n.25
Croft-Murray, Edward 97 n.30
Croft-Murray, Jill xiv
Cromwell, Thomas 17
Crook, J Mordaunt 70
Cross, Thomas 40
Crouzot, François 136 n.19
Crown and Anchor Tavern 119
Crozier, Eric 98 n.41
Crystal Palace Concerts 177 n.40, 177 n.41

Cumberland, Duke and Duchess of 96 n.21
Cummings, William Hayman 159, 169, 176 n.25, 198 n.18; sale 190
Curtis, Henry D 102, 181
Curtis, Spencer H 102, 115
Cusins, Sir William George 115, 159

D., S. 126, 127, 129, 134, 135, 143, 144, 148 n.3, 150 n.41
Dalberg, Baron de 75
D'Almaine & Co 95 n.16, 176 n.10
D'Almaine, Thomas 154
Dance, Henry 152
Dance, William 145, 146
Dando, Joseph 122
Dane, Clemence 98 n.41
Dart, Thurston 30 n.1
Day, John 18, 29
Day, W 92
Day & Haghe 92
Delafosse, Jean Baptiste 61, 71 n.23
Delius, Frederick 187 n.*
Dent, Edward Joseph 68, 72 n.32, 98 n.41, 197 n.1
De Roullède, publisher 73
Desgrave, Louis 14
Deutsch, Otto Erich 69 n.1 n.4, 70 n.4, 71 n.20
Devonshire, Duchess of 78
Dewing's Coffee House 41
Dibdin, Charles the younger 97 n.37
Dibdin, Thomas Frognall 19, 34, 38
Dickons, Maria 122, 142, 149 n.15
Dodsley, Robert 36 n.3
Donaueschingen, Fürstliche Bibliothek 2
Douglas, Keith 163, 175
Dow, T Ramsay 185
Doyle, A Ian 19, 25
Dragonetti, Domenico 153, 176 n.9, 184, 186
Drury Lane Theatre 77
Dubourg, Matthew 110
Duff, Edward Gordon 19
Duncan, William 117 n.16
Dussek, Jan Ladislav 75, 149 n.20
Dussek, Sophia 141, 142, 149 n.20

East India Company's Volunteers 146
East, Thomas 39
Ebers, John 89
Edward VII, King of Great Britain and Ireland 191
Egerton, Seymour, Earl of Wilton 105 n.6
Egerton, Hon. Seymour J G 178, 179, 181
Eglinton, Earl of 58
Einstein, Alfred 99, 101, 103, 104 n.5
Eitner, Robert 50, 192
Eley, – 146
Eley, R T 146 n.*
Elizabeth II, Queen of Great Britain ix, 107
Elkin, Robert 119, 124 n.11, 124 n.12, 124 n.13, 124 n.15, 125 n.16
Elmes, James 124 n.13

Empson, Richard 24, 25
English Folk Song and Dance Society 40
Erasmus, Desiderius 18
Erlebach, Rupert 198 n.20
Esdaile, Arundell 24, 69 n.6
Este, Thomas see East
Eton Manuscript 192
Evans, Charles John 181, 189
Exeter Hall 123

Farmer, Henry George 104 n.5
Farmer, John Stephen 36 n.3
Fauchois, Rene 172
Faulkner, Henry 79
Fédorov, Vladimir 30 n.5, 31 n.11
Ferguson, Frederic Sutherland 28
Fétis, Francois Joseph 15
Field of the Cloth of Gold 16, 18
Fifield, Christopher 183
Fioravanti, Valentino 78, 145
Fischer, Julius 36 n.3
Fishmongers' Hall 192
Fitzgerald, Hon. the Lord Gerald 101, 104 n.6, 178–184
Fitzwilliam Museum, Cambridge 189
Fitzwilliam Virginal Book 191
Flach, Martin 3
Fletcher, W Y 42 n.1
Folk Song Society 192
Folkestone, Viscountess see Helena, Countess of Radnor
Ford (Mr) 154
Forrest, William 18
Forsyth, Michael 125 n.17
Fortescue, George K 24
Fosseyeux, J B 184
Foster, Myles Birkett 150 n.29, 150 n.31, 150 n.37, 160, 161, 172, 176 n.28
Fotheringham, Marion 100, 181, 182
Fotheringham Fotheringham, Miss 100, 182
Fournier, Pierre 11
Franck, César 161
Frankfurt Museum Concerts 170
Freemason's Magazine 71 n.25
Frizzoni, G G-B 71 n.21
Fuller Maitland, John Alexander see Maitland
Fyner, Conrad 6 n.1

G., Mr 145
Garcia, Manuel 97 n.31
Gardiner, William 79, 95 n.11
Gardner, Charles 159, 160, 176 n.23
Garrick, David 18, 32, 35, 37 n.16
Gatti, Madame see Hughes, Maria
Gauci, M 184, 186
Gavarni, Paul 185
Gaye, Arthur 99, 102
Gazzaniga, Giuseppe 95 n.10
Gehring, Franz 31 n.14
Gentleman's Magazine, The 128
George I, King of Great Britain and Ireland 108
George II, King of Great Britain and Ireland 57, 107

George III (as Prince of Wales) 109
George III, King of Great Britain and
  Ireland 108, 109
George V, King of Great Britain 107
Gerber, Ernst Ludwig 74, 111, 117 n.14
Gerson, Jean Charlier de 3, 6 n.1
Gifford, Rev. Andrew 18, 34–6, 56
Gilbert, Alfred 159, 168, 171, 176 n.27, 177 n.47
Gilbert, Sir Alfred 176 n.27
Gilbert, Sir William Schwenk 182, 183
Gladstone, Sir Thomas 159
Gladstone, William Ewart 176 n.20
Gleichen, Countess Valda 181, 186, 191
Globe, The 193
Gloucester, Duke and Duchess of 96 n.21
Gluck, Christoph Willibald von 146
Goldschmidt, Otto 159, 169, 176 n.24
Goldsmith, S O 161, 174
Goodison, Benjamin 109
Goodwin, William 155–7, 164, 170, 174
Goodwin & Tabb 155, 162, 167, 174
Gottron, Adam 76 n.8
Gough, John 7, 19, 22
Goulding, D'Almaine 75, 80, 83, 148 n.1
Gounod, Charles François 161, 184
Grace, Johannes 24, 25
Graichen & Riehl 46, 49
's-Gravenhaegse Vrijdagse Courant 7 n.20
Gray, E Ker 185
Greeting, Thomas 40
Greg, Sir Walter Wilson 19, 22, 24, 33, 36
Gresham, Sir Thomas 39
Grey, Robin 198 n.2
Griffin, George Eugene 137, 139, 143, 148 n.8, 153, 175 n.4
Griglietti, Miss (singer) 137, 140, 143, 145, 147
Gronow, Rees Howell 95 n.8
Grosvenor Hall, Buckingham Palace Road 179, 186
Grove, Sir George 151, 171, 177 n.40, 189
Guérin, printer 17
Guido, d'Aretino 14

Hagenauer, Lorenz 57
Haghe, Charles 90, 92, 94
Hales, Stephen 96 n.26
Hallé, Sir Charles 171, 177 n.48
Halliwell, James Orchard 36 n.3
Hamburg City Library 112
Han, Ulrich 3
Handel, George Frideric 77, 80, 108; autographs 110–7; MSS 193
Hanhart, Michael 178, 184
Hanhart, Nicholas 178, 184, 185
Hanover Square Rooms 121, 123, 137, 142, 143, 154, 157, 174
Harley, Robert, Earl of Oxford 38
Harmonic Society 126
Harmonicon, The 126, 129, 133, 137, 139, 147
Harper, Samuel 56, 146 n.★
Harper, Thomas 123, 145, 146 n.★
Harris, George Frederick 123

Harris, James 57–9, 68
Harrison, Frank Ll., 135 n.7
Haultin, Pierre 11, 15, 19, 33
Haward, Lawrence 198 n.1
Hawes, William 89, 91, 92
Hawkins, Sir John 14, 66, 72 n.28, 110, 111, 134
Hawkins, Laetitia Matilda 110
Hawley, Stanley 160, 161
Haydn, Franz Joseph 75, 80, 123, 126, 148 n.8, 168
Hayward, Thomas 147, 148
Hayward, Thomas & Co 144
Head, Mr (dress designer) 94
Heartz, Daniel 14, 31 n.10, 37 n.5
Heath, Mr 170
Heath, H B 99, 102
Heaton House, Manchester 184
Hecht, Mr 170
Heckel, K Ferdinand 96 n.20
Heinicke, Hartmut 72 n.31
Helena, Countess of Radnor 181, 193
Henry VIII, King of England 16, 23
Herbert, William 34
Heredia sale 190
Herkomer, Hubert 185
Heywood, John 18
Hirsch, Paul 73, 148 n.4
Hirt, F J 71 n.16
Historical Music Loan Exhibition 191
Hoft, Brigitte 96 n.20
Hogan, Charles Beecher 150 n.35
Hogarth, George 172, 174
Hogarth, William 184
Holbein, Hans 18
Hooke, Robert 56
Hopkins, J H 37 n.15
Hopwood, James the elder 83–7, 94, 96 n.6
Hopwood, James the younger 83
Horn, Charles Edward 141, 142, 145, 147, 149 n.16, 149 n.22, 149 n.27
Horsley, William 153, 176 n.6
Horton, J 157, 174
Horwood, Richard 124 n.3
Hughes, Maria 137, 140, 146, 147, 149 n.10
Hughes-Hughes, Augustus 65, 190
Humphries, Charles 107, 190, 198 n.6, and Smith, William C 31 n.29, 31 n.29, 42, 95 n.16
Husk, William Henry 189
Hutchings, Arthur 97 n.27
Huys, Bernard 31 n.35
Hynkes, Wyllyam 24

Illustrated London News 121
International Association of Music Libraries xii
International College, Spring Grove, Isleworth 187, n.★
International Exhibition, Vienna, 1873 46
International Fine Art Congress, Paris 193
International Inventions Exhibition, London, 1885 43
International Musicological Society, London Congress 192

Irving, Sir Henry 171
Isaac, Frank 36 n.1
Isidore, Saint 2

Janiewicz, Feliks 75
Janiowicz, Feliks *see* Janiewicz
Jelinek, F X 104 n.5
Jenkinson, Mr 152
Jones, John Winter 194
Jupp, William 119, 121 n.*

Keller, Ambros 2
Kellway, Joseph 110
Kelly, Michael 147, 150 n.39
Kent, Duchess of 96 n.21
Kerslake, Thomas 116
Kerslake, John F 98 n.55
Keyte, Arthur E R x
Kidson, Frank 42
King, Alec Hyatt 174
King's Band of Music 74
King's Theatre, Haymarket 77, 80, 87, 121, 154
Kininger, Vincenz Georg 97 n.27
Kinsky, George 71 n.20
Kirby, Frances 128
Kirchner, Theodor 43
Knight, Gowin 56
Köchel, Ludwig von 99, 101, 103
Kockx sale 190
Kraus, Felicitas von 117 n.20
Kraus, Felix von 112, 113, 115, 116
Kreusser, Adam 75, 76 n.7
Kreusser, George Anton 75, 76 n.7
Kreusser, Peter Anton 73-6
Kreusser, Johann Matthäus 75
Kriehuber, J 184
Krummel, Donald 29, 30 n.1
Krusemann, G 184
Kurthen, Wilhelm 70 n.14

L., H 39
Laborde, Jean Benjamin François de 14
Lampadius, Auctor 30
Landon, H C Robbins 127
Langley, Leanne 135 n.1, 135 n.22, 135 n.24
Lanza, Gesaldo 141, 142
Latour, Henry John 73
Laurence, Frederick 162, 174
Leeds Public Library 109
Lees, Mrs G M *see* Andrews, Hilda
Lefevre 31 n.30
Leighton-Thomas, A F xii
Leinster, Duke of 178
Lesure, François 14, 30 n.5, 72 n.30
Levien, John Mewburn 163, 177 n.35
Leyden, Lucas van den 185
Lillywhite, Bryant 124 n.4
Linacre, Thomas 17
Lind, Jenny 176 n.24
Lindley, Robert 186
Lister (of the British Museum bindery) 190
Lister, T Villiers 185

Liszt, Franz 167
Little, James Hyatt 87, 97 n.33
Livingston, Arthur 148 n.5
Loewenberg, Alfred 137, 141-5, 148 n.2, 148 n.3, 148 n.4, 148 n.6
London Academy of Music 160
London & County Bank 160
London Tavern 121, 140-3
Lonsdale, Charles 62
Lowinsky, Edward 31 n.36
Lownes, Mathew 39
Lucas, Stanley 157
Lucas Brothers 180
Luff, George 98 n.53
Lully, Jean Baptiste 111
Lyceum, The 89, 91, 98 n.50
Lyon, Elizabeth Sarah 140, 142, 146

Macfarren, Walter Cecil 171, 177 n.44
Mackenzie, Sir Alexander Campbell 171, 177 n.46, 177 n.47
Mackeson, Charles 125 n.23
Mackworth-Young, Sir Robin 76 n.4
Maclise, Daniel 184
Madrigal Society 58, 70 n.14
Magpie Madrigal Society 181, 192
Magpie Minstrels 179, 181, 186
Mainz Psalter 4
Maitland, John Alexander Fuller 100, 181, 183 n.3, 187, 191, 193, 198 n.10
Malmesbury, 1st Earl of 70 n.13
Manns, Sir August 171, 177 n.42
Manson, E 102, 103
Mapleson, Alfred 158-61, 164, 167, 168, 171, 172, 174
Mapleson, James Henry 158
March, Earl of 58
Marlborough, Duchess of 78
Marshall, George William 34
Marshall, Julian 2nd sale 190
Martin, William 117 n.3
Martineau, Russell 118 n.23
Martineau, Mr and Mrs Russell 115
Martini, Giovanni Battista 14
Mary, Princess 16
Mason, Nicholas 129
Maty, Matthew 54, 56, 57, 69 n.3
Maurer, Ludwig 98 n.50
Mayr, Simon 145
Mazzinghi, Joseph ix, 80, 81, 83, 87, 96 n.17, 96 n.21
Mechel, Christian von 62, 71 n.23, 72 n.31
Mee, John H 150 n.33
Melton Mowbray, Corn Exchange 178
Mendelssohn, Felix 122, 167, 183
Merbecke, John 18
Meyer, Henry 97 n.30
Meyer-Baer, Kathi 2
Meyerbeer, Giacomo 184
Miarteni, Signor (singer) 137, 138, 139-141, 149 n.12
Michel, F 30 n.5

Mikado, The 182
Mitford, Algernon Bertram 178, 180, 184
Mitjana, Rafael 197
Moffat, Alfred 75
Montagu House 55, 66, 71 n.20 *see also* British Museum
Monthly Magazine, The 83, 95 n.1
Monthly Musical Record, The 112
Monzani and Hill 79
Moore, John, Bishop of Ely 38
More, Sir Thomas 16–18
Mores, Edward 29
Morison, Stanley 31 n.21
Morris, Val 178
Morshead, Sir Owen 118 n.21
Morton, Charles 57
Moscheles, Felix 170
Moser, Hans Joachim 112, 113
Mount, George 185
Mount Edgcumbe, Lord 79
Mozart, Anna Maria 52, 54, 56, 70 n.11
Mozart, afterwards Nissen, Constanze 63
Mozart, Karl 99, 102, 103
Mozart, Leopold 52–4, 57–62, 67–9, 70 n.11, 71 n.20, 75, 110, 185
Mozart, Maria Anna ('Nannerl') in London 52–4, 60, 62, 67, 70 n.11; in Salzburg 63
Mozart, 'Nannerl' *see* Mozart, Maria Anna
Mozart, Wolfgang Amadeus 122, 126, 129; in London 52–69, 70 n.11, 71 n.20;
—works, vocal: canons K508a 99, 180, 185; *La Clemenza di Tito* 79–83, 85, 144, 146; *Conservati fedele* 62; *Così fan tutte* 79–83, 85, 98, 129, 144, 147; as *Tit for Tat* 89–94, 98 n.49; *Don Giovanni* 77–93, 126, 137–47; *God is our Refuge* ix, 52, 58–60, 63–6, 68, 69, 71 n.25; *Le nozze di Figaro* 79–84, 140, 147; *Va dal furor portata* 61; *Die Zauberflöte (Il flauto magico)* 79–83, 86, 90, 144, 147
—works, instrumental: piano quartet in E flat 99, 101, 180, 185; 'ten' string quartets 190; sonatas K6-K15 60, 65, 110; symphony K19a 60
Music & Letters xii
Musical World, The 123

Nägeli, Hans Georg 112
Nalbach, Daniel 94 n.3, n.4, n.5
Naldi, Giuseppe 87
Napier, Hampden 91, 98 n.50
Nash, John 95 n.7
Nash, Ray 31 n.18
Nasolini, Sebastiano 78
National Cave of Harmony 185
National Portrait Gallery, Trustees xiv
Neate, Charles 123, 170, 173, 177 n.37
New London Tavern *see* City of London Tavern
New Zealand House 95 n.7
Newman, Robert 159
Newton, William 119, 121, n.*, 122
Nicholson, Laura 198 n.8, 198 n.9, 198 n.*
Nicholson, Watson 94 n.1

Nicolay, Bernard Underwood 117 n.5
Nicolay, Caspar 109
Nicolay, Christian Frederick 109, 117 n.5
Nicolay, Frederick 107–9, 117 n.14
Nicolay, Sapphira 109
Nicolini, Giuseppe 141
Nicoll, Allardyce 98 n.51
Niger, Franciscus 5
Nissen, George Nikolaus von 54, 55, 62, 63, 69 n.4, 71 n.20, 99
Nixon, Howard Millar 30 n.1
Noblemen and Gentlemen's Catch Club 58, 59, 70 n.12, 71 n.18, 179
Northcott, Richard 136 n.21
Novello, Mary Sabilla 62
Novello, Vincent 62–5, 189
Novello & Co xii, 115 n.*
Novosielski, Michael 78, 95 n.6

Oates, John C T 31 n.30
Obrecht, Jacob 18
Ogden, Elizabeth 187
Old Hall Manuscript 192
Oldman, Cecil Bernard x, 76 n.2, 99, 101, 103; as Hon. Librarian of Royal Philharmonic Society 163, 179
Oliphant, Thomas 63–5, 70 n.14, 189, 190
opera libretti, in British Library catalogue 193
Or, Dr de 53
Ouseley, Sir Frederick Gore 178
Overton, Thomas 152
Oxford Music Room 146

Pacini, Giovanni 136
Paer, Ferdinando 98 n.50
Paez, Karl (?) 44, 50
Paganini, Nicolo 184
Page, John 70 n.17
Paget, P L C 178
Painter, George D 6 n.1
Paisiello Giovanni 145
Pantheon, The 77, 95 n.6
Papendiek, Charles 110
Papendiek, Charlotte Luisa Henrietta 110
Papworth, J B 95 n.7
Partridge, John 89–9, 97 n.30
Pattison, Bruce 22
Pawlett, Robert 41
Pawzett, Robert *see* Pawlett
Pearce, Ernest Harold, Bishop of Worcester 31 n.31
Pearson, William 40
Pembroke College, Cambridge 187, 193, 198 n.29
Penneck, Rev. Richard 56
Percy, Thomas 37 n.16
Perry, George 91
Peters, Edith 74 n.*
Peters Edition 45
Petre, F Loraine 135 n.17
Petrucci, Ottaviano 5, 30 n.3
Petter, Alfred 98 n.42

Pfannhauser, Karl 58, 70 n.16
Philharmonic Society, afterwards Royal
    Philharmonic Society 126–9, 134, 151–75
Phillips, Henry 91, 98 n.49
Philosophical Transactions 57
Phyllyp, Thomas 24, 25
Pickering, Danby 94 n.1
Pieter de Jode I 185
Pigot's Directory 135 n.6
Pilgrim Trust 163
Pilot, The 193
Pitt, Mr (scene painter) 94
Planché, John Robinson 98 n.48
Planta, family of 57
Planta, Rev. Andrew 53, 54, 56, 60, 61, 68
Planta, Duriges 71 n.21
Planta, Joseph 71 n.21
Planta, Peter von 70 n.10, 71 n.21
Plantinga, Leon 132, 133, 135 n.12, 135 n.14, 135 n.15, 135 n.18
Plath, Wolfgang 67–71, 72 n.9
Playford, Henry 41
Playford, John 40, 41
Pleyel, Ignaz 75, 122, 161
Plomer, Henry Robert 17, 31 n.20
Pogue, Samuel 14
Pohl, Carl Ferdinand 62, 65, 66, 68
Pointer, John 161, 174, 177 n.33
Pollard, Alfred William 24, 42 n.1
Polytechnic Institute, Regent Street 160
Ponte, Lorenzo da 148 n.5
Ponte, Paolo da 148 n.5
Portogallo, Marcus Antonio da Fonseca 78
Potter, Cipriani 161
Powell, Thomas 122
Power, James 87
Pozzorato, L 185
Pressler, Karl xii
Preston (publisher) 91
Procter, Robert 2, 34, 37 n.11, 92
Prussian State Library, Berlin 112
Public Advertiser, The 56
Public Record Office 108
Puccitta, Vincenzo 79
Pugin, Augustus Charles 95 n.7
Pugno, Raoul 161
Pulley, John 19, 23, 33
Purcell, Henry 108, 109
Purcell Society 191
Puttick & Simpson 156

Quaritch, Messrs 162
Queen's Concert Rooms, Hanover Square, *see*
    Hanover Square Rooms
Queen's Hall 159, 160, 174

Rastell, Elizabeth 18
Rastell, John ix, x, 7–35
Rawle, Samuel 124 n.4
Redesdale, Earl of 117 n.24
Redford, John 18
Redgrave, Samuel 28

Reed, Arthur William 16, 32, 33
Reeves' Musical Directory 176 n.18
Rehm, Wolfgang 73
Renouard 31 n.11
Rentsch, Max 45
Ricks, Christopher 29
Riemann, Hugo 42
Riley, E 75
Rivers, W P 161, 174
Roberts, Julian 18 n.*, 30 n.1
Robyns, Wyllyam 24
Rockstro, William S 189
Röder, Carl Gottlieb 43–50
Romberg, Andreas Jakob 161
Rosa, Carl 171, 177 n.43
Rosenberg, F 186
Rosenberg, W F 186
Rosenthal, Albi 71 n.24
Rosenthal, Ludwig (Antiquariat) 24
Rossini, G 79, 80, 89, 123, 183, 184
Round House, Calais 16
Rovedino, Carlo 146
Rovedino, G 146, 150 n.34
Rovedino, Stefania 146
Royal Academy of Music 175, 177 n.31
Royal College of Music 163, 192
Royal Festival Hall 177 n.32
Royal Institute of British Architects 124 n.9
Royal Philharmonic Society *see* Philharmonic
    Society
Royal Society of Musicians 109, 117 n.7, 162
Rudall & Carte 160
ryuteki (Japanese flute) 185

S., J R 134
Saint-Foix, Count Georges de 58
St. James's Hall 123, 158, 159, 174
Salabert, F 184
Salieri, Antonio 146
Salmon, Eliza 122
Salomon, Johann Peter 75
Salzburger Zeitung 54, 57, 59, 66, 69 n.4
Sarti, Giuseppe 146
Satchell, James 134
Saturday Review, The 193
La Scala, Milan 78
Scarlatti, Alessandro 111
Schenk, Erich 58, 70 n.15
Schilling, Gustav 74
Schick & Co 127
Schick, Anthony & Co, 127
Schick, Anton 123, 126, 148
Schieferdecker, A 185
Schlesinger, Maurice 96 n.20
Schnapper, Edith 95 n.9
Schoelcher, Victor 112, 116
Schökh, Anton *see* Schick
Scholderer, Victor 2
Scholes, Percy 4, 117 n.11, 172
Schroeter, Johann Samuel 110
Schultz, J R 134
Schumann, R A 170, 171

Schurig, Arthur 68
Schwenke, Friedrich Gottlob 145
Schwenninger (doctor) 112
Sclater, Claud Edward Lutley xiv
Scotcher, Mr
Scott, Sir Walter 98 n.53
Searle, Arthur 164, 174, 175 n.2
Shaw, Harold Watkins 109
Shepherd, George 124 n.4
Shepherd, Thomas Hosmer 119, 120, 124 n.13
Sheppard, F H W 95 n.7
Sherrington, William 154, 176 n.10
Siboni, Giuseppe 140, 147, 149 n.18
Sigl, G 45
Simpson (oboe-player) 110
Sitwell, Sir Osbert 198 n.24
Sloane, Sir Hans 38, 57
Smart, Sir G 98 n.48, 122, 170, 177 n.38
Smith, D Ritson 163, 174
Smith, John Christopher 112
Smith, John Stafford 111
Smith, William Charles 94 n.4, 95 n.14, 100–3, 107, 149 n.10, 149 n.12, 149 n.24, 150 n.28, 150 n.34, 190, 198 nb, *see also* Humphries, Charles
Solander, Daniel C 56
Sonneck, Oscar George Theodore 197
Sorensen, Scott 146 n.*
Spagnoletti, Paolo 137, 140, 141–3, 147, 149 n.14, 150 n.40
Speyer, Edward 198 n.7
Spohr, Ludwig 122, 156, 161, 170
Springer, Hermann 192
Spydernell, *see* Spyderswell
Spyderswell, Andrew 24
Squire, William 187
Squire, William Barclay ix, x, 19, 24, 39, 65, 100, 101, 103 n.3, 107, 108, 111, 117 n.24, 117 n.25, 181, 182, 187–99
Stainer & Bell xii
Stanford, Sir Charles Villiers 187, 189
Steele, Robert 15, 19, 22, 36 n.1, 42 n.1, 192
Steffani, Agostino 14, 108
Steffens, Mr (of Schott's) 116
Stephen, Sir Leslie 189
Stephens, Charles Edward 159, 176 n.2
Stephens, Kitty (Countess of Essex) 176 n.22
Sterland, John x, 119–24, 126–135, 147, 148, 152
Stevens, Miss (singer) 122
Stevens, John 22, 31 n.28
Stevenson, Allan 2
Stillman, Mrs (dress designer) 94
Stockhausen, Julius 117 n.19
Strang, Sir William 188
Stratton, Stephen 150 n.38, 172
Strauss, Johann the elder 123
Sullivan, Sir Arthur 171, 176 n.28, 182
Swain, Thomas 41

Tabb, Mr 163
Taphouse, Thomas William sale 190
Tartini, Giuseppe 185
Taylor, William 77, 89

Tedder, Henry Richard 159
Temperley, Nicholas 124 n.1, 125 n.18, 131, 135 n.2, 135 n.10, 136 n.21
Tenniel, Sir John 173
Tenschert, Roland 69 n.3
Theatre Royal, English Opera House *see* Lyceum, The
Tholoze, Michel 5
Thudy *see* Tschudi
Thurlow, Edward, 2nd Baron 145
Timbs, John 121
Times, The 122
Tomkins, Mr (scene painter) 134, 136 n.24
Tree, Sir Beerbohm 172
Trinity College of Music 160
Tschudi, Berkard 54, 60
Tübingen, University Library 1
Turner, W L 184
Tyson, Alan 72 n.29, 73, 132, 134

Utley, Francis Lee 28

Valentin, Erich 72 n.32
Vaughan, Thomas 122
Victoria, Queen of Great Britain and Ireland 192: private band 158
Victoria and Albert Museum, theatre collection 98 n.42, 98 n.56
Villebois, H 83
Volkert, Charles 115, 118 n.22

Wagner, Richard 162, 163, 177 n.30, 185
Waldie, Charlotte Ann 148 n.4
Waldie, John 148 n.4
Walker, G (music publisher) 195
Wallace, Janet 69 n.2, 70 n.13, 71 n.22, 72 n.25, 177 n.34
Wallace, William 162, 163
Wallis, William 124 n.13
Walton, Sir William 198 n.24
Wandering Minstrels, the 99–103, 178–186
Warren, afterwards Warren-Horne, Edward Thomas 59
Watts, William 128, 145, 146, 150 n.40, 153, 176 n.12
Webb, John 146 n.*
Weber, Carl Maria von 98 n.48, 122, 167, 170
Weckerlin, Jean-Baptiste Theodore 197
Weingartner, Felix 171
Weippert (composer) 122
Westminster Abbey 24, 25; library 192, 196
Westminster Gazette, The 193
Westminster School 24
Whethamsted, Thomas 24, 25
White, G H 150 n.30
White Lyon Tavern 119
Wickham, Glynne 31 n.16
Willetts, Pamela Joan 30 n.1, 98 n.48, 125 n.27, 174 n.2
Williamson, Thomas 185
Willis's Rooms 146
Willman, Thomas Lindsay 145

Wilson, Albert Edward 98 n.57
Wilton, Lord Grey de 178
Windsor, Castle Hotel 178; Theatre Royal 178
Windsor Castle, Royal Archives 74, 108
Winter, Peter von 98 n.50, 145
Witt, William 44
Wolff, L Hugo 45
Wolfheim, Werner 192
Wotquenne, Alfred 197
Wouwere, Claes van den 29
Würtz, Roland 96 n.20
Würzburg, Theodor of 5

Wyatt, James 95 n.6
Wyzewa, T de 58

X, Mr 59–62

Young, John 40
Young, Percy Marshall 124 n.1

Zainer, Guenther 2
Zainer, Johann 3
Zavertal, Vaclav Hugo 99, 102, 105 n.5
Zuckert, John Frederick 110